BEST RESUMES
FOR $75,000+
EXECUTIVE JOBS

BEST RESUMES FOR $75,000+ EXECUTIVE JOBS

Second Edition

William E. Montag

John Wiley & Sons, Inc.

New York • Chichester • Weinheim • Brisbane • Singapore • Toronto

This book is printed on acid-free paper. ∞

Copyright © 1999 by William E. Montag. All rights reserved.

Published by John Wiley & Sons, Inc.
Published simultaneously in Canada.

This publication is designed to provide accurate and
authoritative information in regard to the subject matter
covered. It is sold with the understanding that the publisher is
not engaged in rendering professional services. If professional
advice or other expert assistance is required, the services of a
competent professional person should be sought.

Library of Congress Cataloging-in-Publication Data

Montag, William E., 1947–
    Best resumes for $75,000+ executive jobs / by William E. Montag.—2nd ed.
       p.   cm.
    ISBN 0-471-29720-8
    1. Résumés (Employment)   2. Cover letters.   3. Executives.   I. Title.
    HF5383.M59   1999
    650.14'024658—dc21   98-8156
                                                                      CIP

Printed in the United States of America.

10 9 8 7 6 5 4 3 2 1

Acknowledgments

To my wonderful Debbie for her heart and soul—and for putting up with mine

To my parents—who did a great job—and my brother whose goodness is
immeasurable

To my wonderful and loving grandmother Billy whose absence has left an
inconsolable void

To Carol for three decades of unwavering friendship, caring, and encouragement

To my grandfather, Uncle Lyle, Aunt Madeline, Aunt Pat, and Uncle Ronnie who
gave a little redheaded kid the best summers of his life

To Uncle Raymond who deserves a special place in the next world for handling a
lifetime of hardship with dignity and courage

To Dr. Patrick McGrath who literally saved my life

To Mary Lou, Patty, Betty, Junie, Jack, and Joe for sharing many fun times and pot
roasts in the past and in years to come

To Kim Harlow, a fellow rebel and writer, and her beloved Carl who will live on
in the memories of those who had the privilege of knowing him

To Lou and Maddie DiBari and their wonderful children whose friendship
means everything

To Aunt Mary who gave much joy to her young nephew

To Dr. Gagnon whose counsel and listening genius are very much appreciated

To my professors, James Hall and Scott Ball, who taught me the discipline and
joy of writing

To my wonderful clients over the past decade: RZ, RG, DJ, KH, MB, PS, VD, LD,
GR, WT, RM, NB, TC, NC, JH, ND, SK, SC, IN, LT, RL, MH, PH, JR, PM,
and countless others

To Paulette, Tom, and Gary who brought much joy and heart even when "Rome
was burning"

To Adam Boyd whose entrepreneurial spirit is surpassed only by his good and
generous heart

To Tom Comer who helped make IMCO North an unforgettable and rewarding
experience

To Henry Wallace whose long-ago friendship is missed

And to Michael Hamilton, my esteemed senior editor at Wiley, whose support
and encouragement have once again made the dream come true

Contents

BEST RESUMES
FOR $75,000+
EXECUTIVE JOBS

Introduction

In this revised and expanded second edition of our original best-seller, I have added some new chapters and appendixes that will help you launch your search with the same competitive edge held by clients of Montag Associates: They have enjoyed a placement success rate that far surpasses even the best performance of the outplacement industry. As demonstrated through real-life case histories featured throughout the text, clients who combined our power packaging in Part I with our market-tested search theories in Part II have repeatedly outmarketed, outsmarted, and outclassed the competition. This new edition is intended to help you achieve the same results.

ABOUT PART I: MARKET-TESTED POWER PACKAGING

As you, the intelligent manager, pick up and browse through yet another resume book, just as I have done for the past two decades, your doubts and skepticism are understandable. The universe of resume books on the market is hardly populated with Pulitzer Prize candidates.

As a Fortune 100 manager, veteran writer, and executive career consultant, I've been an outspoken critic of the past and current crop of generally weak and outdated resume books. The acute shortage of quality, marketing-oriented resume books in the increasingly hostile circa 2000 job market creates a serious void at a time when effective self-marketing is critical. I wrote this book to demonstrate how resumes can be written better, based on an intense decade of successfully packaging and marketing discriminating management-level clients into a wide spectrum of companies ranging from international growth companies (e.g., General Electric, Daimler-Benz, and Lotus Development Corporation) to mid-size and emerging start-up companies.

Since virtually every resume book on the market says that it is either good, better, or best, how can you objectively differentiate and identify those books that can really help you with the critical job search self-marketing process as we enter the twenty-first century?

Let's demonstrate how and why this book *is* superior.

To assist you within an economic environment characterized by corporate downsizing, rapid turnover, zero job security, and perpetual job searches, this workbook offers the following critically important *features and advantages* that clearly separate and distinguish it:

▶ *Superior Quality Sample Resumes and Cover Letters.* Based directly on more than 60 real-life client case histories, the market-tested and proven samples in this book successfully generated quality interviews and six-figure career moves. These are samples of unmatched quality from which to extract, borrow, and adapt key words, phrases, sentences, and paragraphs as you develop your own power package.

▶ *A Uniquely Strong Focus on Defining and Packaging Marketable Skills and Achievements.* Unlike almost all other resume books on the market, this workbook deemphasizes and subordinates the narrative job descriptions (*often misrepresented as achievements* by many books) that clutter most resumes; it also totally eliminates other nonselling information.

The market has responded favorably to the skills and achievement-oriented resumes featured in this workbook—the very types of resumes that *BusinessWeek* (7 October 1991), in a hard-hitting cover story on white-collar layoffs, proclaimed as "The New Twenty-First-Century Resume."

▶ *An Unparalleled Emphasis on the Marketing Cover Letter.* Unlike the majority of resume books on the market, this workbook treats the cover letter and resume as *coequal* and *totally insepa-*

rable components of the total marketing package. While other books frequently highlight the importance of the letter, they often undermine this importance by merely tacking on a chapter near the end of the book that contains a *few* mediocre to poor sample letters, *none* of which are related to the sample resumes.

Every sample resume in this book has a corresponding cover letter—*no* other books on the market can make this claim. Based on a frequently heard comment from my management clients, "The cover letter got me the interview," I have no doubts about the importance of the letter.

▶ *A More Representative Cross Section of Sample Resumes and Cover Letters.* By deliberately excluding many highly specialized, often irrelevant job positions that provide "filler" for countless resume books, this workbook concentrates on presenting the several mainstream categories and subcategories of management-level positions into which most managers fall.

▶ *An Intense Focus on Real-Life Success Stories.* The narrative and samples in this book reflect the market-tested and proven methods and techniques that resulted in successful career moves for satisfied clients.

▶ *A Respect for the Intelligence and Experience of the Reader / Manager.* This workbook steadfastly avoids the insultingly simplistic advice that permeates the universe of resume books: There are no references to paper size, paper color, typos, spelling, or photocopying.

▶ *A Respect for and Focus on Market Response.* Simply stated, the power-packaging techniques and real-life samples in this book achieved the desired results for managers just like you—they produced positive interviews and job offers in an increasingly tough and selective marketplace which is, of course, the *ultimate* and only relevant judge of quality.

If you have not been in the job market for some time and / or have not prepared or updated your resume in recent years, I have included, for your convenience, two data-gathering chapters. They will help you recall, organize, and document the necessary information to complete your marketing resume and cover letter. In particular, Chapters 2 and 3 will help you focus on and define your marketable skills and achievements, which are the major components of your resume and cover letter package.

ABOUT PART II: LAUNCHING A JOB SEARCH CAMPAIGN IN THE TWENTY-FIRST CENTURY

REALITY CHECK

In comparing restrictive search theories to our patented Expansionist Theory, remember this simple truth: You can never be guilty of making too many contacts, but you can certainly be guilty of making too few. Widespread failure to heed this fact has ceded a big competitive edge to our clients who beat the competition with high-volume marketing that wins job offers.

Armed with the market-tested resume and cover letter packages drafted in Part I, you already hold a competitive edge that will facilitate and expedite your search. The combination of power packaging and our patented Expansionist Theory continues to be a winning formula for clients who repeatedly outmarket their peers by at least 1,000%—achieving a placement success rate that buries the competition. Chapter 8 is a provocative new chapter that documents the impact of predatory greed on a stressed-out workforce—a workforce that can take control of their careers by executing a *multistep, high-volume* job search process that distinguishes the Expansionist Theory discussed in Chapter 10. While the rest of the populace dawdles, clients and readers get results. So will you.

PART I

Market-Tested Power Packaging

_____ **REALITY CHECK** _____

In the career and job search game, the only thing that really matters is results. As demonstrated through real-life case histories, clients who combined our market-tested resume and cover letter packages with our patented Expansionist Theory have enjoyed a placement success rate that far surpassed the outplacement industry norm.

1

Frequently Asked Questions with Market-Tested Answers

Your most important job search/marketing tools are your resume and cover letter. As you think through the following questions and answers, please remember three market-tested philosophies that guided the development of this workbook:

Philosophy 1. Conventional, simplistic, and dogmatic how-to advice published in the past has helped to produce a 99% nationwide rejection rate for resumes—hardly a ringing endorsement for perpetuating past practices and advice.

Philosophy 2. The only opinion that really matters in judging the quality and effectiveness of your marketing resume and cover letter package is the opinion and response of the marketplace. The real-life sample resume and cover letter packages in this workbook were well-received by the marketplace, resulting in successful career moves up to six-figure salaries at the senior vice-president level.

Philosophy 3. Individuals need to be professional marketeers in planning their job search campaigns and developing their marketing presentation packages. The increasingly volatile, hostile, and challenging white-collar job market of the twenty-first century will require and demand nothing less.

Q: Why doesn't my resume generate more *quality* interviews and multiple quality offers?

A: The marketing resume and cover letter package should, but rarely does, present your strongest possible case so as to increase your chances of landing on the "potential candidate" pile rather than on the "no" pile allotted to 99% of all resumes. Most resumes reach the "no" pile for a sadly legitimate reason—they utterly fail to market and sell the individual.

Resumes are, of course, rejected for other reasons (e.g., a true nonmatch or lack of needed technical skills or credentials). However, based on two decades of experience, I have concluded that the overriding reason for the nationwide rejection rate of 99% is that most resumes simply do not achieve their intended goal of marketing and selling the candidate.

Q: How then do I present my strongest possible case?

A: By focusing on and presenting, in your resume and cover letter, a well thought out, well-crafted, and hard-hitting presentation of your marketable skills and achievements. When you cut through all the superficial theories postulated about resume content, the undeniable fact is that you will (and should) ultimately be judged by the reader/decision maker based on your applicable skills and past accomplishments.

Few decision makers care much about the extended and detailed job descriptions that fill most resumes. While the resume and cover letter packages that you develop here will include brief job descriptions as secondary data, the primary emphasis will be on developing the strongest possible achievement statements (i.e., "success stories") and skills definition sections of the resume and cover letter.

Strong, hard-hitting achievement statements convey this message: "Since I directed these successful efforts, accomplished these management goals, resolved these major problems, and achieved these targeted results for my past companies, I can do the same for you."

Q: Should my resume be no longer than one page? How critical is the cover letter?

A: Epitaph for the One-Page Resume Theory: Once and for all, let's put this "overaged turkey" of a theory to rest.

A key principle behind the oft-quoted "one-page resume" theory is indeed a sound one, stating that your presentation must be succinct and to the point because you only have 15 seconds of the reader's review time to make your best case. So far, so good.

It is the interpretation and application of this principle, namely, that the resume must therefore be one page, that is all wet. In fact, the principle that you must present your best case as succinctly as possible for a 15-second review process leads instead to the following conclusion: If you don't first sell the reader with your marketing cover letter, you are not likely to sell the reader at all!

As detailed in Chapter 5, the marketing cover letter is the single most critical document that you will produce. While the resume must be as strong as the letter, the cover letter must do 98% of the initial marketing. I can state this unequivocally, based on my experience in the marketplace and on feedback from clients.

The cover letter is a chance to "speak" to the reader/interviewer. By developing the type of skills and achievement-oriented letters outlined in Chapter 5, you give yourself the same competitive edge that led to my clients' successful career moves into international growth companies as well as emerging mid-size and start-up companies. Failure to develop a hard-hitting, creative, achievement and skills-oriented cover letter results in a missed opportunity.

As for the resume, by using the recommended combination format (see next question), which positions your skills and achievements on page one (functional format) and all employer names, dates, and job descriptions on page two (chronological format), you accomplish the following: All the marketing (i.e., communication of your skills and achievements) is indeed contained on the first page of the resume so that if the reader only reviews page one, that is ok.

The cover letter and first page of your two-page resume should and (by applying this book's techniques) will contain 99% of your marketable selling points. This is a sound application of the principle behind the outmoded one-page resume theory. Decades of firsthand experience and the success of my white-collar clients, 98% of whom had two-page resumes, indicate that the rule that the resume must absolutely not exceed one page is simplistic tripe.

Q: What resume format should I use?

A: The typical analysis of the chronological versus functional versus combination formats is frequently characterized by lengthy lists of simplistic pros and cons that complicate the decision-making process and divert attention from the most critical factors to consider in determining the optimum format, namely, the impact of and market response to the various format styles.

Based on a busy decade of measuring market response through clients who made successful career moves, my experience has been that the format producing the greatest market impact is the one that best highlights and sells your most marketable assets—your accomplishments and skills. I, therefore, recommend (and demonstrate throughout this book) the combination functional (page one) and chronological (page two) format, which is, in most instances, the most marketing-driven format for presenting your skills and achievements.

Grouping and presenting your skills and achievements on page one of the resume while presenting your reverse chronological listing of employers (with dates, job titles, and job descriptions) on page two has several marketing advantages:

First of all, and most importantly, by grouping your skills and achievements together on page one of the resume, you are presenting your most marketable and highest impact information first—a sound application of fundamental marketing principles. Remember you are the product, and the resume and cover letter package is your chief preinterview sales tool. You should, therefore, develop your chief sales tool using the same proven marketing principles and techniques that apply to any product.

Second, by using this recommended combination format, you are demonstrating your respect for the employer's valuable and limited time by not forcing the reviewer to read and sort through a bunch of job descriptions, dates, and other low-impact, nonselling data better presented in the chronological section (page two).

If for reasons of convention (remember that conventional methods have helped produce a 99% rejection rate), you choose to use the chronological format, refer to Appendix I for an example of how to convert from the combination format to chronological format.

Q: Should my resume always include an objective statement?

A: An objective statement should always be included somewhere in your resume and cover letter marketing package but not necessarily in the resume itself. In fact, safe rules of thumb are that:

1. An objective statement will *always* be included in the marketing cover letter.
2. An objective statement will be included *less frequently* or *not at all* in the resume.

Q: Why is this so?

A: Including an objective statement in *both* the resume and cover letter is unnecessarily redundant.

Since the recipient of the marketing package will, in most instances, read the cover letter first, the objective statement must always appear in the letter, which is developed as a high-powered marketing tool in Chapter 5. It is, therefore, not necessary also to include an objective statement in the resume. Moreover, by not including the objective statement on the resume, you make the resume less restrictive, thereby leaving the door open to targeting multiple objectives each of which can be readily expressed by simply modifying the objective statements in the cover letter.

It is obviously not forbidden also to include the objective statement on the resume. However, if you decide to include it, have a better reason than "the Sunday newspaper supplement says the objective should always be on the resume." Such Sunday-supplement advice has been a major contributor to the extremely high rejection rate for resumes.

2

Defining Your "Success Stories" and Skills

Chapters 2 and 3 are designed for those of you who have not been on the job market for some time and/or who have not prepared or updated your resume in recent years. These chapters will help you recall, organize, and document the important information needed to complete your marketing resume and cover letter package in Chapters 4 and 5.

In particular, these chapters will help you to focus on and define your marketable credentials, skills, and achievements, which are, of course, the major components of your resume and letter packages. When you have completed these sections, you will have a database of information from which to effectively communicate your credentials, skills, and achievements both in the marketing resume and during interviews when you verbally "tell your story of accomplishment."

WRITING YOUR SUCCESS STORIES/ ACCOMPLISHMENT STATEMENTS

"Success stories" emphasizing and communicating results achieved are the most effective way to demonstrate that you are a leader and an achiever who can assume a leadership role in the new company's organization. They convey the message: "Since I directed these successful efforts, accomplished these management goals, resolved these major problems, and achieved these targeted results for my past companies, I can do the same for you."

Describe, and whenever possible quantify, your success stories focusing on the bottom-line impact of your accomplishments. Describe what you personally accomplished either individually or as a member of the management team, in areas such as these: measurable contributions to survival and profits during recessionary times; improvements to ROI (return on investment) and ROA (return on assets); specific management goals achieved; major roadblocks overcome; serious problems turned around; major projects completed; tough challenges met; contributions to revenue and/or profit growth; productivity improvements instituted; efficiencies implemented; cost reductions achieved; staffs upgraded or turned around.

Think through the specific goals or objectives you were to achieve and/or the problems you were to overcome and describe the steps you specifically executed to help achieve the goals or overcome the problems. Write out the specific accomplishments and the bottom-line impact of these accomplishments on the operating performance of your company, division, or department.

Remember to let your ego flow. Also remember that understatement of facts and achievements is just as bad as overstatement. If you don't fully communicate your achievements to prospective companies, another management candidate who did will very likely get the interview and offer. Do not worry at this point about writing quality or style—simply describe your achievements/success stories (i.e., "tell your story") using your individual style and phraseology.

Following are real-life examples of success story notes, followed by the strong achievement statements developed from them. These achievement statements, excerpted from resumes that generated six-figure-salary job interviews, are similar to the ones you will develop in Chapter 4.

EXAMPLE 1

Corporate Director of Admin. & Property Services; consolidated/co-located facilities: Examples: 29 warehouses consolidated into 4—annual savings $5.8 million; reduced HQ space by lease buyout—reduced from 90,000 square feet to 62,000 square feet = 30% reduction—saved $4.6 million over term of lease; negotiated buy-out of redundant space—cost avoidance of $48,000 × 6 years—yield $250K cash in hand; developed facilities standards program for corporation that aids in identifying requirements, budget levels, and establishing space standards—yielded a 20% reduction in space requirements over previous planning methods—yielded annual savings of $3,400,000.

Written Achievement Statement

• Consolidated 29 Acme warehouses down to 4, generating annual savings of $5.8 million; saved $4.6 million by reducing headquarters space 30%; introduced uniform facility standards that reduced total space requirements 20% saving another $3.4 million annually.

EXAMPLE 2

Vice President International Banking Group; comprised of California and Europe; responsibilities: consolidate; asset sales; capital markets; project financing; thrust of group—toward investment banking; emphasis—lucrative fees and deal-making; in 1994 generated $6.5 million revenue; 270 banking relationships; 1/3 or 90 at-risk; only lost 8; saved over 90% of the business that could have been lost; new transaction business; new corporate clients generated—international clients—Fortune 500 Domestic Deals.

Written Achievement Statement

• As Vice-President of the International Banking Group, produced revenue of $6.5 million in 1994 through aggressive client development and by saving 90% of the seriously at-risk accounts: accelerated the ROA by focusing on corporate finance, investment banking, and asset sales.

Note the emphasis on using strong, descriptive, hard-hitting, and market-tested words and phrases to describe the accomplishments extracted from the success story notes. High-impact words and phrases, such as *turned around, accelerated, executed, generated, initiated, created, instituted, restructured, upgraded, negotiated, expanded, resolved,* are critical components in expressing the importance and impact of your accomplishments.

Use the following list of high-impact words and phrases—extracted from real-life resumes and letters—as a guide in selecting the strongest and most accurate terms to describe, define, and convey the impact of your accomplishments.

As you write your own success story achievement statements both here and in Chapter 4, be sure to refer to Chapters 6 and 7 for a cross section of sample resumes and cover letters. Feel free to borrow and extract from these well-written, well-received success stories and achievement statements.

HIGH-IMPACT WORDS AND PHRASES FROM REAL-LIFE RESUMES AND LETTERS

abated
abolished
accelerated
achieved
actively participated
aggressively
applied
assumed a key role
authored
built
chaired
closed
codeveloped
codirected
cofounded
cold-called
collected
comanaged
communicated
completed
computerized
conducted
consolidated
contributed
controlled
convinced
coordinated
corrected
cost-effectively
created
critiqued
dealt effectively
defined
delivered
designed
developed and applied
directed
doubled
earned
eliminated
emphasized

enforced
established
exceeded
executed
exercised
expanded
expedited
facilitated
filled
focused
formulated
fostered
founded
gained
generated
ground-breaking
helped
implemented
improved
increased
initiated
instituted
instructed
integrated
interviewed
introduced
investigated
lectured
led
leveraged
maintained
managed
marketed
motivated
negotiated
orchestrated
organized
outmaneuvered
overcame
oversaw
penetrated

performed
permitted
persuaded
planned
played a key role
played an early and
   central role
played a pivotal role
positioned
prepared
presented
prevented
produced
profitably
project managed
promoted
proposed
prospected
protected
provided
published
quadrupled
ranked
received
recommended
recruited
reduced
removed
renegotiated
replaced
researched
resolved
restored
restructured
satisfied
saved
saving
scoped out
selected
selected by
self-financed

set up	taught	was able to
signed	tightened	was awarded
significantly	took the lead in	was chosen
sold	trained	was requested
staffed	tripled	was selected
started	troubleshooted	was singled out
stopped	turned around	well-received
substituted	uncovered	withstood
supervised	upgraded	yielded

DEFINING YOUR SKILLS, KNOWLEDGE, AND FUNCTIONAL EXPERTISE

Thinking through your management responsibilities in light of the preceding success stories (and referring to the following list of possible skills, knowledge, and functional expertise), list your skills and areas of knowledge applied in your highest impact positions. Think of your marketable skills and knowledge as the "tools" used to achieve your success stories. Be exhaustive in listing your skills, knowledge, and functional expertise; do not be concerned about prioritizing and editing them until later.

_____ _____ _____

_____ _____ _____

_____ _____ _____

_____ _____ _____

_____ _____ _____

_____ _____ _____

_____ _____ _____

_____ _____ _____

_____ _____ _____

Refer to Chapters 6 and 7 for a cross section of sample cover letters and resumes that include well-worded, well-organized, and well-received skills definition sections. Feel free to borrow and extract directly from these samples.

SKILLS, KNOWLEDGE, AND FUNCTIONAL EXPERTISE

General management

Sales/marketing executive

Sales/marketing management
Client development
Major account development
Quota achievement strategies
Proposals/presentations
Marketing materials/brochure development
Group marketing/seminars/speeches
Trade show participation
Closing skills
Customer service
Marketing
Strategic planning
Market research skills
Advertising/media

Operations executive

Research and development
Product research
Product development
Engineering
Manufacturing
Materials management
Production and inventory control
Procurement operations
Distribution operations
Receiving operations
Warehousing operations
Facilities operations

Finance/administration

Administrative services
Mergers and acquisitions
Finance/accounting
Controller operations
Accounting operations
Budgeting
Capital appropriations
Auditing operations

Cost reduction strategies
Credit operations

Treasury operations

Cash management
Investment/borrowing strategies
Basis point reductions
Foreign exchange strategies
Securities industry
Banking relations

Human resources management

Recruiting strategies
Training and development
Organizational development
Benefits administration
Labor relations
Outplacement
Public relations

Management information systems (MIS)

MIS/IT executive
Computer operations
Software applications/development
Spreadsheets/MS Excel/Lotus 1-2-3
Graphics/MS PowerPoint

Brokerage executive

Investment banking
Asset management
Real estate/property management
Leasing executive

Entrepreneurial

Start-up operations
Financing/capitalization

Turnaround strategies

Project management
Planning skills

Problem-solving
Staff supervision/development
Coordination skills

Communications

Chief Information Officer (CIO)
Negotiating skills
Verbal communication
Written communication
Multilingual (specify)

3

Defining Other Vital Information

As previously discussed, this chapter and Chapter 2 have been included for those of you who have not been on the job market for some time and/or who have not prepared or updated your resume in recent years. These chapters will help you recall, organize, and document the important information needed to complete your marketing resume and cover letter package in Chapters 4 and 5.

While the success stories and marketable skills defined in Chapter 2 are the most important components of your resume and cover letter package, the information gathered here may well further strengthen your marketing package and overall marketability.

DATA COLLECTION: INTERNATIONAL CREDENTIALS, LICENSES, ACTIVITIES, ETC.

What foreign languages do you speak?

_____ Fluent _____ Knowledgeable _____ Weak _____

_____ Fluent _____ Knowledgeable _____ Weak _____

_____ Fluent _____ Knowledgeable _____ Weak _____

What foreign languages do you read and/or write?

_____ Fluent _____ Knowledgeable _____ Weak _____

_____ Fluent _____ Knowledgeable _____ Weak _____

_____ Fluent _____ Knowledgeable _____ Weak _____

Where have you traveled and/or worked internationally? List all countries visited, with approximate dates and reason for the visit:

Since we operate in an increasingly global economy, citing international work assignments, languages, and other global activities may well have substantial market value.

Marketable licenses and/or other certifications (e.g., Real Estate, Brokerage, Private Pilot):

Marketable business-related group memberships, chairmanships, and other elected or appointed positions (including relevant skills acquired and accomplishments):

Marketable volunteer activities that might be applicable (i.e., have some market impact) to your career move:

Documents authored and/or published; government-issued patents or copyrights:

Potentially marketable avocations including sports-related activities, licensed activities, serious hobbies, and other nonwork-related pastimes:

CAUTIONARY NOTE: Whether or not you will actually include any of the preceding licenses, volunteer activities, or avocations in your final marketing package depends on the answer to the following question: Does this information really contribute to marketing myself? Do *not* include obviously superfluous or filler information in your resume marketing package. Almost everybody does it, but the 99% nationwide rejection rate for resumes is hardly an endorsement for perpetuating past practices in developing marketing resumes and cover letters.

DATA COLLECTION: EDUCATION AND MARKETABLE TRAINING

Undergraduate and graduate level education:

Undergraduate College _____ From _____ To _____

City, State _____

Degree _____ Year _____

Major/Minor Course Study _____

Still-marketable academic honors/achievements (cumulative GPA, GPA in major, ranking, special honors, scholarships, etc.)

_____

_____

Still-marketable leadership activities/sports achievements

_____

Other marketable accomplishments (e.g., well-received studies/projects, international studies)

_____

_____

Graduate School _____ From _____ To _____

City, State _____

Degree _____ Year _____

Major/Minor Course Study _____

Still-marketable academic honors/achievements (cumulative GPA, GPA in major, ranking, special honors, scholarships, etc.)

_____

Other marketable accomplishments (e.g., well-received papers, international studies)

_____

Other institution (e.g., additional undergraduate or graduate school attended):

Name _____ From _____ To _____

City, State _____

Degree _____ Year _____

Major Course Study _____

Still-marketable academic honors/achievements (cumulative GPA, GPA in major, ranking, special honors, scholarships, etc.)

_____

_____

Still-marketable leadership activities/sports achievements:

_____

Other marketable accomplishments (well-received papers/studies/projects, international studies, etc.)

_____

_____

List other marketable training courses and /or seminars completed:

1. _____
2. _____
3. _____
4. _____
5. _____
6. _____
7. _____
8. _____

DATA COLLECTION: MILITARY EXPERIENCE
(IF APPLICABLE AND STILL MARKETABLE)

Branch _____

Dates: From _____ To _____

Final Rank _____

Number of Promotions _____

Formal Honors (including reasons)

_____

_____

_____

Describe three to five significant achievements during your military service:

1.

2.

3.

4.

5.

DATA COLLECTION: CHRONOLOGICAL EMPLOYMENT HISTORY

Provide the following information for *each* company by which you were employed starting with your current or most recent employer. This chronological information will assist you in completing page two of your combination functional and chronological formatted resume, which contains skills and accomplishments on page one (extracted from Chapter 2) and chronological work history, including job descriptions, on page two (extracted from this chapter).

Company Name _____ City _____ State _____

Dates of Employment: From _____ To _____

Company's Products or Services _____

Most Recent Job Title _____ Dates in position: From _____ To _____

Describe the scope and responsibilities of this position. Include major projects and/or functional work responsibilities for which you are accountable; number of employees under your direct supervision; amount of your revenue, expense, and capital budgets; other relevant data.

Your *Previous* Job Title _____ Dates in position: From _____ To _____

Describe the scope and responsibilities of this position:

Your *Previous* Job Title _____ Dates in position: From _____ To _____

Describe the scope and responsibilities of this position:

4

Developing and Writing Your Marketing Resume

As you, the sophisticated manager, start the process of developing your updated resume, please keep in mind that my approach to developing the marketing resume is based on an intense decade of successfully packaging and marketing discriminating management-level clients into a wide spectrum of companies ranging from international growth companies to mid-size and emerging start-up companies.

To facilitate and accelerate the process of developing the strongest possible resume package, this book includes (what the marketplace has characterized as) superior quality sample resumes from which to develop your own high-impact resume. Based directly on more than 50 real-life client case histories, the market-tested and proven samples featured in this chapter and in Chapters 6 and 7 provide unmatched quality resumes from which to extract, borrow, and adapt key words, phrases, sentences, and paragraphs as you develop your own power package.

As you generate your marketing package following the techniques outlined in this chapter, you will also note a uniquely strong focus on defining your marketable skills and achievements. Unlike almost all other resume texts, this workbook plays down and subordinates the narrative job descriptions (often misrepresented as achievements by many books) that clutter most resumes; it also totally eliminates other nonselling information.

Remember that the marketplace has responded favorably to the skills and achievement-oriented resumes featured here—the very type of resumes that *BusinessWeek* (7 October 1991), in a hard-hitting cover story on corporate downsizing, proclaimed as "The New Twenty-First-Century Resume." The power-packaging techniques in this book achieved the desired results for managers just like you—they produced positive interviews and job offers in an increasingly tough and selective marketplace, which is, of course, the ultimate and only relevant judge of quality.

HOW TO DEVELOP YOUR MARKETING RESUME

Those of you who have not been on the job market for some time and/or who have not updated your resume in recent years have probably, as suggested earlier, completed Chapters 2 and 3. You have written out and documented your marketable skills, success stories/accomplishments, experiences, honors, and education. Armed with this database, you have at your fingertips all the information that you will need to complete your resume marketing package and marketing cover letter.

The challenge now is to sort through this material to select the most marketable facts. You can select and group together your most marketable skills delineated in Chapter 2. You can likewise review, select, and rewrite for presentation your most marketable achievements based on your success stories, formulated in Chapter 2.

Before you start putting together the marketing resume, let me reiterate a point about format. In developing the resume package, this chapter will be demonstrating and recommending the previously discussed combination format, which positions Career Skills/Knowledge and Career Achievements on page one (functional format) and the chronological employment data on page two (chronological format).

As discussed earlier, I strongly recommend the combination format. The marketplace has responded very favorably to this marketing-driven format. However, should you choose to develop a purely chronological resume, refer to Appendix I, which demonstrates how to convert to the chronological format.

As you develop the resume, feel free to refer to the more than 50 real-life, market-tested, and proven sample resumes in Chapters 6 and 7:

▶ Directly borrow and adapt for your own use key words, phrases, and/or sentences from the real-life samples most closely resembling your field, background, and objectives.

▶ Modify the borrowed phrases and sentences to fit your own experiences and background.

PAGE ONE

Education/Credentials

First of all, let's briefly address the issue of where to position your education and related credentials. Many how-to books advise you to place education at the end of the resume, particularly if you have several years of experience beyond graduation. Well, whether education is positioned first or last is hardly the biggest issue in the world—it certainly will not make or break your resume marketing package.

Having said that, it is my marketing-driven opinion that the education information should, in most cases, be positioned up front on page one unless there are concrete reasons, such as the lack of a degree, to position education information at the end. My recommendation is based on the premise that education and related credentials are *always* a key component of your overall profile even if you are a veteran manager with 30 years experience. While your accumulated job skills and achievements should and do become the most important factors in marketing yourself, your education credentials will follow you and be a part of your total profile for your whole life.

Devoting a few lines to your education at the beginning of the resume doesn't take up much space and instantly informs the reader that you have the baseline academic credentials. Remember that even in classified ads for executive level positions, companies almost always include academic requirements along with the other qualifications to fill the job.

If you ultimately choose to position your education and related credentials toward the end, do it for a logical reason and not because conventional how-to books and other simplistic advice say you should. Remember that conventional methods and simplistic and dogmatic how-to advice from the past have helped produce a 99% nationwide rejection rate for resumes.

The following examples and the resumes in Chapters 6 and 7 include other types of credentials including (relevant and marketable) languages, international travel, licenses, publications, and business memberships. When going through your notes from Chapters 2 and 3, if you feel that certain credentials have some market value (the key criteria) include them in the resume at this point. You can always edit them out later after you see the complete resume package come together.

The following real-life examples of Education/Credentials sections are taken from resumes that generated quality interviews and successful career moves up to the six-figure-salary, senior vice-president level.

EXAMPLE 1

EDUCATION

B.S.   Honors   Finance   Georgetown University   1980

EXAMPLE 2

EDUCATION/CREDENTIALS

M.B.A.   Honors   University of Paris Graduate School of Business   1985

International: Bilingual French and English; solid knowledge of Mideastern languages; traveled to over 60 nations

Certifications: Commercial Pilot's License; Black Belt Karate; Championship Skier

EXAMPLE 3

EDUCATION

| M.B.A. | Finance/Marketing | University of Virginia | 1976 |
| B.S. | Statistics | UCLA | 1974 |

EXAMPLE 4

EDUCATION/CREDENTIALS

| B.S. | Electrical Engineering | International University | Comprehensive Six-Year Program |
| B.A. | Business Administration | Lehman College | Managerial Studies |

International: Traveled throughout Europe, Asia, South America, and North America
Languages: Fluent French and Spanish

EXAMPLE 5

EDUCATION

B.A.   Kent State University   1962

(In this last example, the Education section was positioned at the end of the resume to subordinate the graduation date.)

Career Skills/Knowledge

This section focuses on presenting the relevant, transferable, and marketable skills and knowledge that you documented in Chapter 2. These are the tools that you have accumulated and applied to achieve the bottom-line results and accomplishments that we will address after we have completed the Skills section. By presenting multiple primary and secondary skills, you provide the future employer with a succinct listing of valuable (and therefore marketable) skills and talents that you will apply to achieve bottom-line results for your future company.

Presenting your primary and secondary skills and knowledge also allows you to demonstrate the diversity and multiplicity of talents and abilities in your arsenal of experience. This critical advantage helps avoid the simplistic and narrow-minded stereotyping that frequently accompanies the resume review process (e.g., "he/she is a manufacturing type" or "he/she is a technical type"). Such premature and superficial stereotyping during the critical 15- to 30-second resume review cycle frequently results in a quick trip to the terminal "no" pile. This simplistic stereotyping is particularly costly and frustrating since most veteran managers possess multiple, diverse, and transferable talents and experiences that permit them to market themselves toward as many as three to five different (albeit sometimes related) objectives.

Like the successfully placed clients whose Skills/Knowledge sections are shown here, use this section to show your diversity of talents. As demonstrated, you will extract and develop a two-column list of skills: the left column should reflect your primary skills (aimed at your primary objective); the right column should reflect your secondary skills, which may be just as strong as your primary skills but are designated as secondary because they are not quite as relevant to your primary objective.

As also shown in the following examples, you may well develop a second (and possibly third, fourth, etc.) version of your resume (and Skills section) to market yourself to different objectives. For example, the primary skills in Version 1 may become the secondary skills in Version 2, whereas the secondary skills in Version 1 may become the primary skills in Version 2.

As you develop your Skills section, refer to your Chapter 2 notes and feel free to borrow directly from the examples provided here. Also refer to and borrow from the sample resumes in Chapters 6 and 7, which contain a cross section of well-worded, well-organized, and well-received Skills sections. Remember that you do not have to get it perfect the first time; through several drafts, you can and will perform the editing changes necessary to present your skills in the most marketable way.

Following are examples of the Skills/Knowledge sections of resumes that generated quality interviews and successful career moves up to the six-figure-salary, senior vice-president level.

EXAMPLE 1: JOHN Q. SAMPLE

Career Move Achieved	Vice-President of a major Fortune 500 high-tech company/industry leader
Background	Six-figure-salary executive with multiple objectives: Version 1 below reflects the first objective aimed at securing a Finance/Administration Executive position. Version 2 reflects a second objective aimed at securing a corporate Property Management Executive position.

Version 1

CAREER SKILLS/KNOWLEDGE

- o Finance/administration management
- o General management
- o Strategic/operational planning
- o General/administrative services
- o Financial planning & analysis
- o Procurement operations
- o Facilities/telecommunications
- o Training operations
- o Logistics services
- o Global transportation

- o Property management
- o Development/construction
- o Occupancy growth strategies
- o Premium rate strategies
- o Consolidation strategies
- o Lease management/negotiations
- o Site selection/space planning
- o Budgeting/accountability
- o Government regulations
- o Environmental guidelines

Version 2

CAREER SKILLS/KNOWLEDGE

- o Property management
- o Development/construction
- o Occupancy growth strategies
- o Premium rate strategies
- o Consolidation strategies
- o Lease management/negotiations
- o Site selection/space planning
- o Budgeting/accountability
- o Government regulations
- o Environmental guidelines

- o Finance/administration management
- o General management
- o Strategic/operational planning
- o General/administrative services
- o Financial planning & analysis
- o Procurement operations
- o Facilities/telecommunications
- o Training operations
- o Logistics services
- o Global transportation

EXAMPLE 2: DAVID Q. SAMPLE

Career Move Achieved	Senior Vice-President of major European-based financial institution
Background	Six-figure-salary executive with multiple fast-track objectives: Version 1 below reflects goal of securing a Senior Investment Banking position; Version 2 reflects second goal of securing a corporate Marketing/Sales Executive position.

Version 1

CAREER SKILLS/KNOWLEDGE

o Banking executive
o International banking
o Investment banking
o Corporate/capital markets
o Acquisitions/joint ventures
o Subsidiary recapitalization
o Project financing/syndicates
o Trade financing/foreign exchange

o Marketing/sales executive
o General management
o Start-up operations
o Major client development
o Competitive maneuvering
o Expansion/turnaround strategies
o Revenue/profit growth
o Organizational development

Version 2

CAREER SKILLS/KNOWLEDGE

o Marketing/sales executive
o General management
o Start-up operations
o Major client development
o Competitive maneuvering
o Expansion/turnaround strategies
o Revenue/profit growth
o Organizational development

o Financial executive
o International banking
o Investment banking
o Corporate/capital markets
o Acquisitions/joint ventures
o Subsidiary recapitalization
o Project financing/syndicates
o Trade financing/foreign exchange

EXAMPLE 3: MATTHEW Q. SAMPLE

Career Move Achieved   Executive position within the transportation industry

Background   Over-50 executive under intense pressure to find a position: Version 1 reflects Product Management/Sales objective; Version 2 reflects Strategic Planning objective.

Version 1

CAREER SKILLS/KNOWLEDGE

o Marketing/sales management
o Revenue/profit turnaround
o Product management/market development
o National accounts programs
o Sales productivity growth
o Competitor intelligence systems
o Business ownership/leveraged buyouts
o Advertising/promotions
o Operations turnaround

o Strategic planning
o Business plans/market research
o Market growth/segmentation
o ROI growth strategies
o Profit/investment optimization
o Economic modeling/pricing
o Supply/demand analysis
o Finance/controller operations
o Cash-flow/financing/bank relations

Version 2

CAREER SKILLS/KNOWLEDGE

o Strategic planning
o Business plans/market research
o Market growth/segmentation
o ROI growth strategies
o Profit/investment optimization
o Economic modeling/pricing
o Supply/demand analysis
o Finance/controller operations
o Cash-flow/financing/bank relations

o Marketing/sales management
o Revenue/profit turnaround
o Product management
o National accounts programs
o Sales productivity growth
o Competitor intelligence systems
o Business ownership/leveraged buyouts
o Advertising/promotions
o Operations turnaround

EXAMPLE 4: WILLIAM Q. SAMPLE

Career Move Achieved — General Management position with a European-based company

Background — Over-50 executive with broad-based international experience: Version 1 reflects International Sales/Marketing objective; Version 2 reflects International Operations objective.

Version 1

CAREER SKILLS/KNOWLEDGE

- o Sales/marketing executive
- o International sales/markets
- o European relations
- o Strategic/marketing plans
- o Market share strategies
- o Major client development
- o Competitive maneuvering
- o Exchange rate strategies
- o Organizational development
- o Staff supervision/development

- o Operations/materials/engineering
- o Purchasing operations
- o Cost controls/reductions
- o Global distribution/logistics
- o Heavy industry clients
- o Aircraft engine market
- o Engineering operations
- o Electrical/systems engineering
- o New product design
- o Plant operating systems design

Version 2

CAREER SKILLS/KNOWLEDGE

- o Operations/materials/engineering
- o Purchasing operations
- o Cost controls/reductions
- o Global distribution/logistics
- o Heavy industry clients
- o Aircraft engine market
- o Engineering operations
- o Electrical/systems engineering
- o New product design
- o Plant operating systems design

- o Sales/marketing executive
- o International sales/markets
- o European relations
- o Strategic/marketing plans
- o Market share strategies
- o Major client development
- o Competitive maneuvering
- o Exchange rate strategies
- o Organizational development
- o Staff supervision/development

Career Achievements

More than any other single factor, your achievements (see Chapter 2) help sell you to prospective employers. Here you want to convey the message, "Since I directed these successful efforts, accomplished these management goals, resolved these major problems, and achieved these targeted results for my past companies, I can do the same for you."

Armed with the information assembled in Chapter 2 and the real-life samples from Chapters 6 and 7 (for reference throughout the writing process), you can proceed with confidence to write up the strongest possible list of major achievements. At this stage, you should not yet be concerned with prioritizing or judging whether ultimately to include or exclude any particular achievement. As you systematically go through your Chapter 2 notes and borrow from the samples in Chapters 6 and 7, you should write achievement statements for *all* your success stories. You can and will play editor later.

Consider the following examples of effective, interview-generating achievement statements developed from the type of raw success story notes formulated in Chapter 2.

EXAMPLE 1: SUCCESS STORY NOTES

Executive Vice-President Administration—Prototype Corporation: Direct annual budget—expense—of $65 million plus control additional $15 million in expenses allocated to other cost centers—equals total operating budget of $80 million; $80 million organization; direct 12 major functions including property management; profitably oversee 56 global locations—2 million sq. ft.—office, manufacturing, distribution, field offices. Annual lease expense/facility contracts—$50,000,000; most leased except some mfg. and R&D—contract negotiations critical. Manage assets—company owned—with asset value of approximately $100 million—located worldwide.

Written Achievement Statement Based on Notes

• As Executive Vice-President of Administration at Prototype Corporation, profitably directed an $80 million operation spanning 56 international locations representing over two million square feet: responsibilities executed in directing twelve major departments include the management of $100 million in company assets and the negotiation of $50 million in facility contracts related to properties located worldwide.

EXAMPLE 2: SUCCESS STORY NOTES

Milestones as Exec. V.P. of Administration: (1) Completed 300K sq. ft. research facility—months ahead of schedule—several million $ under budget of 52 million—8.4% under. (2) Also took lead in consolidating 15 locations/sites down to 4—primarily included research and administrative types of facilities; estimated annual savings of at least 5 million $—savings based on reducing sq. ft., rental $, and some infrastructure cost reductions. (3) Also consolidated & relocated—mfg. and branch offices; forcefully renegotiated leasehold agreements; eliminated duplication, improved communication, productivity, and efficiencies. Integrated and consolidated operations to gain efficiencies and productivity worldwide—total savings of $50 million over several years and significant increase in productivity.

Written Achievement Statements Based on Notes

- Generated multiyear savings of $50 million and accelerated productivity growth through a major consolidation of Prototype's manufacturing and branch office network: aggressively renegotiated expensive leasehold agreements, eliminated redundant operations, and instituted global efficiencies.
- Consolidated 15 research and administrative sites into four, generating an annual savings of $5 million for Prototype through reductions in square footage and rental expense; also directed the successful completion of an important 300,000 square foot research facility which was finished well ahead of schedule and several million dollars under budget.

EXAMPLE 3: SUCCESS STORY NOTES

Corporate Director of Admin. & Property Services; consolidated/colocated facilities: Examples: 29 warehouses consolidated into 4— annual savings $5.8 million; reduced HQ space by lease buyout— reduced from 90,000 square feet to 62,000 square feet = 30% reduction—saved $4.6 million over term of lease; negotiated buyout of redundant space—cost avoidance of $48,000 × 6 years—yield $250K cash in hand; developed facilities standards program for corporation that aids in identifying requirements, budget levels, and establishing space standards—yielded a 20% reduction in space requirements over previous planning methods—yielded annual savings of $3,400,000.

Written Achievement Statement Based on Notes

- Consolidated 29 Acme warehouses down to 4, generating annual savings of $5.8 million; saved $4.6 million by reducing headquarters space 30%; introduced uniform facility standards that reduced total space requirements 20%, saving another $3.4 million annually.

EXAMPLE 4: SUCCESS STORY NOTES

Vice President International Banking Group; comprises California and Europe; responsibilities: consolidate; asset sales; capital markets; project financing. Thrust of group—toward investment banking; emphasis—lucrative fees and deal-making; in 1994 generated $6.5 million revenue; 270 banking relationships; 1/3 or 90 at-risk; only lost 8; saved over 90% of the business that could have been lost; new transaction business; new corporate clients generated—international clients—Fortune 500 Domestic Deals.

Written Achievement Statement Based on Notes

• As Vice-President of the International Banking Group, produced revenue of $6.5 million in 1994 through aggressive client development and by saving 90% of the seriously at-risk accounts: accelerated the ROA by focusing on corporate finance, investment banking, and asset sales.

Note again the emphasis on using strong market-tested words and phrases to describe the accomplishments extracted from the success story notes. High-impact terms such as *turned around, accelerated, executed, generated, initiated, created, instituted, restructured, upgraded, negotiated, expanded, resolved* are critical components in expressing the importance and dimension of your accomplishments. Use the word list on pages 15 and 16 as a guide in selecting the strongest and most accurate terms to describe, define, and convey the impact of your accomplishments.

Refer to the following examples and the resumes in Chapters 6 and 7:

▶ Directly borrow and adapt for your own use the action words, phrases, and/or sentences from the real-life samples most closely resembling your field, background, and objectives.

▶ Modify the borrowed phrases and sentences to fit your own experience and background.

Following are examples of the Career Achievements sections of resume packages that generated quality interviews and successful career moves up to the six-figure-salary, senior vice-president level.

EXAMPLE 1: JOHN Q. SAMPLE

Career Move Achieved   Vice-President of a Fortune 500
high-tech company/industry leader

CAREER ACHIEVEMENTS

o As Corporate Director of Administration & Property Services, assumed a central role in Acme's turnaround to profitability: generated tens of millions of dollars in cost reductions and cash flow through aggressive property consolidations, upgraded services and procurement, and enforced management accountability.

o Promoted five grade levels during my last four years at ABC Company based on achieving all major P&L goals in directing the $19 million Corporate Administration and Property Management Department.

o Consolidated 29 Acme warehouses down to 4, generating annual savings of $5.8 million; saved $4.6 million by reducing corporate headquarters space 30%; introduced uniform facility standards which reduced total space requirements 20%, generating another $3.4 million in annual cost savings.

o As head of Acme's $230 million purchasing operation, introduced an aggressive multiple-sourcing program which improved the margins of two major product lines by 7% and 9% respectively.

o Overcame powerful organizational resistance to produce over $3 million cash and annual savings of $2.1 million by persuading the chairman to sell off Acme's corporate yacht.

o Generated annual cost savings of over $800,000 by installing a Novell network and upgrading ABC Company's distribution, travel, and other corporate services.

o Productively managed ABC Company's property holdings, achieving 97% occupancy of 800,000 square feet at premium rates; developed a sophisticated model which helped save $7 million on the cost of an out-of-control $40 million building project at ABC.

EXAMPLE 2: DAVID Q. SAMPLE

Career Move Achieved   Senior Vice-President of major
international financial institution

CAREER ACHIEVEMENTS

o As Vice-President of ABC's International Banking Group, produced revenue of $6.5 million in 1994 through aggressive client development and by saving 90% of the at-risk accounts: accelerated the ROA by focusing on corporate finance, investment banking, and asset sales.

o As Vice-President of Corporate Banking at ABC's Southern California headquarters, leveraged my international contacts to market corporate and capital market products generating $5 million in added net income: achieved 250% growth in fees from capital market products.

o Was recruited away and promoted by ABC to start and manage the new International Energy Group: established and directed the lending operation generating over $500 million in new client bookings in only 18 months with an ROA of over 1%.

o As head of Commercial Development in charge of ABC's International Energy Group, initiated and closed several profitable deals including a hard-to-close $600 million project with an international energy company: created and directed a syndicate of major international lenders.

o As Group Officer at Acme International Bank, established and directed operations of a new North American office: achieved and exceeded an aggressive operating plan generating new lending of $300 million and profitability in five months instead of the forecasted ten months.

EXAMPLE 3: MATTHEW Q. SAMPLE
(Over-50 Client)

Career Move Achieved   Executive position within the
transportation industry

<u>CAREER ACHIEVEMENTS</u>

o Upon promotion to Southwestern Sales Director, accelerated sales productivity and major account development achieving a critically needed 35% growth in sales at a pivotal time for the struggling Acme Corporation, which had lost huge market shares due to poor product pricing strategies: achieved highest sales growth and won a major nationwide sales award.

o As Southeastern Sales Director for a troubled division of Acme, turned around profitability becoming the top-ranked Sales Director in the division: instituted aggressive market expansion, national account programs, and strategic planning increasing revenue from $5 million to $23 million in four years; converted a $3 million loss into a $3 million profit.

o Upon being promoted to Product Manager at Acme, created a product management system which accelerated the decision-making process for the pricing, promotion, and distribution of products: increased profits 30% through saturation marketing to growth industries.

o Based on a track record of achievements in sales management and strategic planning, was recruited by corporate headquarters to manage a major group's business evaluation function as part of the restructuring of the strategic planning process: improved declining ROIs by upgrading the pricing structure; saved tens-of-millions of dollars by demonstrating the marginal payback of proposed expenditures.

o Upon promotion to Business Planning Director, orchestrated a multibillion-dollar asset reallocation program which helped triple profits within five years: reallocated over a billion dollars of production assets to growth products; proposed a half-billion-dollar plant conversion which was implemented at half the cost of constructing a new plant.

o Negotiated and closed the leveraged buyout of a $3 million service business formerly owned by the Avery Company: developed a solid business plan which was successfully marketed to major financial institutions with whom I negotiated over a million dollars in financing.

o As owner of a Texas-based venture, turned around sales and operations overcoming most roadblocks except the company's lack of liquidity in a recessionary economy: increased sales 60% in 15 months by upgrading service and promotional programs; restructured cash management; reduced aged receivables 75%; negotiated a 20% reduction in product costs; achieved a 60% increase in productivity.

EXAMPLE 4: WILLIAM Q. SAMPLE
(Over-50 Client)

Career Move Achieved   General Management position with
European-based Company

CAREER ACHIEVEMENTS

o Earned multiple promotions up to Executive Vice-President of Sales at a U.S. Division of Acme International, one of Europe's largest industrial corporations: created a highly productive sales organization and achieved a fivefold increase in revenue turning the U.S. Division into a $20 million business which now accounts for almost 40% of the subsidiary's global sales.

o In spite of high turnover and chronically unfavorable exchange rates, which adversely impacted the U.S. Division's pricing structure, generated a 500% increase in Acme's customer base through an accelerated client development program which emphasized quality and service to offset the unfavorable pricing.

o In spite of global competition, closed multimillion-dollar clients including Western Electric, AT&T, Boeing, and John Deere: accelerated the AT&T account from zero to $9 million representing half of total sales; generated a ninefold sales increase from the Harvester Division of John Deere; produced an eightfold increase in the Western Electric and Boeing accounts.

o Significantly reduced overhead and logistics expenses and all but eliminated aged receivables and write-offs by creating and enforcing conservative credit policies at Acme; in order to meet scheduled delivery dates through on-time shipments from Europe, also established a first-rate logistics function.

o Earned several promotions up to Director within the Engineering Department of a Florida-based division of Essex Corporation: directed high-quality product designs, upgraded operating systems critical to the production process, and effectively troubleshot the complex power supply systems.

Once you have completed the preceding process, you will probably have written out somewhere between 8 and 15 bulleted accomplishment/achievement statements depending on your years and breadth of experience. You can now go through and edit, rework, and reword the bulleted sentences, combine related achievements wherever appropriate and eliminate less important achievements as you prioritize and reorder the achievements based on their relative importance.

In executing the editing process, remember to borrow and adapt key words, phrases, and/or sentences from the proven, marketing-driven samples in Chapters 6 and 7. Develop and pattern your own achievement statements based on these sample resume packages that generated quality interviews and job offers for clients.

PAGE TWO

Career Experience

This section is (normally) a reverse chronological listing of the companies/organizations where you have been employed. This information appears on page two of your combination functional (page one: Skills and Achievements sections) and chronological resume.

Use your Chapter 3 notes to record dates of employment, job titles, job descriptions, relevant military experience, and relevant education/training/credentials not included on page one. Be sure to augment your job descriptions with any accomplishments not designated for inclusion in the CAREER ACHIEVEMENTS section.

Following (for your adaptation) are real-life examples of the experience sections of resumes that generated interviews leading to successful career moves. Also refer to Chapters 6 and 7 for a cross section of sample resumes and cover letters representing a full complement of fields, backgrounds, and objectives.

EXAMPLE 1: JOHN Q. SAMPLE

CAREER EXPERIENCE

ACME CORPORATION, Any Town, CA   3/88–Present

Corporate Director of Administration & Property Services
Direct the overall management, planning, site selection, lease negotiations, consolidations, and disposition for property totaling two million square feet. Additionally direct the $230 million purchasing operation and all corporate administrative services.

ABC COMPANY, Any Town, CA   6/80–3/88

Director of Services & Property   3/85–3/88
Directed services with a staff of 63 and a budget of $19 million: included property management, purchasing, communications, systems, mail, and office equipment placement and maintenance. Reviewed and approved all facilities and construction contracts. Audited almost $100 million in operating expense budgets.

Manager of Administration   2/83–3/85
Developed policies and procedures, negotiated property transactions, and created a model which turned around a $40 million building project.

Senior Facilities Consultant   8/81–2/83
Developed well-received proposals that resulted in the creation of a $12 million Facilities Group.

Senior Consultant   6/80–8/81
Introduced the much needed zero-based budgeting concept to seven major operations.

REFERENCES PROVIDED UPON REQUEST

EXAMPLE 2: DAVID Q. SAMPLE

CAREER EXPERIENCE

ABC BANK, Any Town, CA   3/88–Present

INTERNATIONAL BANKING GROUP, Any Town, CA   2/91–Present

Vice-President
Responsible for major account development emphasizing high-margin corporate finance and investment banking: acquisitions, recapitalization, and collateralized financing. Upgraded asset quality by addressing and restructuring below-par debt.

CORPORATE BANKING, Any Town, CA   3/88–2/91

Vice-President
Created and marketed corporate and capital market products and services to global clients.

ACME INTERNATIONAL BANK, Any Town, Europe   6/85–3/88

Group Officer (Assistant Vice-President), Any Town, British Columbia   4/87–3/88
Managed start-up of a new operation: directed staffing, property selection, facility planning, contract negotiations, and purchasing. Also developed marketing policies and operating procedures.

Officer, Any Town, CA   5/86–4/87
Accelerated global account development quadrupling pre-tax net income to over $4 million.

Officer, Any Town, Europe   6/85–5/86
Established a Credit Group generating over $2 million in fees from new business development.

REFERENCES PROVIDED UPON REQUEST

EXAMPLE 3: MATTHEW Q. SAMPLE

CAREER EXPERIENCE

ACME CORPORATION, Any City, TX   1976–1992

Business Planning Director—XYZ Division   1989–1992
Designated to orchestrate the development of corporate strategies and upgrade the planning process.

Business Evaluation Director—ABC Division   1986–1989
Designated to reorganize and turn around strategic planning.

Southwestern Sales Director—ABC Division   1982–1986
Developed and directed a high-producing sales team responsible for national account development.

Product Manager—XYZ Division   1978–1982
Created a product management system which accelerated the decision-making process for the pricing, promotion, and distribution of products.

Southeastern Sales Director—XYZ Division   1977–1978
Implemented a Major Account Program; expanded into growth markets; instituted effective competitor data-gathering procedures; created Division's first comprehensive strategic plan.

Senior Marketing Analyst   1976–1977
Executed comprehensive feasibility studies which resulted in the formation of critically needed account development departments. Developed a well-received business plan for a beleaguered venture.

ESSEX COMPANY, Any City, TX   1992–1994

Senior Consultant
Determined the feasibility of a client's expansion into major European markets: executed comprehensive product demand and competitive studies as a basis for decision-making.

SERVICE VENTURE, Any City, TX   1994–Present

Founder: Directed Marketing, Advertising, Sales, Operations, Finance, and Customer Service.

INTERNATIONAL: Traveled throughout South America and Europe
LANGUAGES: Fluent French, Italian, and Spanish

EXAMPLE 4: WILLIAM Q. SAMPLE

CAREER EXPERIENCE

ACME INTERNATIONAL CORPORATION, Any Town, NJ   1984–Present

Executive Vice-President of Sales   1987–Present
Direct the Sales Organization with responsibility for direct sales, marketing, strategic planning, client development, import operations, logistics, distribution, and credit.

Vice-President of Sales   1984–1987
Directed sales, marketing, strategic planning, and related functions.

ESSEX CORPORATION, Any Town, FL   1975–1984

Director of Engineering   1980–1984
Earned several promotions based on engineering achievements in directing low-tolerance design and systems engineering projects. Also successfully planned and executed high-visibility manufacturing projects.

MILITARY EXPERIENCE

European Military: Honorably Discharged

Affiliations: Society of U.S. Engineers; Production Engineers of the Northeast
Citizenship: U.S. Citizen

REFERENCES AVAILABLE UPON REQUEST

Note that the preceding page two Experience Sections are what most people prepare and use as their complete resume. The resultant failure aggressively and succinctly to focus on and highlight your marketable skills and achievements is the single biggest contributor to the nationwide 99% rejection rate. While the chronological Experience section should be included to complete the informational database (and satisfy bureaucratic tendencies to track employment dates), you will not, for the most part, be evaluated and judged based on your ability to write the detailed job descriptions that fill most resumes. You will rather be evaluated and judged on your ability to communicate and highlight your past skills and accomplishments (just as you have done here) as key indicators of your potential to achieve similar bottom-line results for your future employer.

EDITING THE RESUME

Now that the resume package is complete, you may decide to conduct a final review and editing so that you can make editorial changes, reorganize, and refine your total resume package. During the final editing process, continue to borrow freely and to adapt key words, phrases, and/or sentences from the proven, marketing-driven samples in Chapters 6 and 7. Develop and pattern your own achievement statements based on these resume packages that generated quality interviews and job offers for clients.

Use patience and care because the resume combined with the cover letter (discussed in Chapter 5) is the primary, and often only, means of communicating to potential employers and creating your first impression. Remember the old, but nonetheless true, cliche: "You will NOT get a second chance to create a first impression."

BRINGING IT ALL TOGETHER

Following are real-life examples of complete resume packages (assembled from the preceding examples) that generated quality interviews and successful career moves up to the senior vice-president level and six-figure salary range.

Note that these examples include, for your optional application, my trademark "headers" which appear on the same line as your name and provide the reader with a brief two- to five-word description of your background/discipline. These headers have been well-received by the marketplace.

EXAMPLE 1

JOHN Q. SAMPLE   **Administration/Finance Executive**

123 Any Street, Any City, CA XXXXX (619) 555-1234

B.S.   Honors   Finance   Georgetown University   1980

CAREER SKILLS/KNOWLEDGE

o Finance/administration management
o General management
o Strategic/operational planning
o General/administrative services
o Financial planning & analysis
o Procurement operations
o Facilities/telecommunications
o Training operations
o Logistics services
o Global transportation

o Property management
o Development/construction
o Occupancy growth strategies
o Premium rate strategies
o Consolidation strategies
o Lease management/negotiations
o Site selection/space planning
o Budgeting/accountability
o Government regulations
o Environmental guidelines

CAREER ACHIEVEMENTS

o As Corporate Director of Administration & Property Services, assumed a central role in Acme's turnaround to profitability: generated tens of millions of dollars in cost reductions and cash flow through aggressive property consolidations, upgraded services and procurement, and enforced management accountability.

o Promoted five grade levels during my last four years at ABC Company based on achieving all major P&L goals in directing the $19 million Corporate Administration and Property Management Department.

o Consolidated 29 Acme warehouses down to 4, generating annual savings of $5.8 million; saved $4.6 million by reducing corporate headquarters space 30%; introduced uniform facility standards which reduced total space requirements 20%, generating another $3.4 million in annual cost savings.

o As head of Acme's $230 million purchasing operation, introduced an aggressive multiple-sourcing program which improved the margins of two major product lines by 7% and 9% respectively.

o Overcame powerful organizational resistance to produce over $3 million cash and annual savings of $2.1 million by persuading the chairman to sell off Acme's corporate yacht.

o Generated annual cost savings of over $800,000 by installing a Novell network and upgrading ABC Company's distribution, travel, and other corporate services.

o Productively managed ABC Company's property holdings, achieving 97% occupancy of 800,000 square feet at premium rates; developed a sophisticated model which helped save $7 million on the cost of an out-of-control $40 million building project at ABC.

JOHN Q. SAMPLE

CAREER EXPERIENCE

ACME CORPORATION, Any Town, CA   3/88–Present

Corporate Director of Administration & Property Services
Direct the overall management, planning, site selection, lease negotiations, consolidations, and disposition for property totaling two million square feet. Additionally direct the $230 million purchasing operation and all corporate administrative services.

ABC COMPANY, Any Town, CA   6/80–3/88

Director of Services & Property   3/85–3/88
Directed services with a staff of 63 and a budget of $19 million: included property management, purchasing, communications, systems, mail, and office equipment placement and maintenance. Reviewed and approved all facilities and construction contracts. Audited almost $100 million in operating expense budgets.

Manager of Administration   2/83–3/85
Developed policies and procedures, negotiated property transactions, and created a model which turned around a $40 million building project.

Senior Facilities Consultant   8/81–2/83
Developed well-received proposals that resulted in the creation of a $12 million Facilities Group.

Senior Consultant   6/80–8/81
Introduced the much needed zero-based budgeting concept to seven major operations.

REFERENCES PROVIDED UPON REQUEST

EXAMPLE 2

DAVID Q. SAMPLE   **International Sales/Finance**

123 Any Street, Any City, CA XXXXX (619) 555-1234

M.B.A.	Honors	University of Paris Graduate School of Business	1985

International: Bilingual French and English; solid knowledge of Mideastern languages; traveled to over 60 nations

Certifications: Commercial Pilot's License; Black Belt Karate; Championship Skier

CAREER SKILLS/KNOWLEDGE

o Marketing/sales executive
o General management
o Start-up operations
o Major client development
o Competitive maneuvering
o Expansion/turnaround strategies
o Revenue/profit growth
o Organizational development

o Financial executive
o International banking
o Investment banking
o Corporate/capital markets
o Acquisitions/joint ventures
o Subsidiary recapitalization
o Project financing/syndicates
o Trade financing/foreign exchange

CAREER ACHIEVEMENTS

o As Vice-President of ABC's International Banking Group, produced revenue of $6.5 million in 1994 through aggressive client development and by saving 90% of the at-risk accounts: accelerated the ROA by focusing on corporate finance, investment banking, and asset sales.

o As Vice-President of Corporate Banking at ABC's Southern California headquarters, leveraged my international contacts to market corporate and capital market products generating $5 million in added net income: achieved 250% growth in fees from capital market products.

o Was recruited away and promoted by ABC to start and manage the new International Energy Group: established and directed the lending operation generating over $500 million in new client bookings in only 18 months with an ROA of over 1%.

o As head of Commercial Development in charge of ABC's International Energy Group, initiated and closed several profitable deals including a hard-to-close $600 million project with an international energy company: created and directed a syndicate of major international lenders.

o As Group Officer at Acme International Bank, established and directed operations of a new North American office: achieved and exceeded an aggressive operating plan generating new lending of $300 million and profitability in five months instead of the forecasted ten months.

DAVID Q. SAMPLE

CAREER EXPERIENCE

ABC BANK, Any Town, CA   3/88–Present

INTERNATIONAL BANKING GROUP, Any Town, CA   2/91–Present

Vice-President
Responsible for major account development emphasizing high-margin corporate finance and investment banking: acquisitions, recapitalization, and collateralized financing. Upgraded asset quality by addressing and restructuring below-par debt.

CORPORATE BANKING, Any Town, CA   3/88–2/91

Vice-President
Created and marketed corporate and capital market products and services to global clients.

ACME INTERNATIONAL BANK, Any Town, Europe   6/85–3/88

Group Officer (Assistant Vice-President), Any Town, British Columbia   4/87–3/88
Managed start-up of a new operation: directed staffing, property selection, facility planning, contract negotiations, and purchasing. Also developed marketing policies and operating procedures.

Officer, Any Town, CA   5/86–4/87
Accelerated global account development quadrupling pre-tax net income to over $4 million.

Officer, Any Town, Europe   6/85–5/86
Established a Credit Group generating over $2 million in fees from new business development.

REFERENCES PROVIDED UPON REQUEST

EXAMPLE 3

MATTHEW Q. SAMPLE   **Product Management/Strategic Planning/Sales**

123 Any Street, Any Town, TX XXXXX (214) 555-1234

M.B.A.	Finance/Marketing	University of Virginia	1976
B.S.	Statistics	UCLA	1974

CAREER SKILLS/KNOWLEDGE

- o Marketing/sales management
- o Revenue/profit turnaround
- o Product management/market development
- o National accounts programs
- o Sales productivity growth
- o Competitor intelligence systems
- o Business ownership/leveraged buyouts
- o Advertising/promotions
- o Operations turnaround

- o Strategic planning
- o Business plans/market research
- o Market growth/segmentation
- o ROI growth strategies
- o Profit/investment optimization
- o Economic modeling/pricing
- o Supply/demand analysis
- o Finance/controller operations
- o Cash-flow/financing/bank relations

CAREER ACHIEVEMENTS

o Upon promotion to Southwestern Sales Director, accelerated sales productivity and major account development achieving a critically needed 35% growth in sales at a pivotal time for the struggling Acme Corporation, which had lost huge market shares due to poor product pricing strategies: achieved highest sales growth and won a major nationwide sales award.

o As Southeastern Sales Director for a troubled division of Acme, turned around profitability becoming the top-ranked Sales Director in the division: instituted aggressive market expansion, national account programs, and strategic planning increasing revenue from $5 million to $23 million in four years; converted a $3 million loss into a $3 million profit.

o Upon being promoted to Product Manager at Acme, created a product management system which accelerated the decision-making process for the pricing, promotion, and distribution of products: increased profits 30% through saturation marketing to growth industries.

o Based on a track record of achievements in sales management and strategic planning, was recruited by corporate headquarters to manage a major group's business evaluation function as part of the restructuring of the strategic planning process: improved declining ROIs by upgrading the pricing structure; saved tens-of-millions of dollars by demonstrating the marginal payback of proposed expenditures.

o Upon promotion to Business Planning Director, orchestrated a multibillion-dollar asset reallocation program which helped triple profits within five years: reallocated over a billion dollars of production assets to growth products; proposed a half-billion-dollar plant conversion which was implemented at half the cost of constructing a new plant.

o Negotiated and closed the leveraged buyout of a $3 million service business formerly owned by the Avery Company: developed a solid business plan which was successfully marketed to major financial institutions with whom I negotiated over a million dollars in financing.

o As owner of a Texas-based venture, turned around sales and operations overcoming most roadblocks except the company's lack of liquidity in a recessionary economy: increased sales 60% in 15 months by upgrading service and promotional programs; restructured cash management; reduced aged receivables 75%; negotiated a 20% reduction in product costs; achieved a 60% increase in productivity.

MATTHEW Q. SAMPLE   Page 2

CAREER EXPERIENCE

ACME CORPORATION, Any City, TX   1976–1992

Business Planning Director—XYZ Division   1989–1992
Designated to orchestrate the development of corporate strategies and upgrade the planning process.

Business Evaluation Director—ABC Division   1986–1989
Designated to reorganize and turn around strategic planning.

Southwestern Sales Director—ABC Division   1982–1986
Developed and directed a high-producing sales team responsible for national account development.

Product Manager—XYZ Division   1978–1982
Created a product management system which accelerated the decision-making process for the pricing, promotion, and distribution of products.

Southeastern Sales Director—XYZ Division   1977–1978
Implemented a Major Account Program; expanded into growth markets; instituted effective competitor data-gathering procedures; created Division's first comprehensive strategic plan.

Senior Marketing Analyst   1976–1977
Executed comprehensive feasibility studies which resulted in the formation of critically needed account development departments. Developed a well-received business plan for a beleaguered venture.

ESSEX COMPANY, Any City, TX   1992–1994

Senior Consultant
Determined the feasibility of a client's expansion into major European markets: executed comprehensive product demand and competitive studies as a basis for decision-making.

SERVICE VENTURE, Any City, TX   1994–Present

Founder: Directed Marketing, Advertising, Sales, Operations, Finance, and Customer Service.

INTERNATIONAL: Traveled throughout South America and Europe
LANGUAGES: Fluent French, Italian, and Spanish

EXAMPLE 4

WILLIAM Q. SAMPLE   **International Sales Executive**

123 Any Street Address, Any Town, NJ XXXXX (201) 555-1234

B.S.	Electrical Engineering	International University	Comprehensive Six-Year Program
B.A.	Business Administration	Lehman College	Managerial Studies

International: Traveled throughout Europe, Asia, South America, and North America
Languages: Fluent French and Spanish

CAREER SKILLS/KNOWLEDGE

- o Sales/marketing executive
- o International sales/markets
- o European relations
- o Strategic/marketing plans
- o Market share strategies
- o Major client development
- o Competitive maneuvering
- o Exchange rate strategies
- o Organizational development
- o Staff supervision/development

- o Operations/materials/engineering
- o Purchasing operations
- o Cost controls/reductions
- o Global distribution/logistics
- o Heavy industry clients
- o Aircraft engine market
- o Engineering operations
- o Electrical/systems engineering
- o New product design
- o Plant operating systems design

CAREER ACHIEVEMENTS

o Earned multiple promotions up to Executive Vice-President of Sales at a U.S. Division of Acme International, one of Europe's largest industrial corporations: created a highly productive sales organization and achieved a fivefold increase in revenue turning the U.S. Division into a $20 million business which now accounts for almost 40% of the subsidiary's global sales.

o In spite of high turnover and chronically unfavorable exchange rates, which adversely impacted the U.S. Division's pricing structure, generated a 500% increase in Acme's customer base through an accelerated client development program which emphasized quality and service to offset the unfavorable pricing.

o In spite of global competition, closed multimillion-dollar clients including Western Electric, AT&T, Boeing, and John Deere: accelerated the AT&T account from zero to $9 million representing half of total sales; generated a ninefold sales increase from the Harvester Division of John Deere; produced an eightfold increase in the Western Electric and Boeing accounts.

o Significantly reduced overhead and logistics expenses and all but eliminated aged receivables and write-offs by creating and enforcing conservative credit policies at Acme; in order to meet scheduled delivery dates through on-time shipments from Europe, also established a first-rate logistics function.

o Earned several promotions up to Director within the Engineering Department of a Florida-based division of Essex Corporation: directed high-quality product designs, upgraded operating systems critical to the production process and effectively troubleshooted the complex power supply systems.

CAREER EXPERIENCE

ACME INTERNATIONAL CORPORATION, Any Town, NJ   1984–Present

Executive Vice-President of Sales   1987–Present
Direct the Sales Organization with responsibility for direct sales, marketing, strategic planning, client development, import operations, logistics, distribution, and credit.

Vice-President of Sales   1984–1987
Directed sales, marketing, strategic planning, and related functions.

ESSEX CORPORATION, Any Town, FL   1975–1984

Director of Engineering   1980–1984
Earned several promotions based on engineering achievements in directing low-tolerance design and systems engineering projects. Also successfully planned and executed high-visibility manufacturing projects.

MILITARY EXPERIENCE

European Military: Honorably Discharged

Affiliations: Society of U.S. Engineers; Production Engineers of the Northeast
Citizenship: U.S. Citizen

REFERENCES AVAILABLE UPON REQUEST

5

Developing and Writing Your Marketing Cover Letter

THE STRATEGIC MARKETING DOCUMENT

As discussed and detailed in previous chapters, the marketing cover letter combined with a hard-hitting resume is the most critical document that you will produce. Since you have only 15 to 30 seconds of the reviewer's time to market yourself and make your case, if you don't sell the reader with the cover letter, you will very likely not sell the reader at all.

Based on extensive feedback directly from the marketplace and from executive-level clients who have repeatedly stated, "The cover letter got me the interview," I have firmly concluded that the failure to develop a strong, creative achievement and skills-oriented letter results in a missed opportunity.

Unlike the vast majority of resume books on the market, this workbook treats the cover letter and resume as *coequal* and *inseparable* components of the total marketing package. While other books frequently highlight the importance of the letter, they often undermine this importance by merely tacking on a chapter near the end of the book with a few mediocre-to-poor sample letters, *none* of which are related to the sample resumes.

By developing the type of market-tested and proven letters outlined in this chapter and demonstrated through the more than 60 case histories contained in this book, you give yourself the same competitive edge that led to my clients' successful career moves into international growth companies as well as emerging mid-size and start-up companies.

DEVELOPING THE COVER LETTER TEXT

While developing the text of the letter, refer to the sample letters in Chapters 6 and 7, which provide a full complement of fields, backgrounds, and objectives.

- ▶ Directly borrow and adapt for your own use key words, phrases, and/or sentences from the real-life samples most closely resembling your field, background, and objectives.
- ▶ Modify the borrowed phrases and sentences to fit your own experiences and background.

The Introductory Paragraph: A Modular Approach

The introductory paragraph must "grab" the reader to make him or her want to read further. It should include a fact-oriented, hard-hitting capsule overview of your achievements and skills extracted from your already-developed resume.

By *substituting* words and phrases that apply to *you and your experience* for the words in parentheses, you can modify the following introductory paragraphs to fit your own situation. Once you have initially modified the paragraph, then insert additional changes *to reflect your own personality and style*—make sure your final version fits you.

The following modular paragraphs were excerpted from letters that generated quality interviews and job offers:

As a central figure in (Acme Corporation's massive restructuring), I applied executive skills in (finance), (administration), (property management), and (purchasing) to (facilitate Acme's turnaround to profitability). I likewise produced (multimillion-dollar profits for the ABC Company) through (productive management of its administration and property management services) receiving (accelerated promotions up to Director of a $19 million operation).

I have combined (a top business degree, global experience), and executive skills in (sales), (finance), (banking), and (general management) to (establish and direct new operations which have generated millions in revenue for well-respected international companies). Bottom-line contributions to profit have been rewarded with (accelerated promotions, job security, and a six-figure salary package).

I have combined (a top school M.B.A.) with executive skills in (marketing), (sales management), (product management), (strategic planning), and (general management) to (orchestrate a leveraged buyout), (head up a $3 million business), (strategically reposition troubled operations), and (turn around and accelerate sales for weak divisions of the Acme Corporation).

As (Executive Vice President of Sales for the U.S. Division of a European-based corporation), I have applied proficient skills in (international sales), (marketing), (client development), and (operations) to (outmaneuver the competition), (deal with volatile exchange rates), (accelerate growth of the corporate client base), and (achieve a five-fold increase in sales)—(a revenue level that now accounts for 40% of worldwide sales).

I have developed and applied skills in (sales), (marketing), and (operations) to (successfully sell products), (direct plant operations), (generate cost reductions), (achieve quotas), and (upgrade product quality) for (two Seattle-based companies). Results achieved have been rewarded with (promotions and substantial pay raises).

I have (profitably) applied skills in (sales), (marketing), (client development), (real estate brokerage), and (property management) to (sell $10 million worth of product), (earn Million-Dollar-Club status), (profitably manage several apartment buildings), and (generate $5 million in sales in a two-year period).

I have applied skills in (sales), (marketing), (operations), and (project management) to (start up a multimillion-dollar electronics company), (generate half of its total sales), (expand the client base of another high-tech company), and (coordinate total administration of a $300 million project for a major electronics firm).

I have formulated and executed expert (sales and marketing strategies) to (outmaneuver the competition), (penetrate new markets), and (generate record sales in the Los Angeles marketplace) during (the past 15 years with a subsidiary of Acme Industries). This has been rewarded with (up to a six-figure income) and (number one ranking nationally).

The Letter's Second Paragraph: A Modular Approach

In the second paragraph, you tell the reader why you are writing to the company/firm. Use the same basic approach that you used to develop the introductory paragraph. By substituting words and phrases that apply to you and your experience for the words in parentheses, you can modify the following paragraphs to fit your own situation. Once you have initially modified the paragraph, insert additional changes *to reflect your own personality and style*—make sure your final version fits you.

Following are modular paragraphs from letters that achieved quality interviews and job offers:

I am presenting for your review my skills, achievements, and (talent for accelerating profit margins and turning around unprofitable organizations) so that we can discuss my joining _____ as a member of your (senior management) team.

I am bringing to your attention my skills, achievements, (strategic brainpower), (global network), and (talent for exceeding profit goals under negative economic conditions) so that we can discuss my joining _____ as a member of your (senior management) team.

I am bringing to your attention my skills, achievements, (talent for stimulating sales productivity), and (ability to achieve bottom-line results under the most intense pressure) so that we can discuss my joining _____ as a member of your (senior sales management) team.

I am presenting for your review my skills, achievements, (technical degree), (global contacts), and (talent for creating productive sales forces and achieving aggressive revenue and profit goals) so that we can discuss my joining _____ as a member of your (senior sales management) team.

I am bringing to your attention my skills, achievements, (high energy), (talent for improving job candidate quality), and (track record of cost reductions) so that we can discuss my joining _____ as a member of your (HR Management) Team.

I am bringing to your attention my skills, achievements, (nationwide network of electronics industry contacts), and (ability to produce results under crisis management conditions) so that we can discuss my joining _____ as a member of your (R&D Management) Team.

I am bringing to your attention my skills, achievements, (leasing industry expertise), and (talent for generating bottom-line results within problem operations) so that we can discuss my joining _____ as a member of your (management) team.

Writing the Second Paragraph Objective Statements

Your objective statements should not be so restrictive that you are easily eliminated from contention for alternative job opportunities. For example, you can use generic or organizational objectives as alternatives to job titles:

> . . . so that we can discuss my joining the Acme Corporation as a member of your
> Senior Management team.
> General Management team.
> Sales/Marketing Management team.
> Financial or Treasury Management team.
> Operations/Manufacturing Management team.
> Research & Development Management team.
> Human Resources Management team.
> Engineering Management team.

It is not unusual for people realistically and legitimately to define as many as three to five different objectives. This is an excellent way to broaden your options and create as many different job opportunities as possible by marketing yourself toward multiple objectives.

Multiple objectives require the creation and use of multiple objective statements (and multiple versions of the cover letter and resume package) for marketing and dissemination to multiple functional contacts within the corporate structure.

The Letter's Third Paragraph

To develop the letter's third paragraph, simply select and extract some of the major bulleted achievements directly from the already-developed resume to reinforce and support the achievements summarized in the first paragraph. The deliberate and necessary redundancy created by including bulleted achievement statements in both the cover letter and resume has met with unqualified success in the marketplace.

The all-important cover letter must be developed as a stand-alone document based on the assumption that the reader will only review the letter—remember that you only get 15 to 30 seconds to make your case; therefore, the reader may well not get past the letter. To be a stand-alone document, the cover letter must necessarily contain key information extracted from and deliberately redundant with the resume.

The success of my clients in the marketplace has proven that intelligent decision makers are impressed by candidates who create comprehensive stand-alone letters that contain vital information excerpted from the resume. Such letters send a positive message to the reader that the candidate is a good communicator who understands and respects the reader's limited review time.

Following are examples of third paragraphs from letters that generated quality interviews and job offers:

EXAMPLE 1: JOHN Q. SAMPLE

Results achieved to date include:

o Promoted five grade levels during my last four years at ABC Company based on achieving all major P&L goals in directing the $19 million Corporate Administration and Property Management Department.

o As Acme's Corporate Director of Administration & Property Services, generated tens of millions of dollars in cost reductions and cash flow through aggressive property consolidations, upgraded services and procurement, and enforced management accountability.

o Consolidated 29 Acme warehouses down to 4, generating annual savings of $5.8 million; saved $4.6 million by reducing corporate headquarters space 30%; introduced uniform facility standards which reduced total space requirements 20%, generating another $3.4 million in annual cost savings.

o As head of Acme's $230 million purchasing operation, introduced an aggressive multiple-sourcing program which improved the margins of two major product lines by 7% and 9% respectively.

o Productively managed ABC Company's property holdings, achieving 97% occupancy of 800,000 square feet at premium rates; developed a sophisticated model which helped save $7 million on the cost of an out-of-control $40 million building project at ABC.

EXAMPLE 2: DAVID Q. SAMPLE

Major accomplishments to date include:

o As Vice-President of ABC's International Banking Group, produced revenue of $6.5 million in 1994 through aggressive client development and by saving 90% of the seriously at-risk accounts: accelerated the ROA by focusing on corporate finance, investment banking, and asset sales.

o As Vice-President of Corporate Banking at ABC's Southern California headquarters, leveraged my international contacts to market corporate and capital market products generating $5 million in added net income: achieved 250% growth in fees from capital market products.

o Was recruited away and promoted by ABC to start and manage the new International Energy Group: established and directed the lending operation generating over $500 million in new client bookings in only 18 months with an ROA of over 1%.

o As head of Commercial Development in charge of ABC's International Energy Group, initiated and closed several profitable deals including a hard-to-close $600 million project with an international energy company: created and directed a syndicate of major international lenders.

EXAMPLE 3: MATTHEW Q. SAMPLE

Results achieved to date include:

o Upon promotion to Southwestern Sales Director, accelerated sales productivity and major account development achieving a critically needed 35% growth in sales at a pivotal time for the struggling Acme Corporation, which had lost huge market shares due to poor product pricing strategies: achieved highest sales growth and won a major nationwide sales award.

o As Southeastern Sales Director for a troubled division of Acme, turned around profitability becoming the top-ranked Sales Director in the division: instituted aggressive market expansion, national account programs, and strategic planning increasing revenue from $5 million to $23 million in four years; converted a $3 million loss into a $3 million profit.

o Based on a track record of achievements in sales management and strategic planning, was recruited by corporate headquarters to manage a major group's business evaluation function as part of the restructuring of the strategic planning process: improved declining ROIs by upgrading the pricing structure; saved tens-of-millions of dollars by demonstrating the marginal payback of proposed expenditures.

o Negotiated and closed the leveraged buyout of a $3 million service business formerly owned by the Avery Company: developed a solid business plan which was successfully marketed to major financial institutions with whom I negotiated over a million dollars in financing.

o As owner of a Texas-based venture, turned around sales and operations overcoming most roadblocks except the company's lack of liquidity in a recessionary economy: increased sales 60% in 15 months by upgrading service and promotional programs; restructured cash management; reduced aged receivables 75%; negotiated a 20% reduction in product costs; achieved a 60% increase in productivity.

EXAMPLE 4: WILLIAM Q. SAMPLE

Results achieved during the past decade with Acme International include:

o Earned multiple promotions up to Executive Vice-President of Sales at a U.S. Division of Acme International, one of Europe's largest industrial corporations: created a highly productive sales organization and achieved a fivefold increase in revenue turning the U.S. Division into a $20 million business which now accounts for almost 40% of the subsidiary's global sales.

o In spite of high turnover and chronically unfavorable exchange rates, which adversely impacted the U.S. Division's pricing structure, generated a 500% increase in Acme's customer base through an accelerated client development program which emphasized quality and service to offset the unfavorable pricing.

o In spite of global competition, closed multimillion-dollar clients including Western Electric, AT&T, Boeing, and John Deere: accelerated the AT&T account from zero to $9 million representing half of total sales; generated a ninefold sales increase from the Harvester Division of John Deere; produced an eightfold increase in the Western Electric and Boeing accounts.

o Significantly reduced overhead and logistics expenses and all but eliminated aged receivables and write-offs by creating and enforcing conservative credit policies at Acme; in order to meet scheduled delivery dates through on-time shipments from Europe, also established a first-rate logistics function.

The Closing Paragraph

The letter should end with an affirmative statement indicating that you would be interested in discussing how you might be able to contribute to the future success of the company.

Examples of closing paragraphs that worked:

I look forward to meeting and discussing how I can help accelerate or turn around your company's revenue and profit growth.

It should be mutually beneficial to meet and assess how I can help accelerate or turn around revenue and profit growth contributing to your company's future success.

I will work hard to achieve bottom-line results and look forward to discussing how I can contribute to your company's future success.

I look forward to discussing how I can help accelerate or turn around the performance of your international operations.

I will work hard to achieve sales objectives and look forward to discussing how I can contribute to your company's future success.

It should be to our mutual benefit to meet and determine how I can contribute to your company's future profitability.

It should be to our mutual benefit to meet and determine how I can help accelerate or turn around company performance, contributing to your future success.

Should we reach a mutually beneficial agreement, I will work hard to help accelerate or turn around your company's international operations and overall operating performance.

I look forward to discussing how I can contribute to your company's future success.

Following are real-life examples of complete cover letters (assembled from the preceding examples) that generated quality interviews and successful career moves up to the senior vice-president level and six-figure salary range.

Note that these examples include, for your optional application, my trademark "headers" which appear on the same line as your name and provide the reader with a brief two- to five-word description of your background/discipline. These headers have been well-received by the marketplace.

EXAMPLE 1

JOHN Q. SAMPLE   **Administration/Finance Executive**

123 Any Street, Any City, CA XXXXX (619) 555-1234

Contact Name   Date
Title
Company
Address
City, State Zip

Dear Mr/Ms. _____:

As a central figure in Acme Corporation's massive restructuring, I applied executive skills in finance, administration, property management, and purchasing to facilitate Acme's turnaround to profitability. I likewise produced multimillion-dollar profits for the ABC Company through productive management of its administration and property management services, receiving accelerated promotions to Director of a $19 million operation.

I am presenting for your review my skills, achievements, and talent for accelerating margins and turning around unprofitable organizations so that we can discuss my joining _____ as a member of your senior management team.

Results achieved to date include:

o Promoted five grade levels during my last four years at ABC Company based on achieving all major P&L goals in directing the $19 million Corporate Administration and Property Management Department.

o As Acme's Corporate Director of Administration & Property Services, generated tens of millions of dollars in cost reductions and cash flow through aggressive property consolidations, upgraded services and procurement, and enforced management accountability.

o Consolidated 29 Acme warehouses down to 4, generating annual savings of $5.8 million; saved $4.6 million by reducing corporate headquarters space 30%; introduced uniform facility standards which reduced total space requirements 20%, generating another $3.4 million in annual cost savings.

o As head of Acme's $230 million purchasing operation, introduced an aggressive multiple-sourcing program which improved the margins of two major product lines by 7% and 9% respectively.

o Productively managed ABC Company's property holdings, achieving 97% occupancy of 800,000 square feet at premium rates; developed a sophisticated model which helped save $7 million on the cost of an out-of-control $40 million building project at ABC.

I look forward to meeting and discussing how I can help accelerate or turn around your company's revenue and profit growth.

                                                    Sincerely,

Enclosure: John Q. Sample

EXAMPLE 2

DAVID Q. SAMPLE   **International Sales/Finance**

123 Any Street, Any City, CA XXXXX (619) 555-1234

Contact Name   Date
Title
Company
Address
City, State Zip

Dear Mr./Ms. _____ :

I have combined a top business degree, global experience, and executive skills in sales, finance, banking, and general management to establish and direct new operations which have generated millions in revenue for well-respected international companies. Bottom-line contributions to profit have been rewarded with accelerated promotions, job security, and a six-figure salary package.

I am bringing to your attention my skills, achievements, strategic brainpower, global network, and talent for exceeding profit goals under negative economic conditions so that we can discuss my joining _____ as a member of your senior sales management team.

Major accomplishments to date include:

o As Vice-President of ABC's International Banking Group, produced revenue of $6.5 million in 1994 through aggressive client development and by saving 90% of the seriously at-risk accounts: accelerated the ROA by focusing on corporate finance, investment banking, and asset sales.

o As Vice-President of Corporate Banking at ABC's Southern California headquarters, leveraged my international contacts to market corporate and capital market products generating $5 million in added net income: achieved 250% growth in fees from capital market products.

o Was recruited away and promoted by ABC to start and manage the new International Energy Group: established and directed the lending operation generating over $500 million in new client bookings in only 18 months with an ROA of over 1%.

o As head of Commercial Development in charge of ABC's International Energy Group, initiated and closed several profitable deals including a hard-to-close $600 million project with an international energy company: created and directed a syndicate of major international lenders.

It should be mutually beneficial to meet and assess how I can help accelerate or turn around revenue and profit growth contributing to your company's future success.

                                        Sincerely,

Enclosure: David Q. Sample

EXAMPLE 3

MATTHEW Q. SAMPLE   **Product Management/Strategic Planning/Sales**

123 Any Street Address, Any Town, TX XXXXX (214) 555-1234

Contact Name   Date
Title
Company
Street Address
City, State Zip

Dear Mr./Ms. _____:

I have combined a top school M.B.A. with executive skills in marketing, sales management, product management, strategic planning, and general management to orchestrate a leveraged buyout, head up a $3 million business, strategically reposition troubled operations, and turn around and accelerate profit growth for weak divisions of the Acme Corporation.

I am bringing to your attention my skills, achievements, talent for stimulating sales productivity, and ability to achieve bottom-line results under the most intense pressure so that we can discuss my joining _____ as a member of your senior sales management team.

Results achieved to date include:

o Upon promotion to Southwestern Sales Director, accelerated sales productivity and major account development achieving a critically needed 35% growth in sales at a pivotal time for the struggling Acme Corporation, which had lost huge market shares due to poor product pricing strategies: achieved highest sales growth and won a major nationwide sales award.

o As Southeastern Sales Director for a troubled division of Acme, turned around profitability becoming the top-ranked Sales Director in the division: instituted aggressive market expansion, national account programs, and strategic planning increasing revenue from $5 million to $23 million in four years; converted a $3 million loss into a $3 million profit.

o Based on a track record of achievements in sales management and strategic planning, was recruited by corporate headquarters to manage a major group's business evaluation function as part of the restructuring of the strategic planning process: improved declining ROIs by upgrading the pricing structure; saved tens-of-millions of dollars by demonstrating the marginal payback of proposed expenditures.

o Negotiated and closed the leveraged buyout of a $3 million service business formerly owned by the Avery Company: developed a solid business plan which was successfully marketed to major financial institutions with whom I negotiated over a million dollars in financing.

o As owner of a Texas-based venture, turned around sales and operations overcoming most roadblocks except the company's lack of liquidity in a recessionary economy: increased sales 60% in 15 months by upgrading service and promotional programs; restructured cash management; reduced aged receivables 75%; negotiated a 20% reduction in product costs; achieved a 60% increase in productivity.

I will work hard to achieve bottom-line results and look forward to discussing how I can contribute to your company's future success.

Sincerely,

Enclosure: Matthew Q. Sample

EXAMPLE 4

WILLIAM Q. SAMPLE   **International Sales Executive**

123 Any Street, Any Town, NJ XXXXX (201) 555-1234

Contact Name   Date
Title
Company
Street Address
City, State Zip

Dear Mr. /Ms. _____:

As Executive Vice-President of Sales for the U.S. Division of a European-based corporation, I have applied executive skills in international sales, marketing, client development, and operations to outmaneuver the competition, deal with volatile exchange rates, accelerate growth of the corporate client base, and achieve a fivefold increase in sales—a revenue level which now accounts for 40% of worldwide sales.

I am presenting for your review my skills, achievements, technical degree, global contacts, and talent for creating productive sales forces and achieving aggressive revenue and profit goals so that we can discuss my joining _____ as a member of your senior sales management team.

Results achieved during the past decade with Acme International include:

o Earned multiple promotions up to Executive Vice-President of Sales at a U.S. Division of Acme International, one of Europe's largest industrial corporations: created a highly productive sales organization and achieved a fivefold increase in revenue turning the U.S. Division into a $20 million business which now accounts for almost 40% of the subsidiary's global sales.

o In spite of high turnover and chronically unfavorable exchange rates, which adversely impacted the U.S. Division's pricing structure, generated a 500% increase in Acme's customer base through an accelerated client development program which emphasized quality and service to offset the unfavorable pricing.

o In spite of global competition, closed multimillion-dollar clients including Western Electric, AT&T, Boeing, and John Deere: accelerated the AT&T account from zero to $9 million representing half of total sales; generated a ninefold sales increase from the Harvester Division of John Deere; produced an eightfold increase in the Western Electric and Boeing accounts.

o Significantly reduced overhead and logistics expenses and all but eliminated aged receivables and write-offs by creating and enforcing conservative credit policies at Acme; in order to meet scheduled delivery dates through on-time shipments from Europe, also established a first-rate logistics function.

I look forward to discussing how I can help accelerate or turn around the performance of your international operations.

                                                     Sincerely,

Enclosure: William Q. Sample

6

Market-Tested
Sample Resumes
and Cover Letters
for Executives

INTRODUCTION

The real-life, market-tested samples in Chapter 6 produced results for executives with 15 to 30-plus years of experience. This chapter offers the following unique features designed to give you the same competitive edge that produced quality interviews and job offers for executives just like you:

1. *Superior Quality Sample Resumes and Cover Letters.* Taken directly from almost 30 real-life client case histories, the market-tested and proven samples in this chapter successfully generated quality interviews and career moves. These samples of unmatched quality enable you to extract, borrow, and adapt key words, phrases, sentences, and paragraphs as you develop your own power package.

2. *A Strong Focus on Packaging Marketable Skills and Achievements.* This workbook subordinates the narrative job descriptions that clutter most resumes. The market has responded favorably to the skills and achievement-oriented resumes featured in the following pages.

3. *An Unparalleled Emphasis on the Marketing Cover Letter.* This workbook treats the cover letter and resume as *coequal* and *inseparable* components of the total marketing package. Based on a frequently heard comment from my management clients, "The cover letter got me the interview," I have no doubts about the letter's importance. Every sample resume in this book has a corresponding cover letter—*no* other book on the market can make this claim.

4. *A Representative Cross Section of Sample Resumes and Letters.* As reflected in the Chapter Index, I have deliberately excluded many highly specialized, often irrelevant, job positions that provide "filler" for countless resume books. This chapter, instead, presents *eight* major categories and several additional subcategories of mainstream executive-level positions into which most managers fall.

5. *An Intense Focus on Market Response.* Simply stated, the following samples achieved the desired results for veteran managers just like you: They produced positive interviews and job offers in an increasingly tough and selective marketplace, which is, of course, the *ultimate* and *only relevant* judge of quality.

THE RESUME AND COVER LETTER HEADERS

As discussed earlier, the sample resume and cover letter packages include, for your optional application, my trademark "headers" which provide the reader with a brief two- to five-word description of your background/discipline. For your convenience and ease in referencing the samples, I have elevated and boxed in these descriptive headers which are cross-referenced in the Index on pages 71 and 72. Should you choose to include the header in your own resume and cover letter package, you will, of course, position it on the same line as your name.

A WORD ABOUT CLIENT CONFIDENTIALITY

While retaining the full impact and integrity of the real-life marketing packages in this chapter, I have selectively modified and/or otherwise blinded certain confidential information including client names, company names, addresses, specific job titles, employment dates, and other identifying narrative. While education information has also been blinded, colleges and graduate schools of equivalent ranking were substituted where appropriate.

CHAPTER 6 RESUME INDEX

WILLIAM Q. SAMPLE (Version 1)

123 Any Street, Any Town, NJ XXXXX (201) 555-1234

Contact Name   Date
Title
Company
Street Address
City, State Zip

Dear Mr./Ms. _____:

As Executive Vice-President of Sales for the U.S. Division of a European-based corporation, I have applied executive skills in international sales, marketing, client development, and operations to outmaneuver the competition, deal with volatile exchange rates, accelerate growth of the corporate client base, and achieve a fivefold increase in sales—a revenue level which now accounts for 40% of worldwide sales.

I am presenting for your review my skills, achievements, technical degree, global contacts, and talent for creating productive sales forces and achieving aggressive revenue and profit goals so that we can discuss my joining _____ as a member of your senior sales management team.

Results achieved during the past decade with Acme International include:

o Earned multiple promotions up to Executive Vice-President of Sales at a U.S. Division of Acme International, one of Europe's largest industrial corporations: created a highly productive sales organization and achieved a fivefold increase in revenue turning the U.S. Division into a $20 million business which now accounts for almost 40% of the subsidiary's global sales.

o In spite of high turnover and chronically unfavorable exchange rates, which adversely impacted the U.S. Division's pricing structure, generated a 500% increase in Acme's customer base through an accelerated client development program which emphasized quality and service to offset the unfavorable pricing.

o In spite of global competition, closed multimillion-dollar clients including Western Electric, AT&T, Boeing, and John Deere: accelerated the AT&T account from zero to $9 million representing half of total sales; generated a ninefold sales increase from the Harvester Division of John Deere; produced an eightfold increase in the Western Electric and Boeing accounts.

o Significantly reduced overhead and logistics expenses and all but eliminated aged receivables and write-offs by creating and enforcing conservative credit policies at Acme; in order to meet scheduled delivery dates through on-time shipments from Europe, also established a first-rate logistics function.

I look forward to discussing how I can help accelerate or turn around the performance of your international operations.

Sincerely,

Enclosure: William Q. Sample

International Sales Executive

WILLIAM Q. SAMPLE

123 Any Street Address, Any Town, NJ XXXXX (201) 555-1234

B.S.   Electrical Engineering   International University   Comprehensive Six-Year Program
B.A.   Business Administration   Lehman College   Managerial Studies

International: Traveled throughout Europe, Asia, South America, and North America
Languages: Fluent French and Spanish

CAREER SKILLS/KNOWLEDGE

- Sales/marketing executive
- International sales/markets
- European relations
- Strategic/marketing plans
- Market share strategies
- Major client development
- Competitive maneuvering
- Exchange rate strategies
- Organizational development
- Staff supervision/development

- Operations/materials/engineering
- Purchasing operations
- Cost controls/reductions
- Global distribution/logistics
- Heavy industry clients
- Aircraft engine market
- Engineering operations
- Electrical/systems engineering
- New product design
- Plant operating systems design

CAREER ACHIEVEMENTS

- Earned multiple promotions up to Executive Vice-President of Sales at a U.S. Division of Acme International, one of Europe's largest industrial corporations: created a highly productive sales organization and achieved a fivefold increase in revenue turning the U.S. Division into a $20 million business which now accounts for almost 40% of the subsidiary's global sales.

- In spite of high turnover and chronically unfavorable exchange rates, which adversely impacted the U.S. Division's pricing structure, generated a 500% increase in Acme's customer base through an accelerated client development program which emphasized quality and service to offset the unfavorable pricing.

- In spite of global competition, closed multimillion-dollar clients including Western Electric, AT&T, Boeing, and John Deere: accelerated the AT&T account from zero to $9 million representing half of total sales; generated a ninefold sales increase from the Harvester Division of John Deere; produced an eightfold increase in the Western Electric and Boeing accounts.

- Significantly reduced overhead and logistics expenses and all but eliminated aged receivables and write-offs by creating and enforcing conservative credit policies at Acme; in order to meet scheduled delivery dates through on-time shipments from Europe, also established a first-rate logistics function.

- Earned several promotions up to Director within the Engineering Department of a Florida-based division of Essex Corporation: directed high-quality product designs, upgraded operating systems critical to the production process, and effectively troubleshooted the complex power supply systems.

CAREER EXPERIENCE

ACME INTERNATIONAL CORPORATION, Any Town, NJ   1984–Present

Executive Vice-President of Sales   1987–Present
Direct the Sales Organization with responsibility for direct sales, marketing, strategic planning, client development, import operations, logistics, distribution, and credit.

Vice-President of Sales   1984–1987
Directed sales, marketing, strategic planning, and related functions.

ESSEX CORPORATION, Any Town, FL   1975–1984

Director of Engineering   1980–1984
Earned several promotions based on engineering achievements in directing low-tolerance design and systems engineering projects. Also successfully planned and executed high-visibility manufacturing projects.

MILITARY EXPERIENCE

European Military: Honorably Discharged

Affiliations: Society of U.S. Engineers; Production Engineers of the Northeast
Citizenship: U.S. Citizen

REFERENCES AVAILABLE UPON REQUEST

JOHN A. JONES (Version 1)

123 Any Street, Any City, WA XXXXX (206) 555-1234

Contact Name
Title
Company
Street Address
City, State Zip

Date

Dear Mr./Ms. _____ :

I have combined degrees from Stanford and Wharton with executive skills in sales, marketing, operations, and engineering to build a $20 million company known internationally for its state-of-the-art products, cost-effective production, substantial market shares, and global clients. Achievements were rewarded with growing profits and prestigious awards for delivering vital systems in record time.

I am bringing to your attention my leadership skills, achievements, ability to create cost-effective solutions, and proven talent for accelerating market share and profits to produce financial security for others and myself so that we can discuss my joining _____ as a member of your general management/marketing team.

Results achieved to date include:

o As Founder and Chief Executive of ABC, Inc., started and built this profitable high-tech electronics company known over 20 years for its innovative products and low-cost volume production: negotiated and executed the lucrative sale of the company to a major corporation.

o More than doubled ABC's revenue by marketing breakthrough products to over 40 countries and major Fortune 500 corporations: developed damage-proof and modular products; introduced concept of placing electronics into clothing; developed communications systems for space projects, carriers, train systems, executive aircraft, and bank machines.

o Became one of the world's largest producers of specialized communication devices by focusing on the high volume global market; instituted "people-based" engineering to extend the life of electronic equipment and produce safety-conscious communications for major clients.

o Turned around out-of-control quality and distribution problems at XYZ Technology increasing on-time shipments from 38% to 95%; also turned around purchasing operations generating $3 million a year in cost reductions while reducing inventory $3 million.

Should we reach mutually agreeable terms, I will work hard to help accelerate or turn around operating performance contributing to your future success.

Sincerely,

Enclosure:

John A. Jones

Sales Executive/General Management

JOHN A. JONES

123 Any Street, Any City, WA XXXXX (206) 555-1235

M.B.A.	Management	Wharton	1974
B.S.	Electrical Engineering	Stanford University	1972
B.A.	Economics	Stanford University	1972

CAREER SKILLS/KNOWLEDGE

- o International marketing/sales
- o General management/finance
- o Start-up operations/organization
- o Major client development
- o Product management
- o Competitive maneuvering
- o Expansion/turnaround strategies
- o Profit/market share growth
- o New product marketing/pricing

- o Operations/engineering
- o Manufacturing/Q.C./materials
- o Cost-effective production
- o Labor negotiations
- o Productivity improvements
- o R&D/systems engineering
- o New product development
- o Cost reduction strategies
- o Electronics industry

CAREER ACHIEVEMENTS

o As Founder and Chief Executive of ABC, Inc., started and built this profitable high-tech electronics company known over 20 years for its innovative products and low-cost volume production: negotiated and executed the lucrative sale of the company to a major corporation.

o Awarded a coveted medal by a foreign government for producing and delivering, in less than 60 days, critically needed communications systems vital to their national defense: crash program cut four months off the schedule.

o More than doubled ABC's revenue by marketing breakthrough products to over 40 countries and major Fortune 500 corporations: developed damage-proof and modular products; introduced concept of placing electronics into clothing; developed communications systems for space projects, carriers, train systems, executive aircraft, and bank machines.

o Became one of the world's largest producers of specialized communication devices by focusing on the high volume global market; instituted "people-based" engineering to extend the life of electronic equipment and produce safety-conscious communications for major clients.

o Turned around out-of-control quality and distribution problems at XYZ Technology increasing on-time shipments from 38% to 95%; also turned around purchasing operations generating $3 million a year in cost reductions while reducing inventory $3 million.

o As Director of Procurement at Acme Company, generated $4 million in annual cost savings and reduced inventory $2 million by resolving serious cost control and material control problems.

CAREER EXPERIENCE

ACME COMPANY, Any City, WA   1996–Present

Director of Procurement
Instituted much needed budget systems; upgraded material control, developed off-shore vendors, reduced materials shortages, and stopped downtime; generated cost savings and reduced inventory.

XYZ TECHNOLOGY CORPORATION, Any Town, WA   1995–1996

Project Director
In a series of manufacturing, technical, and procurement assignments, instituted modern management techniques: improved production quality, cut costs, reduced inventory, and established on-time delivery:

o Upgraded Q.C. operations, policies, and procedures.
o Tightened vendor product quality standards.
o Instituted competitive bidding and second sourcing.
o Introduced Japanese methods of inventory stocking.

ABC, INCORPORATED, Any Town, WA   1974–1995

Chief Executive and Founder
Founded and managed a high-tech company which grew to over 150 employees:

o Expanded through innovation, systems engineering, and cost-effective manufacturing.
o Oversaw product development from inception through design, engineering, and production.
o Established and monitored marketing and pricing objectives.
o Developed client relations with major corporations and numerous countries.
o Continuously expanded into new markets.
o Redesigned and improved products to reduce costs.
o Established rigid quality control standards.
o Designed a plant layout which dramatically improved assembly productivity.
o Consistently met tight delivery schedules.

REFERENCES PROVIDED UPON REQUEST

Marketing Executive/General Management

THOMAS A. JOHNSON

123 Any Street, Any City, CA XXXXX (619) 555-1234

Contact Name   Date
Title
Company
Street Address
City, State Zip

Dear Mr./Ms. _____:

I have combined executive skills in marketing, sales, and general management with a first-rate education and military experience to restructure and turn around struggling businesses and accelerate profits and cost controls for Fortune 50 and smaller companies.

Bottom-line results have been rewarded with promotions leading to CEO of a Los Angeles County company which, unfortunately, requires a four-hour commute.

I am presenting for your review my skills, achievements, proven leadership, and no-nonsense ability to get the job done so that we can discuss my joining _____ as a member of your senior sales/marketing management team.

Results achieved to date include:

o As Chief Executive Officer of ABC Energy Company, directed its consolidation and turnaround, streamlining the organization, reducing costs, and doubling pre-tax earnings.

o At ABC, negotiated a separate cost-effective labor agreement for Los Angeles County obtaining substantial wage savings and increased productivity through revised work rules.

o As Marketing Director in charge of retail and wholesale businesses for Avery Energy Company, achieved sales growth of 18% (to $95 million) within a declining total market.

o At a Fortune 100 energy company, earned several major promotions to increasingly responsible Marketing, Sales, Administrative, and Planning positions.

o Promoted to Sales Manager at a Fortune 100 company, achieving sales quota in all major product categories by restructuring the sales area and coordinating over 200 accounts in the San Diego market.

I look forward to a meeting at which we can determine how I can contribute to your company's future success.

Sincerely,

Enclosure: Thomas A. Johnson

Marketing Executive/General Management

THOMAS A. JOHNSON

123 Any Street, Any City, CA XXXXX (619) 555-1234

B.A.   Duke University   1978

CAREER SKILLS/KNOWLEDGE

o Marketing/sales executive
o Revenue growth strategies
o Profit maximization
o Competitive strategies
o New account development
o Product strategies
o Sales promotions
o Territory planning
o Dealer recruiting/relations
o Customer relations
o Real estate development
o Site expansion/divestiture

o General management
o Operations
o Turnaround strategies
o Business restructuring
o Leadership skills
o Staff development
o Labor relations
o Contract negotiations
o Administration
o Strategic planning
o Budget management
o Capital planning/control

CAREER ACHIEVEMENTS

o As Chief Executive Officer of ABC Energy Company, directed its consolidation and turnaround, streamlining the organization, reducing costs, and doubling pre-tax earnings.

o At ABC, negotiated a separate cost-effective labor agreement for Los Angeles County obtaining substantial wage savings and increased productivity through revised work rules.

o As Marketing Director in charge of retail and wholesale businesses for Avery Energy Company, achieved sales growth of 18% (to $95 million) within a declining total market.

o At a Fortune 100 energy company, earned several major promotions to increasingly responsible Marketing, Sales, Administrative, and Planning positions.

o Promoted to Marketing Manager at a Fortune 100 energy company, in charge of preparing five-year plans and evaluating, monitoring, and controlling the $88 million capital budget.

o Promoted to Control Manager at a Fortune 100 company, successfully directing overall administration of the $91 million San Diego District.

o Promoted to Sales Manager at a Fortune 100 company, achieving sales quota in all major product categories by restructuring the sales area and coordinating over 200 accounts in the San Diego market.

o Upon promotion to Site Manager at a Fortune 100 company, researched and added ten highly profitable new business sites and shut down seven unprofitable sites.

BUSINESS EXPERIENCE

ACME ENERGY CORPORATION, Any City, CA   2/95–Present

Chief Executive Officer—ABC Energy Company
Doubled subsidiary's net profit contribution to over $1.3 million:

o Restructured company to streamline operations.
o Negotiated cost-effective labor agreement for Los Angeles County.
o Generate new accounts through direct advertising strategy.
o Increased budget accountability of middle managers.
o Developed incentives for 86 employees.
o Improved client relations through better service.
o Stopped the decline of our existing customer base.
o Manage multimillion-dollar company assets.

AVERY ENERGY COMPANY, Any City, CA   9/89–2/95

Marketing Director
Directed growth and cost control of a $90 million operation.

ESSEX CORPORATION (FORTUNE 100), Any City, CA   8/82–9/89

Marketing Manager   4/87–9/89
Managed capital budget of $88 million: consolidated budgets, presented to management and monitored. Prepared five-year plans and well-received compliance reports for the government.

Control Manager   5/86–4/87
Directed administration for $91 million San Diego District: managed budgeting, controls, facilities, and field support.

Sales Manager   4/84–5/86
Developed staff, restructured territory, and coordinated accounts.

MILITARY EXPERIENCE   (1978–1982)

o Attended Officer Candidate School; served on U.S.S. Kennedy
o Directed 125 service personnel; controlled major logistics operations
o Awarded multiple performance citations

COMMUNITY/VOLUNTEER ACTIVITIES

o Board Member, San Diego County Red Cross and Zoning Commission
o Vice President & Board Member, San Diego Water Council

JOHN A. SMITH (Version 1)

123 Any Street, Any Town, CA XXXXX Home: (619) 555-1234 Office: (619) 555-2345

Contact Name   Date
Title
Company
Street Address
City, State Zip

Dear Mr./Ms. _____:

I have profitably applied executive skills in sales, marketing, major account development, and finance to exceed revenue targets and play a key role in the start-up and marketing of Asset Management Associates, a division of the $2 billion Acme Corporation which has achieved a 35% ROI through the purchase and sale of real estate worth $200 million. I also played a central role in Acme's entry into both the asset management and financial industries.

I am presenting for your review my skills, achievements, proven leadership, work ethic, and straightforward approach to getting the job done so that we can discuss my joining _____ as a member of your sales/marketing management team.

Results achieved to date include:

o As Director of Sales, played a central role in the start-up, marketing, and general management of Asset Management Associates—a venture which has yielded an on-target 35% return through the purchase and resale of over 2,000 foreclosed properties valued at $200 million: codeveloped the start-up business plan, helped staff the company, and assumed a Director position reporting directly to the President.

o Helped generate third-year profits of $2 million on revenue of $7 million at Asset Management Associates: signed the first major banking client accounting for a 50-house management contract; closed deals which contributed to the company managing 400 properties generating $800,000 in fees; signed a major lender accounting for purchased inventory of over $2 million a month; sold 20 additional accounts yielding 8 management and 12 buy-out clients.

o As Major Account Executive at an Acme Division, exceeded revenue targets by maintaining volume, increasing business, and renegotiating contracts with multimillion-dollar accounts.

o Prior to and during my tenure as a Major Account Executive, directly facilitated Acme's subsequent entry into asset management: at the request of the Chairman, executed a feasibility study which recommended entry into asset management; closed a lucrative deal which represented the company's first asset management client and led to the eventual formation of Asset Management Associates.

o As Director of Investment Acquisition at Asset Management Associates, directed development of a $40 million offering package and formed a syndicate of investors to meet our outside borrowing requirements; previously developed and recommended cancellation of a $200 million public offering.

I look forward to discussing how I can help accelerate or turn around revenue and profit growth, contributing to your future success.

                                        Sincerely,

Enclosure: John A. Smith

JOHN A. SMITH

123 Any Street, Any Town, CA XXXXX Home: (619) 555-1234 Office: (619) 555-2345

| M.B.A. | Finance | University of Maine | 1982 |
| B.A. | Accounting | State University of New York | 1980 |

CAREER SKILLS/KNOWLEDGE

- Sales/marketing management
- Quota achievement strategies
- Staff supervision/development
- Client/major account development
- Cold-calling/proposals
- Group marketing/seminars/speeches
- Trade show participation
- Marketing materials/brochures
- Closing/customer service
- Asset management/real estate
- Buy-out/resale/ROI strategies
- Balance sheet management

- Financial/treasury management
- Budgeting/capital appropriations
- Consolidations/financial statements
- Auditing operations
- Credit and collections
- Treasury operations
- Cash management/allocation
- Investment strategies
- Borrowing strategies
- Basis point reductions
- Foreign exchange strategies
- Banking relations

CAREER ACHIEVEMENTS

o As Director of Sales, played a central role in the start-up, marketing, and general management of Asset Management Associates—a venture which has yielded an on-target 35% return through the acquisition and disposition of 2,000 foreclosed properties valued at $200 million: codeveloped the start-up business plan, helped staff the company, and assumed a Director position reporting directly to the President.

o Helped generate third-year profits of $2 million on revenue of $7 million at Asset Management Associates: signed the first major banking client accounting for a 50-house management contract; closed deals which contributed to the company managing 400 properties generating $800,000 in fees; signed a major lender accounting for purchased inventory of over $2 million a month; sold 20 additional accounts yielding 8 management and 12 buy-out clients.

o As a Major Account Executive at an Acme Division, exceeded revenue targets by maintaining volume, increasing business, and renegotiating contracts with multimillion-dollar accounts.

o Prior to and during my tenure as a Major Account Executive, directly facilitated Acme's subsequent entry into asset management: at the request of the Chairman, executed a feasibility study which recommended entry into asset management; closed a lucrative deal which represented the company's first asset management client and led to the eventual formation of Asset Management Associates.

o As Director of Investment Acquisition at Asset Management Associates, directed development of a $40 million offering package and formed a syndicate of investors to meet our outside borrowing requirements; previously developed and recommended cancellation of a $200 million public offering.

o Took the lead in establishing Asset Management Associates first relationship with the FDIC by directly contacting government officials; initiated negotiations for a major purchase from the Resolution Trust Corporation.

o As Treasury Director in charge of treasury operations at a division of Acme, initiated development of financial services which allowed clients to process applications through the mail to bankers with whom we had negotiated contracts: success of the services led to Acme's entry into the financial industry.

CAREER EXPERIENCE

ACME CORPORATION, Any City, CA   1990–Present

ASSET MANAGEMENT ASSOCIATES, Any City, CA   1992–Present

Director of Investment Acquisition   1994–Present
Member of management team responsible for directing business and establishing strategic objectives. While still executing sales responsibilites, directed development of $40 million offering package.

Director of Sales   1993–1994
Developed new business in marketing acquisition and disposition services for foreclosed real estate to savings & loans, banks, the federal government, and other financial institutions.

Director   1992–1993
Member of group formed to assess the need for an Asset Management Company.

ACME DIVISION, Any City, CA   1990–1992

Major Account Executive   1991–1992
Maintained volume, increased business, and renegotiated contracts with established accounts of Acme.

Treasury Director   1990–1991
Instituted a new method of funding bank accounts which yielded a savings of $3 million a year; instituted a system of billing to clients which reduced receivables by $8 million; stopped a 40% increase in headcount by developing a computerized accounts receivable system during a period of rapid growth; computerized several Cash Management reports which accelerated the reimbursement process thereby reducing excess borrowing by $7 million.

AVERY INCORPORATED, Any City, CA   1982–1990

Assistant Treasury Manager   1987–1990
Profitably managed a $400 million portfolio of short-term investments; managed the daily cash position; negotiated basis point reductions; established and directed Currency Exchange review process.

Senior Financial Analyst   1984–1987
Reviewed budget submissions from international subsidiaries. Prepared reports with recommended changes that were routinely accepted.

ADDITIONAL EDUCATION/TRAINING

Professional Courses: o Professional Marketing Series
                         o The Art of Selling Series
                         o Professional Communications Series

MATTHEW Q. SAMPLE (Version 1)

123 Any Street Address, Any Town, TX XXXXX (214) 555-1234

Contact Name   Date
Title
Company
Street Address
City, State Zip

Dear Mr./Ms. _____ :

I have combined a top school M.B.A. with executive skills in marketing, sales management, product management, strategic planning, and general management to orchestrate a leveraged buyout, head up a $3 million business, strategically reposition troubled operations, and turn around and accelerate profit growth for weak divisions of the Acme Corporation.

I am bringing to your attention my skills, achievements, talent for stimulating sales productivity, and ability to achieve bottom-line results under the most intense pressure so that we can discuss my joining _____ as a member of your senior sales management team.

Results achieved to date include:

o Upon promotion to Southwestern Sales Director, accelerated sales productivity and major account development achieving a critically needed 35% growth in sales at a pivotal time for the struggling Acme Corporation, which had lost huge market shares due to poor product pricing strategies: achieved highest sales growth and won a major nationwide sales award.

o As Southeastern Sales Director for a troubled division of Acme, turned around profitability becoming the top-ranked Sales Director in the division: instituted aggressive market expansion, national account programs, and strategic planning increasing revenue from $5 million to $23 million in four years; converted a $3 million loss into a $3 million profit.

o Based on a track record of achievements in sales management and strategic planning, was recruited by corporate headquarters to manage a major group's business evaluation function as part of the restructuring of the strategic planning process: improved declining ROIs by upgrading the pricing structure; saved tens-of-millions of dollars by demonstrating the marginal payback of proposed expenditures.

o Negotiated and closed the leveraged buyout of a $3 million service business formerly owned by the Avery Company: developed a solid business plan which was successfully marketed to major financial institutions with whom I negotiated over a million dollars in financing.

o As owner of a Texas-based venture, turned around sales and operations overcoming most roadblocks except the company's lack of liquidity in a recessionary economy: increased sales 60% in 15 months by upgrading service and promotional programs; restructured cash management; reduced aged receivables 75%; negotiated a 20% reduction in product costs; achieved a 60% increase in productivity.

I will work hard to achieve bottom-line results and look forward to discussing how I can contribute to your company's future success.

Sincerely,

Enclosure: Matthew Q. Sample

MATTHEW Q. SAMPLE

123 Any Street, Any Town, TX XXXXX (214) 555-1234

M.B.A.	Finance/Marketing	University of Virginia	1976
B.S.	Statistics	UCLA	1974

CAREER SKILLS/KNOWLEDGE

- o Marketing/sales management
- o Revenue/profit turnaround
- o Product management/market development
- o National accounts programs
- o Sales productivity growth
- o Competitor intelligence systems
- o Business ownership/leveraged buyouts
- o Advertising/promotions
- o Operations turnaround

- o Strategic planning
- o Business plans/market research
- o Market growth/segmentation
- o ROI growth strategies
- o Profit/investment optimization
- o Economic modeling/pricing
- o Supply/demand analysis
- o Finance/controller operations
- o Cash-flow/financing/bank relations

CAREER ACHIEVEMENTS

o Upon promotion to Southwestern Sales Director, accelerated sales productivity and major account development achieving a critically needed 35% growth in sales at a pivotal time for the struggling Acme Corporation, which had lost huge market shares due to poor product pricing strategies: achieved highest sales growth and won a major nationwide sales award.

o As Southeastern Sales Director for a troubled division of Acme, turned around profitability becoming the top-ranked Sales Director in the division: instituted aggressive market expansion, national account programs, and strategic planning increasing revenue from $5 million to $23 million in four years; converted a $3 million loss into a $3 million profit.

o Upon being promoted to Product Manager at Acme, created a product management system which accelerated the decision-making process for the pricing, promotion, and distribution of products: increased profits 30% through saturation marketing to growth industries.

o Based on a track record of achievements in sales management and strategic planning, was recruited by corporate headquarters to manage a major group's business evaluation function as part of the restructuring of the strategic planning process: improved declining ROIs by upgrading the pricing structure; saved tens-of-millions of dollars by demonstrating the marginal payback of proposed expenditures.

o Upon promotion to Business Planning Director, orchestrated a multibillion-dollar asset reallocation program which helped triple profits within five years: reallocated over a billion dollars of production assets to growth products; proposed a half-billion-dollar plant conversion which was implemented at half the cost of constructing a new plant.

o Negotiated and closed the leveraged buyout of a $3 million service business formerly owned by the Avery Company: developed a solid business plan which was successfully marketed to major financial institutions with whom I negotiated over a million dollars in financing.

o As owner of a Texas-based venture, turned around sales and operations overcoming most roadblocks except the company's lack of liquidity in a recessionary economy: increased sales 60% in 15 months by upgrading service and promotional programs; restructured cash management; reduced aged receivables 75%; negotiated a 20% reduction in product costs; achieved a 60% increase in productivity.

CAREER EXPERIENCE

ACME CORPORATION, Any City, TX   1976–1992

Business Planning Director—XYZ Division   1989–1992
Designated to orchestrate the development of corporate strategies and upgrade the planning process.

Business Evaluation Director—ABC Division   1986–1989
Designated to reorganize and turn around strategic planning.

Southwestern Sales Director—ABC Division   1982–1986
Developed and directed a high-producing sales team responsible for national account development.

Product Manager—XYZ Division   1978–1982
Created a product management system which accelerated the decision-making process for the pricing, promotion, and distribution of products.

Southeastern Sales Director—XYZ Division   1977–1978
Implemented a Major Account Program; expanded into growth markets; instituted effective competitor data-gathering procedures; created Division's first comprehensive strategic plan.

Senior Marketing Analyst   1976–1977
Executed comprehensive feasibility studies which resulted in the formation of critically needed account development departments. Developed a well-received business plan for a beleaguered venture.

ESSEX COMPANY, Any City, TX   1992–1994

Senior Consultant
Determined the feasibility of a client's expansion into major European markets: executed comprehensive product demand and competitive studies as a basis for decision making.

SERVICE VENTURE, Any City, TX   1994–Present

Founder: Directed Marketing, Advertising, Sales, Operations, Finance, and Customer Service.

INTERNATIONAL: Traveled throughout South America and Europe
LANGUAGES: Fluent French, Italian, and Spanish

JOHN Q. SAMPLE (Version 1)

123 Any Street, Any City, CA (619) 555-5678

Contact Name   Date
Title
Company
Address
City, State Zip

Dear Mr./Ms. _____:

As Executive Vice-President responsible for directing an $80 million global operation at Prototype Corporation, I have taken the lead in instituting major competitive changes, cost reductions, and productivity improvements which have accelerated the company's competitiveness while increasing profits $20 million annually.

As a central figure in Acme Corporation's massive restructuring, I applied executive skills in finance, administration, real estate, property management, and procurement to facilitate Acme's turnaround to profitability. I likewise produced multimillion-dollar profits for ABC Company through productive management of its administration and property management, receiving accelerated promotions to Director of a $19 million operation.

I am presenting for your review my skills, achievements, ability to recapture the competitive edge, and talent for accelerating profits and turning around out-of-control operations so that we can discuss my joining _____ as a member of your senior management team.

Accomplishments critical to Prototype recapturing its blue-chip profitability:

o As Executive Vice-President of Administration, profitably direct an $80 million operation spanning 56 international locations representing over two million square feet: responsibilities executed in directing twelve major departments include the management of $100 million in company assets and the negotiation of $50 million in facility contracts related to properties located worldwide.

o Generated multiyear savings of $50 million and accelerated productivity growth through a major consolidation of Prototype's manufacturing and branch office network: aggressively renegotiated expensive leasehold agreements, eliminated redundant operations, and instituted global efficiencies.

o Consolidated 15 research and administrative sites into 4, generating an annual savings of $5 million through reductions in square footage and rental expense; also directed the successful completion of an important 300,000 square foot research facility which was finished well ahead of schedule and several million dollars under budget.

o Positioned Prototype as a pacesetter in instituting worker accident prevention programs: fostered the company's global reputation for valuing human resources while generating a 50% reduction in insurance premiums.

I look forward to meeting and discussing how I can help accelerate or turn around your company's revenue and profit growth.

                                                                   Sincerely,

Enclosure: John Q. Sample

Administration/Finance/General Management

JOHN Q. SAMPLE

123 Any Street, Any City, CA XXXXX (619) 555-5678

B.S. Honors Finance   Georgetown University   1980

CAREER SKILLS/KNOWLEDGE

- o General management
- o Finance/administration
- o Strategic planning
- o Financial planning and analysis
- o Procurement operations
- o Telecommunications
- o Travel/relocation
- o Insurance/risk management
- o Training/security
- o International distribution

- o Global property management
- o Development/construction
- o Occupancy growth strategies
- o Premium rate strategies
- o Consolidation strategies
- o Facilities management
- o Lease management/negotiations
- o Site selection/space planning
- o Budgeting/accountability
- o Governmental regulations

CAREER ACHIEVEMENTS

o As Executive Vice-President at Prototype Corporation, profitably direct an $80 million operation spanning 56 international locations representing two million square feet: responsibilities executed in directing twelve major departments include the management of $100 million in company assets and the negotiation of $50 million in facility contracts related to properties located worldwide.

o Generated multiyear savings of $50 million and accelerated productivity growth through a major consolidation of Prototype's manufacturing and branch office network: aggressively renegotiated expensive leasehold agreements, eliminated redundant operations, and instituted global efficiencies.

o Proposed and instituted lucrative outsourcing programs based on competitive benchmarking: improved Prototype's overall competitiveness by redirecting corporate priorities and eliminating costly redundancies, inefficiencies, and excess expenditures.

o Consolidated 15 research and administrative sites into 4, generating an annual savings of $5 million for Prototype through reductions in square footage and rental expense; also directed the successful completion of an important 300,000 square foot research facility which was finished well ahead of schedule and several million dollars under budget.

o Positioned Prototype as a pacesetter in instituting worker accident prevention programs: fostered the company's global reputation for valuing human resources while generating a 50% reduction in insurance premiums.

o Assumed a central role in Prototype's efforts to address and resolve the industry's billion-dollar counterfeiting problem by instituting comprehensive security programs.

o Generated international recognition for Prototype by initiating and instituting cost-effective environmental programs which are recognized by the global business community as the standard against which to measure future programs.

CAREER EXPERIENCE

PROTOTYPE CORPORATION, Any Town, CA   4/93–Present

Executive Vice-President Administration
Direct Property Management, Travel, Relocation, and Communications. Additional accomplishments:

o Achieved a 10% reduction in absenteeism by creating healthier employees through the implementation of cost-effective fitness programs.
o Reopened negotiations with major transportation carriers yielding a million dollar annual savings.
o Centralized previously decentralized functions generating annual savings of over $500,000.
o Implemented advanced technologies in teleconferencing: shortened the R&D cycle, improved inquiry response time, and reduced expenses.

ACME CORPORATION, Any Town, CA   3/88–4/93

Corporate Director of Administration & Property Services
Directed the overall management, planning, site selection, lease negotiations, consolidations, and disposition for property totaling two million square feet. Additionally directed the $230 million purchasing operation and all corporate administrative services. Major accomplishments:

o Assumed a central role in Acme's turnaround to profitability: generated tens of millions of dollars in cost reductions and cash flow through aggressive property consolidations, upgraded services and procurement, and enforced management accountability.
o As head of Acme's $230 million purchasing operation, introduced an aggressive multiple-sourcing program which improved the margins of two major product lines by 7% and 9% respectively.
o Overcame powerful organizational resistance to produce over $3 million cash and annual savings of $2.1 million by persuading the Chairman to sell off Acme's corporate yacht.

ABC COMPANY, Any Town, CA   6/80–3/88

Director of Services & Property   3/85–3/88
Earned five promotions during my last four years at ABC Company based on achieving all major profit goals in directing this multimillion-dollar operation. Directed services with a staff of 63 and a budget of $19 million: included property management, purchasing, communications, systems, mail, and office equipment placement and maintenance.

Profitably directed company's real estate holdings, achieving 97% occupancy of 800,000 square feet at premium rates; developed a sophisticated model which helped save $7 million on the cost of an out-of-control $40 million building project.

REFERENCES PROVIDED UPON REQUEST

DAVID Q. SAMPLE (Version 1)

123 Any Street, Any City, CA XXXXX (619) 555-1234

Contact Name   Date
Title
Company
Address
City, State Zip

Dear Mr./Ms. _____:

I have combined a top business degree, global experience, and executive skills in finance, banking, sales, and general management to establish and direct new operations which have generated millions in revenue for well-respected international banks. Bottom-line contributions to profit have been rewarded with accelerated promotions, job security, and a six-figure salary package.

I am bringing to your attention my skills, achievements, strategic brainpower, global network, and talent for exceeding profit goals under negative economic conditions so that we can discuss my joining _____ as a member of your senior financial management team.

Results achieved during the past nine years with ABC Bank include:

o As Vice-President of an International Banking Group, produced revenue of $6.5 million in 1994 through aggressive client development and by saving 90% of the seriously at-risk accounts: accelerated the ROA by focusing on corporate finance, investment banking, and asset sales.

o As Vice-President of Corporate Banking at ABC's Southern California headquarters, leveraged my international contacts to market corporate and capital market products generating $5 million in added net income: achieved 250% growth in fees from capital market products.

o Was recruited away and promoted by ABC to start and manage the new International Energy Group: established and directed the lending operation generating over $500 million in new client bookings in only 18 months with an ROA of over 1%.

o As head of Commercial Development in charge of ABC's International Energy Group, initiated and closed several profitable deals including a hard-to-close $600 million project with an international energy company: created and directed a syndicate of major international lenders.

It should be mutually beneficial to meet and assess how I can help accelerate or turn around revenue and profit growth contributing to your company's future success.

Sincerely,

Enclosure: David Q. Sample

DAVID Q. SAMPLE

123 Any Street, Any City, CA XXXXX (619) 555-1234

M.B.A.   Honors   University of Paris Graduate School of Business   1985

International: Bilingual French and English; solid knowledge of Mideastern languages; traveled to over 60 nations
Certifications: Commercial Pilot's License; Black Belt Karate; Championship Skier

CAREER SKILLS/KNOWLEDGE

- Financial executive
- International banking
- Investment banking
- Corporate/capital markets
- Acquisitions/joint ventures
- Subsidiary recapitalization
- Project financing/syndicates
- Trade financing/foreign exchange

- Marketing/sales executive
- General management
- Start-up operations
- Major client development
- Competitive maneuvering
- Expansion/turnaround strategies
- Revenue/profit growth
- Organizational development

CAREER ACHIEVEMENTS

o As Vice-President of ABC's International Banking Group, produced revenue of $6.5 million in 1994 through aggressive client development and by saving 90% of the at-risk accounts: accelerated the ROA by focusing on corporate finance, investment banking, and asset sales.

o As Vice-President of Corporate Banking at ABC's Southern California headquarters, leveraged my international contacts to market corporate and capital market products generating $5 million in added net income: achieved 250% growth in fees from capital market products.

o Was recruited away and promoted by ABC to start and manage the new International Energy Group: established and directed the lending operation generating over $500 million in new client bookings in only 18 months with an ROA of over 1%.

o As head of Commercial Development in charge of ABC's International Energy Group, initiated and closed several profitable deals including a hard-to-close $600 million project with an international energy company: created and directed a syndicate of major international lenders.

o As Group Officer at Acme International Bank, established and directed operations of a new North American office: achieved and exceeded an aggressive operating plan generating new lending of $300 million and profitability in five months instead of the forecasted ten months.

CAREER EXPERIENCE

ABC BANK, Any Town, CA   3/88–Present

INTERNATIONAL BANKING GROUP, Any Town, CA   2/91–Present

Vice-President
Responsible for major account development emphasizing high-margin corporate finance and investment banking: acquisitions, recapitalization, and collateralized financing. Upgraded asset quality by addressing and restructuring below-par debt.

CORPORATE BANKING, Any Town, CA   3/88–2/91

Vice-President
Created and marketed corporate and capital market products and services to global clients.

ACME INTERNATIONAL BANK, Any Town, Europe   6/85–3/88

Group Officer (Assistant Vice-President), Any Town, British Columbia   4/87–3/88
Managed start-up of a new operation: directed staffing, property selection, facility planning, contract negotiations, and purchasing. Also developed marketing policies and operating procedures.

Officer, Any Town, CA   5/86–4/87
Accelerated global account development quadrupling pre-tax net income to over $4 million.

Officer, Any Town, Europe   6/85–5/86
Established a Credit Group generating over $2 million in fees from new business development.

REFERENCES PROVIDED UPON REQUEST

Treasury/Accounting Management

DONALD A. SMITH
---

123 Any Street, Any City, NY XXXXX (212) 555-1234

Contact Name   Date
Title
Company
Street Address
City, State Zip

Dear Mr./Ms. _____:

I have profitably applied skills in general and financial management, treasury, operations, and acquisitions to streamline departments, improve productivity, and increase critically needed cash by 350% at Acme International Corporation.

Based on results achieved during Acme's growth and my contributions during the rapid decline of the energy industry, I have been retained in spite of an unfortunate 85% reduction in staffing.

I would like to discuss the possibility of joining _____ as a member of your financial management team.

Results achieved to date at Acme include:

o As Treasurer, spearheaded a major cost-control and cash-conservation effort which more than quadrupled cash.

o Executed in-depth operational audits of proposed acquisitions: those approved generated over $100 million in revenue; those cancelled included one where the stock value subsequently declined more than 90%.

o Identified and resolved serious product costing problems at the subsidiaries: installed cost systems, corrected inventory records, eliminated marginal products, and increased profits.

o Interacting with subsidiary Presidents, coordinated the annual plan review: introduced zero-based budgeting and a disciplined cycle for approving sales, expense, and capital projections.

o Instituted and enforced a capital budgeting and request cycle which accelerated ROIs to 30% and higher.

Once we determine how I can contribute to the future success of your company, I will work hard to achieve bottom-line results.

Sincerely,

Enclosure: Donald A. Smith

DONALD A. SMITH

123 Any Street, Any City, NY XXXXX (212) 555-1234

ACADEMIC CREDENTIALS

M.B.A.	Finance	Manhattan College	GPA 3.8	1990
B.S.	Mechanical Engineering	Bahrain Institute of Science & Technology	Honors	1985

CAREER SKILLS/KNOWLEDGE

- o Financial management
- o Treasury operations
- o Acquisition studies
- o Capital budgeting
- o Zero-based budgeting
- o S.E.C. reporting
- o Product line analysis
- o Cost accounting

- o General management
- o Annual and long-range plans
- o Internal consulting
- o Project management
- o Cost reduction strategies
- o Systems design/implementation
- o Excel/Lotus 1-2-3 applications
- o MRP implementation

CAREER ACHIEVEMENTS AT ACME INTERNATIONAL

o As Treasurer, spearheaded a major cost-control and cash-conservation effort that increased critically needed cash by 350% in eight months.

o Executed in-depth operational audits of proposed acquisitions: those approved generated over $100 million in revenue; those cancelled included one where the stock value subsequently declined more than 90%.

o Interacting with subsidiary Presidents, coordinated the annual plan review: introduced zero-based budgeting and a disciplined cycle for approving sales, expense, and capital projections.

o Identified and resolved serious product costing problems at the subsidiaries: installed cost systems, corrected inventory records, eliminated marginal products, and increased profits.

o Streamlined and upgraded departmental systems and procedures, increasing productivity and reducing costs in several areas including manufacturing, engineering, and order entry and billing; initiated MRP implementation improving inventory turns by over 30%.

o Instituted and enforced a capital budgeting and request cycle which accelerated ROIs to 30% and higher.

o Designed and implemented a top management reporting system which became the primary source for identifying problems; reports were based on the subsidiaries' financial and operating reports which were upgraded and standardized.

CAREER EXPERIENCE

ACME INTERNATIONAL CORPORATION, Any City, NY   1988–Present

Treasurer   1992–Present
Responsible for cash management, short-term borrowing, bank relations, pension asset management, investments, letters of credit, and foreign exchange. Also coordinate capital budgeting, lease versus buy decisions, and equipment leasing.

Corporate Director of Budgets   1988–1992
Responsibilities executed:

o Directed preparation, review, and consolidation of annual and long-range plans.
o Introduced top management reporting system.
o Evaluated operating results as a basis for corrective actions.
o Troubleshooter and senior consultant to subsidiaries.
o Installed job cost and standard cost systems.
o Directed the $60 million capital expenditure program.
o Executed comprehensive acquisition reviews.
o Audited subsidiaries' operations, systems, and procedures.

Restructured Treasury operations to eliminate duplications, upgrade systems, and reduce costs.

ENERGY SURVEY OF SAUDI ARABIA, Bahrain, Saudi Arabia   1985–1988

Energy Engineer   1986–1988
Managed 120 employees in directing the turnaround of major energy exploration projects.

REFERENCES PROVIDED UPON REQUEST

TIMOTHY A. WILSON

123 Any Street, Any City, CA XXXXX (619) 555-1234

Contact Name   Date
Title
Company
Street Address
City, State Zip

Dear Mr./Ms. _____:

As a key player in delivering 75% of Westar Bank's 1994 profits, as an early entrant into the multi-million-dollar Japanese aircraft leasing industry, and as a member of core teams which pulled off the lucrative sale of a bankrupt company and closed a $60 million portfolio deal, I have proven my ability to generate bottom-line results.

I am bringing to your attention my skills, achievements, creative energy, and talent for getting the job done. Irrespective of your current staffing, there may well be a "fit" between my skills and background and your business needs, namely:

o **Outstanding** Education (**M.B.A./J.D.**)

o 15 Years of Progressive Experience in Fortune 100, Entrepreneurship, Workouts, Turnarounds, Start-ups, Consulting, and **Equipment Leasing**

o Multiple and Diverse Skills:

- **FINANCE** (Corporate; Operations; Leasing)
- **ACCOUNTING** ("Big 6" Quality)
- **LEGAL** (Contracts; Taxation)
- **SYSTEMS** (PC to Mainframe)
- **PORTFOLIO MANAGEMENT**

o A Proven Track Record of Concrete, Measurable, Bottom-line, **Hands-on,** and **Team-Oriented** Accomplishments

I don't possess a "golden Rolodex" or "smoke & mirror" solutions, but I *can* offer a thorough knowledge of corporate finance, equipment leasing, and asset-based lending as well as a track record of achieving quantifiable results through honest and creative approaches.

Please call at your convenience if you would like to discuss further how I can contribute to your company's future success.

Sincerely yours,

Timothy A. Wilson

CFO/Controller/Legal/Taxes/Leasing

TIMOTHY A. WILSON

123 Any Street, Any City, CA XXXXX (619) 555-1234

EDUCATION

M.B.A.	Princeton University	Finance/Marketing	1984
J.D.	University of California	Business/Taxation	1990
B.A.	Princeton University	Economics	1982

SKILLS THAT ACHIEVE SUCCESS

o Finance expertise
o Accounting expertise
o Complex business/tax issues
o Legal analysis
o Staff management
o PC/systems expertise
o Strategic planning

o Lease portfolio evaluation
o Tax shelter analysis
o Financing strategies
o Deal origination/structuring
o Workouts/turnarounds
o Start-up ventures
o Business plan formulation

CAREER ACHIEVEMENTS

o In June 1996, closed one of the few *true* commercial aircraft *operating* lease transactions for a Japanese owner/lessor.

o Member of four-person team that closed—in 30 days—the sale of residual interests in a 4000 lease, multiple investor portfolio, generating $16.2 million in profit; represented more than 75% of Westar Bank's profits for 1994.

o Coexecuted the turnaround and premium price sale of a bankrupt equipment leasing firm with $60 million in assets and $250 million in tax losses; structured and implemented formal profit-planning (cash, tax, and GAAP); modeled and analyzed financing strategies and long-term business growth for equipment leasing.

o Consummated a private placement tax shelter equipment trust by resurrecting "11th hour" negotiations with a major Los Angeles bank and obtaining unsecured note financing for investors.

o On 12/31/93, closed "the deal that died a dozen deaths": a $60 million portfolio in long-term leases (an L-1011, railroad cars, mining and manufacturing equipment, trucks) originally acquired by the seller as a corporate tax shelter.

o Cofounder of personal computer start-up venture; coauthored business plan that resulted in a successful $1 million IPO.

o Financial member of start-up team for Acme Brands' entry into the soft-drink market: analyzed expansion alternatives, developed pricing strategies, established national bottler distribution network, and helped sell new ideas to senior management.

o Financial manager for $80 million business with multi-plant operations at Acme Brands: coexecuted turnaround strategy and start-up of new packaging technology.

CAREER EXPERIENCE

AIRLEASE INTERNATIONAL   12/94–Present
Any City, CA
VICE PRESIDENT—FINANCE & ADMINISTRATION
Full responsibility and accountability for all financial, legal, and administrative functions, from in-house CFO duties to structuring investment deals for clients. Promoted the institutional investment opportunity of the 1990s: "Low-Leverage, Short-Term Operating Leasing of Used Commercial Aircraft."

THE COMLEASE GROUP (WESTAR BANK)   12/91–12/94
Any City, CA
DIRECTOR—FINANCIAL PROJECTS
Reported to CEO. Responsible for profitability analyses, business reviews, trend and portfolio analysis, pricing, mergers and acquisitions, financial modeling, residual forecasting, and competitive analyses. Renegotiated and managed equity syndications, leveraged leases, tax-oriented deals, and special investments. Net worth doubled in less than two years.

ABC LEASING SERVICES, INC.   4/91–12/91
Any City, CA
CONSULTANT TO TRUSTEE
Responsible for analysis and forecasting of business valuation, reorganization alternatives, long-term financing, tax shelter impacts, and accounting issues. Negotiated with several prominent investment groups resulting in a sale price well above the creditors' most optimistic expectations.

PC VENTURE GROUP, INC.   8/90–4/91
Any City, CA
COFOUNDER and DIRECTOR OF BUSINESS ANALYSIS
Start-up venture. Member of three-person team that developed and authored business plan that effected a $1 million IPO. Personal contribution focused on financial projections, ROI/profit analyses, capitalization alternatives, market analysis, and competitive strategies.

ACME BRANDS CORPORATION   11/84–8/90
Any City, CA
BUDGET ANALYST TO FINANCIAL MANAGER
Projects Consultant—Sunset Boulevard Capital Corporation
Financial Manager—Corporate Manufacturing/Operations
Capital Investment Supervisor—Beverage & Breakfast Foods
Financial Associate—Syrup & Pancake Mix
Senior Financial Analyst—Soft-drink Group
EDP/Financial Analyst—Corporate Distribution
Budget Analyst—Corporate Distribution

OTHER QUALIFICATIONS

o Admitted to California State Bar
o Honorable Discharge—U.S. Air Force Finance Corps (2LT)

DAVID Q. SAMPLE (Version 2)

123 Any Street, Any City, CA XXXXX (619) 555-1234

Contact Name   Date
Title
Company
Address
City, State Zip

Dear Mr. /Ms. _____ :

I have combined a top business degree, global experience, and executive skills in banking, sales, finance, and general management to establish and direct new operations which have generated millions in revenue for well-respected international banks. Bottom-line contributions to profit have been rewarded with accelerated promotions, job security, and a six-figure salary package.

I am bringing to your attention my skills, achievements, strategic brainpower, global network, and talent for exceeding profit goals under negative economic conditions so that we can discuss my joining _____ as a member of your senior management team.

Results achieved during the past nine years with ABC Bank include:

o As Vice-President of an International Banking Group, produced revenue of $6.5 million in 1994 through aggressive client development and by saving 90% of the seriously at-risk accounts: accelerated the ROA by focusing on corporate finance, investment banking, and asset sales.

o As Vice-President of Corporate Banking at ABC's Southern California headquarters, leveraged my international contacts to market corporate and capital market products generating $5 million in added net income: achieved 250% growth in fees from capital market products.

o Was recruited away and promoted by ABC to start and manage the new International Energy Group: established and directed the lending operation generating over $500 million in new client bookings in only 18 months with an ROA of over 1%.

o As head of Commercial Development in charge of ABC's International Energy Group, initiated and closed several profitable deals including a hard-to-close $600 million project with an international energy company: created and directed a syndicate of major international lenders.

It should be mutually beneficial to meet and assess how I can help accelerate or turn around revenue and profit growth contributing to your company's future success.

Sincerely,

Enclosure: David Q. Sample

International Investment Banking

DAVID Q. SAMPLE

123 Any Street, Any City, CA XXXXX (619) 555-1234

M.B.A.   Honors   University of Paris Graduate School of Business   1985

International: Bilingual French and English; solid knowledge of Mideastern languages; traveled to over 60 nations

Certifications: Commercial Pilot's License; Black Belt Karate; Championship Skier

CAREER SKILLS/KNOWLEDGE

- o Banking executive
- o International banking
- o Investment banking
- o Corporate/capital markets
- o Acquisitions/joint ventures
- o Subsidiary recapitalization
- o Project financing/syndicates
- o Trade financing/foreign exchange

- o Marketing/sales executive
- o General management
- o Start-up operations
- o Major client development
- o Competitive maneuvering
- o Expansion/turnaround strategies
- o Revenue/profit growth
- o Organizational development

CAREER ACHIEVEMENTS

o As Vice-President of ABC's International Banking Group, produced revenue of $6.5 million in 1994 through aggressive client development and by saving 90% of the at-risk accounts: accelerated the ROA by focusing on corporate finance, investment banking, and asset sales.

o As Vice-President of Corporate Banking at ABC's Southern California headquarters, leveraged my international contacts to market corporate and capital market products generating $5 million in added net income: achieved 250% growth in fees from capital market products.

o Was recruited away and promoted by ABC to start and manage the new International Energy Group: established and directed the lending operation generating over $500 million in new client bookings in only 18 months with an ROA of over 1%.

o As head of Commercial Development in charge of ABC's International Energy Group, initiated and closed several profitable deals including a hard-to-close $600 million project with an international energy company: created and directed a syndicate of major international lenders.

o As Group Officer at Acme International Bank, established and directed operations of a new North American office: achieved and exceeded an aggressive operating plan generating new lending of $300 million and profitability in five months instead of the forecasted ten months.

CAREER EXPERIENCE

ABC BANK, Any Town, CA   3/88–Present

INTERNATIONAL BANKING GROUP, Any Town   2/91–Present

Vice-President
Responsible for major account development emphasizing high-margin corporate finance and investment banking: acquisitions, recapitalization, and collateralized financing. Upgraded asset quality by addressing and restructuring below-par debt.

CORPORATE BANKING, Any Town, CA   3/88–2/91

Vice-President
Created and marketed corporate and capital market products and services to global clients.

ACME INTERNATIONAL BANK, Any Town, Europe   6/85–3/88

Group Officer (Assistant Vice-President), Any Town, British Columbia   4/87–3/88
Managed start-up of a new operation: directed staffing, property selection, facility planning, contract negotiations, and purchasing. Also developed marketing policies and operating procedures.

Officer, Any Town, CA   5/86–4/87
Accelerated global account development quadrupling pre-tax net income to over $4 million.

Officer, Any Town, Europe   6/85–5/86
Established a Credit Group generating over $2 million in fees from new business development.

REFERENCES PROVIDED UPON REQUEST

GEORGE A. JOHNSON

123 Any Street, Any City, CA XXXXX (619) 555-1234

Contact Name   Date
Title
Company
Street Address
City, State Zip

Dear Mr./Ms. _____:

I have profitably applied executive skills in brokerage management, sales, marketing, and client development to become a top five producer, Western Region Vice-President, and a top earner with XYZ Securities. I have consistently demonstrated my talent for directing brokerage operations which generate tens-of-millions of dollars in fees exceeding even the most aggressive revenue targets.

I am presenting for your review my skills, bottom-line achievements, and accelerated experience so that we can initiate discussions about my joining _____ as a member of your senior brokerage management team.

Results achieved by applying my diverse skills include:

o Based on my nationwide ranking, productive management of the San Diego Branch, and turn-around of the Northern Los Angeles Branch, was promoted to Regional Vice-President of XYZ Securities at age 29.

o At XYZ, generate as much as $4,000,000 monthly in "new" money; personally generate as much as $800,000 monthly.

o At Acme Inc., more than doubled the dollar volume generated by fifteen high-dollar accounts.

o Consistently ranked among the top five sales producers at ABC Products, Inc.

I look forward to a face-to-face meeting at which we can determine how I can contribute to your company's future success.

Sincerely,

Enclosure: George A. Johnson

Stock Brokerage Executive

GEORGE A. JOHNSON

123 Any Street, Any City, CA XXXXX (619) 555-1234

BROKERAGE INDUSTRY EXPERIENCE

XYZ SECURITIES, INC., Any City, CA   6/95–Present

Western Region Vice President   6/96–Present
Responsible for Northern Los Angeles:

o Based on top five nationwide ranking, successful management of the San Diego Branch, and turnaround of the Northern Los Angeles Branch, was promoted to Western Region Vice-President at age 29.
o Generate up to $4,000,000 monthly in "new" money; personally generate as much as $800,000 monthly, servicing over 2,000 accounts.

BROKERAGE/MANAGEMENT SKILLS

o Regional executive	o Staff recruiting
o New account development	o Staff development
o Account management	o Advertising
o Underwriting	o NASD/banking rules

SALES EXPERIENCE

ABC PRODUCTS, INC., Any Town, CA   4/93–6/95

Sales Representative
Ranked among the top five producers.

AVERY COMPANY, INC., Any Town, CA   4/92–4/93

Sales Representative
Produced a 100% increase in the territory customer base.

ACME, INC., Any Town, CA   6/90–4/92

Account Representative
More than doubled the dollar volume generated by fifteen high-dollar accounts.

EDUCATION/CREDENTIALS

B.A.	Business Administration	University of San Diego	1990

Honor/Athletics:	o Graduated top quarter; varsity team captain
	o Named a Top Athlete in U.S. Colleges (1989)
Certification:	o Registered Broker Principal (NASD)
	o Registered Full Service Broker Representative (NASD)

MARK A. WILSON

123 Any Street, Any City, WA XXXXX (206) 555-1234

Contact Name   Date
Title
Company
Street Address
City, State Zip

Dear Mr./Ms. _____:

As Division Manager of Acme Corporation's Leasing Subsidiary, directed its turnaround and major contribution to profits in an otherwise disappointing period for the company. Achieved this by instituting a lucrative remarketing program, upgrading financial controls, and turning around out-of-control reporting.

I am presenting for your review my skills, achievements, leasing industry expertise, and talent for generating bottom-line results within problem operations so that we can discuss my joining _____ as a member of your management team.

Results achieved to date include:

o Instituted Acme's lucrative remarketing program for off-lease equipment generating substantial rentals from the over $4 million in equipment leased to date under the program.

o Investigated and uncovered several million dollars of off-lease equipment that had never been returned to inventory recovering $700,000 in fees for Acme.

o Restructured and turned around Acme's third-party leasing portfolio, upgrading the accounting and administrative controls and creating an accurate database of all equipment.

o As Program Director at ABC Computer Leasing, introduced critically needed administrative and accounting controls for an affiliated leasing company; thoroughly analyzed the affiliate's portfolio of leases, loans, sale/leasebacks, and remarketing agreements.

o One of five key veteran managers remaining after the bankruptcy of XYZ Leasing Services, a nationwide company with revenues of $200 million; comanaged its turnaround and better-than-forecasted $30 million sale.

I look forward to discussing how I can contribute to your company's future success.

                                                    Sincerely,

Enclosure: Mark A. Wilson

MARK A. WILSON

123 Any Street, Any City, WA XXXXX (206) 555-1234

B.B.A.   Accounting   University of Seattle   1986

Certified Public Accountant

CAREER SKILLS/KNOWLEDGE

- o Leasing industry expertise
- o Lease financing cycle
- o Division management
- o P&L responsibility
- o Marketing/sales
- o MIS operations
- o Personnel/payroll
- o Staff supervision/development
- o Information security

- o Finance/accounting
- o Controller operations
- o Treasury operations
- o Portfolio management
- o Banking relations
- o Audit operations
- o General accounting
- o Budgeting/controls
- o Collections/taxes

CAREER ACHIEVEMENTS

o As Division Manager of Acme Corporation's Leasing Subsidiary, directed its turnaround and major contribution to profits in an otherwise disappointing period for the corporation.

o Instituted Acme's lucrative remarketing program for off-lease equipment generating substantial rentals from the over $4 million in equipment leased to date under the program.

o Investigated and uncovered several million dollars of off-lease equipment that had never been returned to inventory recovering $700,000 in fees for Acme.

o Restructured and turned around Acme's third-party leasing portfolio, upgrading the accounting and administrative controls and creating an accurate database of all equipment.

o As Program Director at ABC Computer Leasing, introduced critically needed administrative and accounting controls for an affiliated leasing company; thoroughly analyzed the affiliate's portfolio of leases, loans, sale/leasebacks, and remarketing agreements.

o Instituted critically needed Equity Tracking System upgrading and streamlining the calculation and distribution of residual rents to ABC Computer Leasing's equity investors.

o One of five key veteran managers remaining after the bankruptcy of XYZ Leasing Services, a nationwide company with revenues of $200 million; comanaged its turnaround and better-than-forecasted $30 million sale.

CAREER EXPERIENCE

ACME CORPORATION, INC., Any Town, WA   2/95–Present

Division Manager
Responsibilities executed for the Acme Leasing Subsidiary:

o Achieved targeted P&L goals; instituted remarketing program.
o Direct senior staff: Controller, Systems Director, and Operations and Credit Managers.
o Upgraded financial and operational controls and reporting.
o Negotiate, screen, and approve all contracts.
o Upgraded relations with banks.
o Reduced aged receivables; upgraded inventory control.
o Eliminated aged backlog of customer inquiries.

ABC COMPUTER LEASING COMPANY, Any Town, WA   3/94–2/95

Program Director
Audited portfolio of affiliated leasing company from its inception through current status; instituted Equity Tracking System; assisted in transition to new database system.

XYZ LEASING SERVICES, INC., Any Town, WA   6/86–3/94

Treasurer   2/91–3/94
Responsibilities executed:

o Upgraded portfolio management increasing return on $40 million cash.
o Developed relations with major northwestern banks.
o Gained approval for post-bankruptcy exception request.
o Managed Personnel, Payroll, and Collections Departments.

Executed a major systems database project critical to the $30 million sale of the company.

Controller   3/89–2/91
Responsibilities executed:

o Recruited, trained, and supervised several staff accountants.
o Directed the Bookkeeping Department.
o Directed general ledger accounting; prepared consolidations.
o Managed in-depth operational reviews; initiated corrective actions.
o Supervised tax area; reduced equipment property taxes.

Instituted effective post-bankruptcy financial controls returning critically needed credibility to XYZ.

REFERENCES PROVIDED UPON REQUEST

Asset Management Executive

JOHN A. SMITH (Version 2)
---

123 Any Street, Any Town, CA XXXXX Home: (619) 555-1234 Office: (619) 555-2345

Contact Name   Date
Title
Company
Street Address
City, State Zip

Dear Mr./Ms. _____:

I have profitably applied executive skills in asset management, marketing, finance, real estate, and treasury to play a key role in the start-up and marketing of Asset Management Associates, a division of the $2 billion Acme Corporation which has achieved a 35% ROI through the acquisition and disposition of foreclosed real estate worth $200 million. I also played a central role in Acme Corporation's entry into both the asset management and financial industries.

I am presenting for your review my skills, achievements, proven leadership, work ethic, and straight-forward approach to getting the job done so that we can discuss my joining _____ as a member of your Asset Management Team.

Results achieved to date include:

o As Director of Sales, played a central role in the start-up, marketing, and general management of Asset Management Associates—a venture which has yielded an on-target 35% return through the purchase and resale of over 2,000 foreclosed properties valued at $200 million: codeveloped the start-up business plan, helped staff the company, and assumed a Director position reporting directly to the President.

o Helped generate third-year profits of $2 million on revenue of $7 million at Asset Management Associates: signed the first major banking client accounting for a 50-house management contract; closed deals which contributed to the company managing 400 properties generating $800,000 in fees; signed a major lender accounting for purchased inventory of over $2 million a month; sold 20 additional accounts yielding 8 management and 12 buy-out clients.

o Prior to and during my tenure as a Major Account Executive, directly facilitated Acme's subsequent entry into asset management: at the request of the Chairman, executed a feasibility study which recommended entry into asset management; closed a lucrative deal which represented the company's first asset management client and led to the eventual formation of Asset Management Associates.

o Took the lead in establishing Asset Management Associates' first relationship with the FDIC by directly contacting government officials; initiated negotiations for a major purchase from the Resolution Trust Corporation.

o As Treasury Director in charge of treasury operations at a division of Acme, initiated development of financial services which allowed clients to process applications through the mail to bankers with whom we had negotiated contracts: success of the services led to Acme's entry into the financial industry.

I look forward to discussing how I can help accelerate or turn around revenue and profit growth, contributing to your future success.

                                                                    Sincerely,

Enclosure: John A. Smith

JOHN A. SMITH

123 Any Street, Any Town, CA XXXXX Home: (619) 555-1234 Office: (619) 555-2345

| M.B.A. | Finance | University of Maine | 1982 |
| B.A. | Accounting | State University of New York | 1980 |

CAREER SKILLS/KNOWLEDGE

- o Asset management/marketing
- o Sales/marketing management
- o Balance sheet management
- o Real estate foreclosures
- o Collections/work-outs
- o Buy-out negotiations
- o Resale/ROI target strategies
- o Real estate management
- o Mortgage services
- o Cold-calling/client development
- o Proposals/presentations/closing

- o Financial/treasury management
- o Treasury operations
- o Cash management/allocation
- o Investment strategies
- o Borrowing strategies
- o Basis point reductions
- o Foreign exchange strategies
- o Banking relations
- o Budgeting/capital appropriations
- o Consolidations/financial statements
- o Auditing/credit and collections

CAREER ACHIEVEMENTS

o As Director of Sales, played a central role in the start-up, marketing, and general management of Asset Management Associates—a venture which has yielded an on-target 35% return through the acquisition and disposition of 2,000 foreclosed properties valued at $200 million: codeveloped the start-up business plan, helped staff the company, and assumed a Director position reporting directly to the President.

o Helped generate third-year profits of $2 million on revenue of $7 million at Asset Management Associates: signed the first major banking client accounting for a 50-house management contract; closed deals which contributed to the company managing 400 properties generating $800,000 in fees; signed a major lender accounting for purchased inventory of over $2 million a month; sold 20 additional accounts yielding 8 management and 12 buy-out clients.

o Prior to and during my tenure as a Major Account Executive, directly facilitated Acme's subsequent entry into asset management: at the request of the Chairman, executed a feasibility study which recommended entry into asset management; closed a lucrative deal which represented the company's first asset management client and led to the eventual formation of Asset Management Associates.

o As Director of Investment Acquisition at Asset Management Associates, directed development of a $40 million offering package and formed a syndicate of investors to meet our outside borrowing requirements; previously developed and recommended cancellation of a $200 million public offering.

o Took the lead in establishing Asset Management Associates' first relationship with the FDIC by directly contacting government officials; initiated negotiations for a major purchase from the Resolution Trust Corporation.

o As a Major Account Executive at an Acme Division, exceeded revenue targets by maintaining volume, increasing business, and renegotiating contracts with multimillion-dollar accounts.

o As Treasury Director in charge of treasury operations at a division of Acme, initiated development of financial services which allowed clients to process applications through the mail to bankers with whom we had negotiated contracts: success of the services led to Acme's entry into the financial industry.

CAREER EXPERIENCE

ACME CORPORATION, Any City, CA   1990–Present

ASSET MANAGEMENT ASSOCIATES, Any City, CA   1992–Present

Director of Investment Acquisition   1994–Present
Member of management team responsible for directing business and establishing strategic objectives. While still executing sales responsibilities, directed development of $40 million offering package.

Director of Sales   1993–1994
Developed new business in marketing acquisition and disposition services for foreclosed real estate to savings and loans, banks, the federal government, and other financial institutions.

Director   1992–1993
Member of group formed to assess the need for an Asset Management Company.

ACME DIVISION, Any City, CA   1990–1992

Major Account Executive   1991–1992
Maintained volume, increased business, and renegotiated contracts with established accounts of Acme.

Treasury Director   1990–1991
Instituted a new method of funding bank accounts which yielded a savings of $3 million a year; instituted a system of billing to clients which reduced receivables by $8 million; stopped a 40% increase in headcount by developing a computerized accounts receivable system during a period of rapid growth; computerized several Cash Management reports which accelerated the reimbursement process thereby reducing excess borrowing by $7 million.

AVERY INCORPORATED, Any City, CA   1982–1990

Assistant Treasury Manager   1987–1990
Profitably managed a $400 million portfolio of short-term investments; managed the daily cash position; negotiated basis point reductions; established and directed Currency Exchange review process.

Senior Financial Analyst   1984–1987
Reviewed budget submissions from international subsidiaries. Prepared reports with recommended changes that were routinely accepted.

ADDITIONAL EDUCATION/TRAINING

Professional Courses:
- o Professional Marketing Series
- o The Art of Selling Series
- o Professional Communications Series

Property Management/Development Executive

JOHN Q. SAMPLE (Version 2)

123 Any Street, Any City, CA XXXXX (619) 555-1234

Contact Name   Date
Title
Company
Address
City, State Zip

Dear Mr./Ms. _____ :

As a central figure in Acme Corporation's massive restructuring, I applied executive skills in property management, property development, administration, and purchasing to facilitate Acme's turnaround to profitability. I likewise produced multimillion-dollar profits for the ABC Company through productive management of its property management services and administration, receiving accelerated promotions to Director of a $19 million operation.

I am presenting for your review my skills, achievements, and talent for accelerating margins and turning around unprofitable organizations so that we can discuss my joining _____ as a member of your senior management team.

Results achieved to date include:

o As Acme's Corporate Director of Property Services & Administration, generated tens of millions of dollars in cost reductions and cash flow through aggressive property consolidations, upgraded services and procurement, and enforced management accountability.

o Promoted five grade levels during my last four years at ABC Company based on achieving all major P&L goals in directing the $19 million Corporate Property Management and Administration Department.

o Consolidated 29 Acme warehouses down to 4, generating annual savings of $5.8 million; saved $4.6 million by reducing corporate headquarters space 30%; introduced uniform facility standards which reduced total space requirements 20%, generating another $3.4 million in annual cost savings.

o Productively managed ABC Company's property holdings, achieving 97% occupancy of 800,000 square feet at premium rates; developed a sophisticated model which helped save $7 million on the cost of an out-of-control $40 million building project at ABC.

o As head of Acme's $230 million purchasing operation, introduced an aggressive multiple-sourcing program which improved the margins of two major product lines by 7% and 9% respectively.

I look forward to meeting and discussing how I can help accelerate or turn around your company's revenue and profit growth.

                                                                Sincerely,

Enclosure: John Q. Sample

Property Management/Development Executive

JOHN Q. SAMPLE

123 Any Street, Any City, CA XXXXX (619) 555-1234

B.S.   Honors   Finance   Georgetown University   1980

CAREER SKILLS/KNOWLEDGE

o Property management
o Development/construction
o Occupancy growth strategies
o Premium rate strategies
o Consolidation strategies
o Lease management/negotiations
o Site selection/space planning
o Budgeting/accountability
o Government regulations
o Environmental guidelines

o Finance/administration management
o General management
o Strategic/operational planning
o General/administrative services
o Financial planning and analysis
o Procurement operations
o Facilities/telecommunications
o Training operations
o Logistics services
o Global transportation

CAREER ACHIEVEMENTS

o As Corporate Director of Property Services & Administration, assumed a central role in Acme's turnaround to profitability: generated tens of millions of dollars in cost reductions and cash flow through aggressive property consolidations, upgraded services and procurement, and enforced management accountability.

o Promoted five grade levels during my last four years at ABC Company based on achieving all major P&L goals in directing the $19 million Corporate Property Management and Administration Department.

o Consolidated 29 Acme warehouses down to 4, generating annual savings of $5.8 million; saved $4.6 million by reducing corporate headquarters space 30%; introduced uniform facility standards which reduced total space requirements 20%, generating another $3.4 million in annual cost savings.

o Productively managed ABC Company's property holdings, achieving 97% occupancy of 800,000 square feet at premium rates; developed a sophisticated model which helped save $7 million on the cost of an out-of-control $40 million building project at ABC.

o As head of Acme's $230 million purchasing operation, introduced an aggressive multiple-sourcing program which improved the margins of two major product lines by 7% and 9% respectively.

o Overcame powerful organizational resistance to produce over $3 million cash and annual savings of $2.1 million by persuading the Chairman to sell off Acme's corporate yacht.

o Generated annual cost savings of over $800,000 by installing a Novell network and upgrading ABC Company's distribution, travel, and other corporate services.

CAREER EXPERIENCE

ACME CORPORATION, Any Town, CA   3/88–Present

Corporate Director of Property Services & Administration
Direct the overall management, planning, site selection, lease negotiations, consolidations, and disposition for property totaling two million square feet. Additionally direct the $230 million purchasing operation and all corporate administrative services.

ABC COMPANY, Any Town, CA   6/80–3/88

Director of Property & Services   3/85–3/88
Directed services with a staff of 63 and a budget of $19 million: included property management, purchasing, communications, systems, mail, and office equipment placement and maintenance. Reviewed and approved all facilities and construction contracts. Audited almost $100 million in operating expense budgets.

Manager of Administration   2/83–3/85
Developed policies and procedures, negotiated property transactions, and created a model which turned around a $40 million building project.

Senior Facilities Consultant   8/81–2/83
Developed well-received proposals that resulted in the creation of a $12 million Facilities Group.

Senior Consultant   6/80–8/81
Introduced the much needed zero-based budgeting concept to seven major operations.

REFERENCES PROVIDED UPON REQUEST

Real Estate Executive

JANET A. JONES

---

123 Any Street, Any City, CA XXXXX (619) 555-1234

Contact Name   Date
Title
Company
Address
City, State Zip

Dear Mr./Ms. _____:

As Vice-President in charge of XYZ Corporation's real estate referral service, I expanded the net-work from 21 to 264 firms, turned this money-losing operation into a highly profitable one, and re-ferred $550 million in real estate deals to XYZ Realty in 1996.

I am presenting for your review my skills, achievements, and ability to motivate personnel and generate bottom-line results so that we can discuss my joining _____ as a member of your senior management team.

Additional results achieved by aggressively applying my diverse skills include:

o Initiated research and identified serious economic problems with the Warranty Sales Plan; based on my recommendation, XYZ discontinued the program thereby preventing major losses.

o As Director of Relocation Services at XYZ, cost effectively managed the move of transferees in-volved in corporate relocations at General Electric, MCI, and TWA.

o During six years with ABC Realty, Inc., ranked as a top producer selling as much as $3 million in modestly priced real estate annually.

o Recognized at the 1995 Annual Meeting for "Outstanding Service to XYZ."

I look forward to meeting you, at which time we can determine how I can contribute to your com-pany's future success.

Sincerely,

Enclosure: Janet A. Jones

Real Estate Executive

JANET A. JONES

123 Any Street, Any City, CA XXXXX (619) 555-1234

REAL ESTATE ACHIEVEMENTS

o As Vice-President of XYZ Corporation's real estate referral service, developed and executed a marketing plan which expanded the network from 21 to 264 firms in four years.

o Turned around XYZ from a money-losing operation into a highly profitable one generating $2.5 million in fees annually; referred $550 million in real estate deals to XYZ Realty in 1996.

o Recognized at the 1995 Annual Meeting for "Outstanding Service to XYZ."

o Initiated research and identified serious economic problems with the Warranty Sales Plan; based on my recommendation, XYZ discontinued the program thereby preventing major losses.

o As Director of Relocation Services at XYZ, cost effectively managed the move of transferees involved in corporate relocations at General Electric, MCI, and TWA.

o During six years with ABC Realty, Inc., ranked as a top producer selling as much as $3 million in modestly priced real estate annually.

o Developed a homesale program for XYZ to generate additional revenues, currently not captured.

REAL ESTATE EXPERIENCE

XYZ CORPORATION, Any City, CA   5/89–Present

Vice-President   5/94–Present
Develop, expand, and direct overall operations of a full-service referral network:

o Member of the advisory board responsible for developing policies and programs for recruitment, marketing, and productivity.
o Manage development of Relocation Directors and Referral Coordinators; selected as lead instructor at regional meetings.
o In charge of the National Convention: develop all programs and select and contract for featured speakers.
o Member of Planning Committee for Employee Relocations Council's Conference.

Director of Relocation Services   5/89–5/94
In charge of developing and upgrading staffs in company-owned firms nationwide; also developed new revenue-generating programs.

ABC REALTY, INC., Any City, CA   5/83–5/89

Sales Associate: Consistently achieved Million-Dollar-Club status.

REFERENCES PROVIDED UPON REQUEST

Advertising Industry Executive

JOHN A. CUMMINGS

123 Any Street, Any City, CA XXXXX (213) 555-1234

Contact Name   Date
Title
Company
Street Address
City, State Zip

Dear Mr./Ms. _____:

I have applied executive skills in advertising, marketing, new product introductions, and acquisitions to generate multimillion-dollar billings and accelerate the revenue and profit growth of major Fortune 500 clients. Results have been rewarded with stock options and accelerated promotions up to Vice-President from Richard Smith, President of Prestigious Advertising, Inc.

I am bringing to your attention my skills, achievements, and proven ability to accelerate billings so that we can discuss my joining _____ as a member of your senior management team.

Results achieved at Prestigious Advertising, Inc. include:

o Singlehandedly developed the long-range corporate strategy and business plan for the development and acquisition of new products by the ABC affiliate of XYZ; profitably integrated the Essex Baking Company, a several hundred million dollar acquisition, into ABC.

o Initiated and executed aggressive new product introductions by the QRS Division of Acme, Inc.: codirected product development, packaging, market positioning, advertising, and testing; over a dozen high-profit-potential products were put into various stages of development.

o After winning key toy and game accounts of Acme, Inc., comanaged their new product acquisitions and development; coexecuted start-up of the multimillion-dollar Dimensions account.

o After recommending that senior management "kill" the frozen product lines of the Smith Division of Acme, Inc., presented a ten-part proposal that helped save the division; codirected a major new product introduction generating second-year sales of $80,000,000.

o Member of the core team which created, produced, and launched a highly successful cereal campaign featuring what turned into a well-known and nationally popular character; achieved highest persuasion and recall scores and sales gains of over 60% for Acme.

I know that an exploratory meeting to determine how I can, likewise, contribute to your company's future success will be to our mutual benefit.

Sincerely,

Enclosure: John A. Cummings

Advertising Industry Executive

JOHN A. CUMMINGS

123 Any Street, Any City, CA XXXXX (213) 555-1234

B.A. English   University of Massachusetts   1982

CAREER SKILLS/KNOWLEDGE

- o Advertising executive
- o Account management
- o Business reviews
- o Media/copy expertise
- o Market positioning
- o Commercial production
- o Product testing
- o Roll-out strategies
- o Oral/written presentations
- o Staff supervision
- o Budget management/control

- o Marketing executive
- o New business development
- o New product introduction
- o P&L responsibility
- o Acquisitions/mergers
- o Business plan development
- o Marketing strategies
- o Competitive analyses
- o Pricing/margin strategies
- o Financial analyses
- o International marketing

BUSINESS ACHIEVEMENTS AT PRESTIGIOUS ADVERTISING, INC.

o As Vice-President, developed the long-range corporate strategy and business plan for the development and acquisition of new products by the ABC affiliate of XYZ; profitably integrated the Essex Baking Company, a several hundred million dollar acquisition, into ABC.

o Initiated and executed aggressive new product introductions by the QRS Division of Acme, Inc.: codirected product development, packaging, market positioning, advertising, and testing; over a dozen high-profit-potential products were put into various stages of development.

o After winning key toy and game accounts of Acme, Inc., comanaged their new product acquisitions and development; coexecuted start-up of the multimillion-dollar Dimensions account.

o Member of the core team which created, produced, and launched a highly successful cereal campaign featuring what turned into a well-known and nationally popular character; achieved highest persuasion and recall scores and sales gains of over 60% for Acme.

o After recommending that senior management "kill" the frozen product lines of the Smith Division of Acme, Inc., presented a ten-part proposal that helped save the division.

o At a critical strategy meeting of the New Business Division of Acme, candidly assessed a proposed soft drink line as competitively inferior, causing senior management to "kill" it.

o Promoted to Senior Account Executive on the Acme account responsible for management of a main brand and introduction of a major new product; totally redesigned the new product packaging and codirected the overall project generating second-year sales of $80,000,000.

CAREER EXPERIENCE

PRESTIGIOUS ADVERTISING, INC., Any City, CA   9/90–Present

Vice-President, Account Supervisor
Responsibilities executed for major international clients:

o Coordinated long-range strategic planning and business plan development.
o Integral member of new and established products business development team.
o Conducted in-depth product feasibility studies as a basis for marketing decisions.
o Formulated market share growth strategies.
o Established product priorities.
o Established and monitored development schedules.
o Planned for acquisitions and mergers.
o Integrated acquisitions into client's corporate structure.
o Planned and implemented advertising campaigns.

ANOTHER ADVERTISING FIRM, Any City, CA   7/85–9/90

Account Executive
Achieved brand share growth, in spite of aggressive competition, for major clients including Major Brand A (Product 1, Product 2, Product 3) and Major Brand B (Product 1, Product 2, Product 3). Prepared corporate annual report for the CEO and Chairman.

ANOTHER ADVERTISING FIRM, Any City, CA   6/82–7/85

Account Executive
Sole Account Executive assigned to the multimillion-dollar Major Consumer Products Company account. Selected by the President of the Agency to be an on-site representative to a Fortune 50 Corporation.

REFERENCES AVAILABLE UPON REQUEST

> # Broadcast Industry/Sales Executive

JOHN A. DRAKE

123 Any Street, Any Town, CA XXXXX (619) 555-1234

Contact Name   Date
Title
Company
Address
City, State Zip

Dear Mr./Ms. _____:

I have formulated and executed expert sales, marketing, broadcasting, and product strategies to outmaneuver the competition, sell at premium rates, accelerate billings, and exceed revenue targets for the National Broadcasting Company during the past several years. I routinely generate millions in advertising revenue and a high six-figure income.

I am bringing to your attention my skills, achievements, and special talent for penetrating and selling even the toughest decision makers to that we can discuss my joining _____ as a member of your Senior Sales Management Team.

Results achieved during the last 13 years with NBC include:

o Earn a six-figure income by selling and servicing an expanding base of corporate clients for NBC Channel 6 in Los Angeles: generated four-year billings in excess of $60 million ranking as the number two biller the last two years.

o Ranked among the top Account Managers at NBC's Regional Sales Office in Los Angeles; achieved this by penetrating agencies and advertisers to reach decision makers to whom I sold a high percentage of available commercial time at premium prices.

o Developed and sold lucrative entertainment packages and created several well-received programming ideas for telecast over NBC-owned stations, generating millions in advertising revenue.

o Promoted to NBC's Regional Sales Office in Los Angeles in less than two years instead of the normal four to five year cycle.

o Accelerated NBC's Regional Sales Office in Miami from fourth place to second place in billings.

It should be to our mutual benefit to meet and determine how I can help accelerate or turn around sales, thereby contributing to your company's future success.

Sincerely,

Enclosure: John A. Drake

JOHN A. DRAKE

123 Any Street, Any Town, CA XXXXX (619) 555-1234

B.A.   University of Iowa   Self-financed   1977

CAREER SKILLS/KNOWLEDGE

o Broadcast industry sales	o Sales/marketing
o Station operations	o Decision-maker contact
o Advertiser relations	o Market penetration
o Program development	o Competitive strategies
o Automotive advertising expert	o Long-range planning
o Market share strategies	o Staff training/development
o Premium rate strategies	o Systems planning

SALES/MARKETING ACHIEVEMENTS

o Earn a high six-figure income by selling and servicing an expanding base of corporate clients for NBC Channel 6 in Los Angeles: generated four-year billings in excess of $60 million ranking as the number two biller the last two years.

o Ranked among the top Account Managers at NBC's Regional Sales Office in Los Angeles; achieved this by penetrating agencies and advertisers to reach decision makers to whom I sold a high percentage of available commercial time at premium prices.

o Developed and sold lucrative entertainment packages and created several well-received programming ideas for telecast over NBC owned stations generating millions in advertising revenue.

o Promoted to NBC's Regional Sales Office in Los Angeles in less than two years instead of the normal four to five year cycle.

o Accelerated NBC's Regional Sales Office in Miami from fourth place to second place in billings.

o Achieved market shares of 35% plus for BBD&O by outmaneuvering the competition and charging premium rates.

o Ranked as a top producer for Acme Television in Atlanta: achieved market shares of 30% through effective marketing of special programming to major client corporations.

o Promoted to Miami Office Manager for Acme Television after productively representing 83 outlets.

CAREER EXPERIENCE

NATIONAL BROADCASTING COMPANY, Los Angeles, CA   6/84–Present

Executive Account Manager   3/91–Present
Responsibilities executed at the Los Angeles owned station:

o Maintain and accelerate base of corporate clients.
o Create rate cards; review and sign off exceptions.
o Head of Productivity Group formed to improve overall sales productivity.

Executive Account Manager   11/87–3/91
Responsibilities executed at the Regional Sales Office in Los Angeles:

o Optimized commercial time usage and revenue generated per spot.
o Developed entertainment packages and created programming.
o Marketed special programming to major corporate clients.
o Trained and developed new sales recruits.

Account Manager   6/84–11/87
At the Regional Sales Office in Miami, exceeded billing targets and elevated our national ranking.

BBD&O, Miami, FL   2/81–6/84

Account Manager
Consistently exceeded billing targets.

ACME TELEVISION, Miami/Atlanta   1/79–2/81

Sales Manager/Account Manager
Represented some 83 outlets.

CAPITAL CITIES BROADCASTING, Dallas, TX   6/77–1/79

Account Manager
Produced commercials, accelerated the client base, and exceeded revenue targets.

REFERENCES PROVIDED UPON REQUEST

JEFFREY A. CUMMINGS

123 Any Street, Any City, WA XXXXX (609) 555-1234

Contact Name   Date
Title
Company
Street Address
City, State Zip

Dear Mr. /Ms. _____ :

Having developed and applied a command of Executive Hotel Management and the technical and organizational facets of hotel operations, I have proven my ability to achieve bottom-line results. My accelerated experience combined with academic credentials from the top-ranked universities for executive hotel management has prepared me to assume a general management role.

I am very interested in exploring the possibility of joining _____ as a member of your senior management team.

Results achieved by applying the managerial/technical skills detailed on the attached resume include:

o As General Manager, elevated the occupancy rate at a major 1,000 acre hotel and resort from an unsatisfactorily low level to over 90%; significantly improved profit margins.

o Significantly improved our all-important rating by reorganizing and modernizing all departments of the 1,000 acre hotel and resort including the 1,000 seat restaurant, separate celebrity nightclub, villas, theatres, and beach facilities.

o Successfully marketed and expanded lucrative convention operations as General Manager of a top-ranked European hotel.

o As General Manager of a major hotel, developed and directed a separate operation devoted to servicing/catering a major international airline: won this contract in a major "bidding war."

I know that I can achieve similar results for your company. I feel it will be to our mutual benefit to meet and talk face-to-face. You may contact me at the above number to set up an appointment. I look forward to our meeting.

Sincerely,

Enclosure: Jeffrey A. Cummings

JEFFREY A. CUMMINGS

123 Any Street, Any City, WA XXXXX (609) 555-1234

U.S. Citizen

ACADEMIC CREDENTIALS

GRADUATE DEGREE 1980	PRESTIGIOUS INTERNATIONAL INSTITUTE, Europe School for Executive Hotel Management High academic standards; selective; premier institution. Honors graduate.
COLLEGE DEGREE 1978	SCHOOL OF HOTEL PROFESSIONS, Europe Highly respected academic training; selective; prestigious. Honors graduate.
COLLEGE DEGREE 1976	UNIVERSITY OF LONDON Major: English Literature. Honors Graduate
Internships:	Summers during college at major International Hotels
Professional Seminars:	Attended and, in some cases, organized comprehensive training seminars for hotel executives conducted by major institutions: Major U.S. University; European-based Law School; European Center for Productivity
Languages:	Fluent in English, French, and German

HOTEL MANAGEMENT/TECHNICAL SKILLS

- o Executive hotel management
- o Full P&L responsibility
- o Hotel marketing/sales
- o Public relations
- o Food and beverage management
- o Classical French preparation
- o Menu composition
- o Personnel selection/training
- o Banquet management
- o Catering: inside/outside
- o Special catering
- o Hasidic Kosher/other ethnic cuisines
- o Wine expertise
- o Trainer/educator
- o Executive consultant
- o Operational planning
- o Organization and staffing
- o Procurement/product selection
- o Layout/construction
- o Interior decoration
- o Inventory control/storage
- o Interaction with public officials
- o Hotel operations law
- o Tourist/convention management
- o Negotiations with travel organizations
- o Hotel computer applications

EUROPEAN CAREER EXPERIENCE

MAJOR BEACH RESORT HOTEL, Europe   1989–1991

General Manager
Managed 1,000 acre hotel and resort: 1,000 seat restaurant; nightclub with name celebrities; separate villas; theatres; beach resort facilities and sports; other facilities. Major achievements:

o Occupancy rate climbed significantly to over 90%.
o Reorganized and modernized all departments.
o Significantly improved profits and critical rating.

Reason for leaving: to move permanently to the United States

EUROPEAN PALACE HOTEL, Europe   1986–1989

General Manager
Managed top-rated operations: marketing, promotion, and public relations; food and beverage; major conventions including NATO, International Athletic Medicine Association; reservations strategy; negotiations with travel organizations; support services including engineering, housekeeping, and security. Major achievements:

o Marketed/expanded lucrative convention operations; new clients included International Auto Exhibition and several governmental functions negotiated in talks with high officials.
o Developed/directed separate operation to service/cater a major international airline: won this contract in a major "bidding war."
o Named benefactor of a local prestigious hotel school.

HOTEL CONSULTING CORP., Europe   1983–1986

Senior Consultant—Hotel Specialist
Promoted to this position. One of 10 consultants selected to perform key assignments including: reorganization of highly rated hotels; architectural design—maximizing productivity and service; market research studies for developing menus and defining service needs; floor plan layouts, design of hotel machinery and technical specifications; purchasing equipment and materials; supervision of construction; development of policies/procedures.

EUROPEAN CRUISE LINE, Europe   1980–1983

Director of Hotel Services
Promoted to position. Managed hospitality services on large cruise ships. Recipes and menus developed earned accolades.

AMERICAN CAREER EXPERIENCE

NORTHWEST EXECUTIVE HOTEL, Any City, WA   1994–Present

<u>Director of Catering/Executive Maitre d'</u>
Market catering services to corporate clients; plan, schedule, and coordinate execution of banquets.

TOP OF THE HILL RESTAURANT, Any City, WA   1993–1994

<u>Executive Maitre d'</u>
In charge of banquet operations for this prestigious restaurant and caterer; emphasized negotiations with customers, planning, and overall supervision. Successfully managed over 200 wedding receptions and several corporate/social functions.

PORT OF CALL RESTAURANT, Any City, WA   1992–1993

<u>Manager</u>
Upon returning from Europe, was asked by a major lending institution to manage the turnaround of this troubled operation. Converted this low-rated local operation into a profitable, first-class restaurant.

ESSEX INN, Any City, WA   1991–1992

<u>Food and Beverage Director</u>
In charge of: major banquets; marketing/sales; procurement; entertainment lounge; and overall management of personnel. Received excellent feedback from senior management and customers.

REFERENCES PROVIDED UPON REQUEST

LEONARD A. SMITH

123 Any Street, Any City, WA XXXXX (206) 555-1234

Contact Name   Date
Title
Company
Street Address
City, State Zip

Dear Mr./Ms. _____:

I have applied executive skills in systems operations, project management, systems development, and manufacturing to implement multimillion-dollar systems, turn around out-of-control projects, accelerate productivity, and reduce costs for Fortune 500 companies. This has been rewarded with multiple promotions and a reputation for getting the job done.

I am bringing to your attention my skills, achievements, ability to produce under crisis management conditions, and talent for completing projects on time and under budget so that we can discuss my joining _____ as a member of your Systems/Manufacturing Management Team.

Results achieved to date include:

o As Project Director at Acme Corporation, brought critically needed cooperation and discipline to the Essex Manufacturing System, a $5 million MRPII project: instituted project planning, status reporting, and accountability; chaired status meeting; and upgraded relations between Systems and Manufacturing.

o As MIS Director at XYZ Corporation, installed Purchasing, Receiving, and Payables systems: reduced purchase order cycle from four weeks to one, elevated receiving accuracy from 55% to 97%, increased staff productivity 25%, and saved over $100,000 annually in overpayments.

o Promoted to MIS Director at XYZ after implementing the on-line Bill of Material and Inventory Control systems which turned around inventory accuracy from 65% up to 95%.

o Resolved serious vendor delivery problems and increased user involvement to successfully install the IBM 4000 Series and VSE and VM systems software at XYZ; also turned around the out-of-control computer operations.

o Converted ABC, Inc.'s obsolete systems, installing CICS and DL/1 in three months instead of the projected ten; installed Bill of Material and Parts Control systems which helped reduce obsolete inventory by 60%.

I look forward to discussing how I can, likewise, contribute to your company's future success.

Sincerely,

Enclosure: Leonard A. Smith

LEONARD A. SMITH

123 Any Street, Any City, WA XXXXX (206) 555-1234

M.B.A.	Computer Science	Washington State University	1980
B.S.	Computer Science	Washington State University	1978

Member: American Production and Inventory Control Society (APICS)

CAREER SKILLS

- MIS management
- Project management
- Systems development
- Planning/budgeting
- Design/specifications
- Staff supervision/training
- User relations/training
- Testing/implementation
- Major conversions
- Turnaround strategies

- Manufacturing operations
- Customer support/service
- Production systems
- MRP implementation
- Bill of material
- Inventory control
- Quality control
- Purchasing/receiving systems
- Service management systems
- Financial/sales systems

CAREER ACHIEVEMENTS

- As Project Director at Acme Corporation, brought critically needed cooperation and discipline to the Essex Manufacturing System, a $5 million MRPII project: instituted project planning, status reporting, and accountability; chaired status meetings; and upgraded relations between Systems and Manufacturing.

- Led the troubleshooting and resolution of project-threatening problems with vendor software packages on which the above system is based, identifying and correcting 400 major "bugs."

- As MIS Director at XYZ Corporation, installed Purchasing, Receiving, and Payables systems: reduced purchase order cycle from four weeks to one, elevated receiving accuracy from 55% to 97%, increased staff productivity 25%, and saved over $100,000 annually in overpayments.

- Promoted to MIS Director at XYZ after implementing the on-line Bill of Material and Inventory Control systems which turned around inventory accuracy from 65% up to 95%.

- Resolved serious vendor delivery problems and increased user involvement to successfully install the IBM 4000 Series and VSE and VM systems software at XYZ; also turned around the out-of-control computer operations.

- Converted ABC, Inc.'s obsolete systems, installing CICS and DL/1 in only three months versus the projected ten months by developing a conversion program to change the 150 programs.

- Installed ABC's Bill of Material and Parts Control systems which helped reduce obsolete inventory 60% from $4 million down to $1.6 million.

- Implemented, in record time, a comprehensive Service Control system upgrading the management of ABC's $70 million service business.

CAREER EXPERIENCE

ACME CORPORATION, Any Town, WA   6/93–Present

Project Director
Total responsibility for the implementation and support of the Essex Manufacturing System:

o Direct and train the professional staff.
o Interact closely with manufacturing to resolve design issues.
o Coordinate with the software vendor on the next release.

XYZ CORPORATION, Any Town, CA   5/88–6/93

MIS Director
Responsible for budgeting, planning, and staff management and training. Implemented several systems including Procurement/Receiving, Bill of Material, Inventory Control, and Accounts Payable. Instituted Systems Control software to manage systems changes, problems, and networking. Saved well over $100,000 annually by instituting key production cost reports.

ABC, INC., Any Town, CA   5/84–5/88

Senior Analyst
Led the conversion from batch mode to on-line, accelerating the number of computer terminals from only a few to 125; implemented data retrieval system on time-sharing giving users access to key reports within hours instead of days. Initiated and executed feasibility study which led to the cost-saving cancellation of a major systems project.

AVERY COMPANY, Any Town, CA   5/80–5/84

Systems Analyst
Promoted based on the on-time and under-budget implementation of critically-needed financial systems and reporting.

SYSTEMS ENVIRONMENTS

o CICS	o 308X
o IDMS	o 4341
o DL/1	o 3090
o IMS	o 303X
o AS	o MVS
o VSAM	o VSE
o PROFS	o VM

REFERENCES PROVIDED UPON REQUEST

WILLIAM A. JONES (Version 1)

123 Any Street, Any Town, CA XXXXX Home: (619) 555-1234 Work: (619) 555-2345

Contact Name   Date
Title
Company
Address
City, State Zip

Dear Mr. /Ms. _____:

I have applied expert skills in training, development, systems implementation, operations, materials management, and MRP to train and upgrade staffs, teach major quality improvement programs, turn around out-of-control operations, resolve serious inventory problems, implement critically needed MRP systems, and generate crucial project funding for Fortune 500 and smaller companies. Results achieved have been rewarded with promotions and major cross-divisional job offers.

I am bringing to your attention my skills, achievements, talent for teaching complex subject matter, and dedication to producing the best so that we can discuss my joining _____ as a member of your Training Management Team.

Results achieved to date include:

o As Materials Director at ABC Corporation, turned around out-of-control inventory problems within 15 months reducing inventory by 40%: implemented a critically needed IBM-based MRP system in only six months; created a critically needed Master Scheduling function; restructured and upgraded the previously ineffective Excess and Obsolescence process.

o As Director of Production Systems, took the initiative at a critical time for the beleaguered XYZ Company by initiating and executing a military funded study designed to justify and solicit multimillion-dollar military funding for XYZ's MRP II implementation: study led to funding approval.

o As Manager of P&IC at XYZ, accelerated inventory turn rates without impacting product lead times and was selected as an Instructor for the complex Quality Improvement Process: while executing my full-time responsibilities, worked several hours a week overtime to teach this ground-breaking course which impacted every department.

o Chosen from several candidates to direct and execute a high-profile corporate assignment aimed at providing project leadership for the planning and start-up of the Acme MRP II Manufacturing System at XYZ's Systems Division: developed a detailed, 24-month plan and organized a 200-person implementation team earning praise and a major job offer.

I will work hard to achieve bottom-line results and look forward to discussing how I can contribute to your company's future success.

Sincerely,

Enclosure: William A. Jones

WILLIAM A. JONES

123 Any Street, Any Town, CA XXXXX Home: (619) 555-1234 Work: (619) 555-2345

B.A. Honors Pace University Scholarship Recipient 1980

Certifications:
o American Production and Inventory Control Society
o Certified in Production and Inventory Management

CAREER SKILLS/KNOWLEDGE

o Training/development
o Systems consulting
o Quality improvement instructor
o Systems implementation
o Manufacturing systems
o Design/specifications
o Testing/debugging
o Alpha/Beta site testing
o Government guidelines
o Vendor/user relations

o Operations/materials management
o MRP systems expertise
o IBM/Acme MRP systems
o Commercial versions
o Production and inventory control
o Made/engineered to order/stock
o Master scheduling/forecasting/planning
o Excess/obsolescence control
o Procurement/distribution operations
o Service operations

CAREER ACHIEVEMENTS

o As Materials Director at ABC Corporation, turned around out-of-control inventory problems within 15 months reducing inventory by 40%: implemented a critically needed IBM-based MRP system in only six months; created a critically needed Master Scheduling function; restructured and upgraded the previously ineffective Excess and Obsolescence process.

o As Director of Production Systems, took the initiative at a critical time for the beleaguered XYZ Company by initiating and executing a military funded study designed to justify and solicit multimillion-dollar military funding for XYZ's MRP II implementation: study led to funding approval.

o As Manager of P&IC at XYZ, accelerated inventory turn rates without impacting product lead times and was selected as an Instructor for the complex Quality Improvement Process: while executing my full-time responsibilities, worked several hours a week overtime to teach this ground-breaking course which impacted every department.

o Chosen from several candidates to direct and execute a high-profile corporate assignment aimed at providing project leadership for the planning and start-up of the Acme MRP II Manufacturing System at XYZ's Systems Division: developed a detailed, 24-month plan and organized a 200-person implementation team earning praise and a major job offer.

o As Project Director for the implementation of the Acme MRP Manufacturing System at XYZ's Printer Division, directed and forced vendor's cooperation in executing design modifications, testing, and debugging of all modules including BOM, INVENTORY, MRP, PURCHASING, and all interfaces to shop floor control, data collection, and accounting: with minimal interruption to business, loaded over 70,000 part numbers and 50,000 bills of material.

o As Materials Manager within a multi-warehousing environment at XYZ, implemented a critically needed on-line order entry system including a time-phased requirements module; planned and directed the on-schedule relocation of a 100,000 sq. ft. warehouse.

CAREER EXPERIENCE

ABC CORPORATION, Any City, CA   4/92–Present

Materials Director
Implemented IBM-based MRP system in only a few months; established Master Scheduling function; formalized the Excess and Obsolescence process.

XYZ COMPANY, VARIOUS DIVISIONS   5/86–4/92

ESSEX DIVISION, Any City, CA   3/91–4/92

Director of Production Systems
Adviser for implementation of the multimillion-dollar Acme MRP II Manufacturing System. Coordinated and controlled all system changes.

AVERY PRINTER DIVISION, Any City, CA   5/86–3/91

Project Director   1/89–3/91
Projected managed implementation of Acme Integrated Manufacturing System.

Project Consultant   2/88–1/89
Executed this critical corporate assignment: provided project leadership for the implementation planning of the Acme MRP implementation.

Manager P&IC   3/87–2/88
Managed master scheduling, forecasting, and inventory. As an Instructor for the Quality Improvement Process, assumed a central role in instituting this ground-breaking program.

Materials Manager   5/86–3/87
Responsible for customer order through shipping process for parts sales in excess of $80 million: managed procurement, inventory, warehousing, and transportation.

SMART PRODUCTS COMPANY, Any City, CA   6/80–5/86

Manager of Production Control   6/83–5/86
Promoted to this position becoming the youngest supervisor in the company; responsible for the planning, master scheduling, and expediting functions; was chosen for a corporate task force which developed the standards for material control.

Master Scheduling Supervisor   8/81–6/83
Worked long hours to bring a lucrative product into production.

Supervisor   6/80–8/81
Redesigned Bill of Material; instituted uniform methods and procedures.

REFERENCES AVAILABLE UPON REQUEST

JOHN A. JONES (Version 2)

123 Any Street, Any City, WA XXXXX (206) 555-1235

Contact Name   Date
Title
Company
Street Address
City, State Zip

Dear Mr./Ms. _____:

I have combined degrees from Stanford and Wharton with executive skills in operations, manu-facturing, engineering, and sales to build a $20 million company known internationally for its state-of-the-art products, cost-effective production, substantial market shares, and global clients. Achievements were rewarded with growing profits and prestigious awards for delivering vital systems in record time.

I am bringing to your attention my leadership skills, achievements, ability to create cost-effective solutions, and proven talent for accelerating market share and profits to produce financial security for others and myself so that we can discuss my joining _____ as a member of your general management/operations/engineering team.

Results achieved to date include:

o As Founder and Chief Executive of ABC, Inc., started and built this profitable high-tech elec-tronics company known over 20 years for its innovative products and low-cost volume produc-tion: negotiated and executed the lucrative sale of the company to a major corporation.

o More than doubled ABC's revenue by marketing breakthrough products to over 40 countries and major Fortune 500 corporations: developed damage-proof and modular products; intro-duced concept of placing electronics into clothing; developed communications systems for space projects, carriers, train systems, executive aircraft, and bank machines.

o Became one of the world's largest producers of specialized communication devices by focusing on the high volume global market; instituted "people-based" engineering to extend the life of electronic equipment and produce safety-conscious communications for major clients.

o Turned around out-of-control quality and distributions problems at XYZ Technology increas-ing on-time shipments from 38% to 95%; also turned around purchasing operations generating $3 million a year in cost reductions while reducing inventory $3 million.

Should we reach mutually agreeable terms, I will work hard to help accelerate or turn around op-erating performance contributing to your future success.

Sincerely,

Enclosure: John A. Jones

Manufacturing/Engineering/General Management

JOHN A. JONES

---

123 Any Street, Any City, WA XXXXX (206) 555-1235

M.B.A.	Management	Wharton	1974
B.S.	Electrical Engineering	Stanford University	1972
B.A.	Economics	Stanford University	1972

CAREER SKILLS/KNOWLEDGE

o Operations/engineering
o Manufacturing/Q.C./materials
o Cost-effective production
o Labor negotiations
o Productivity improvements
o R&D/systems engineering
o New product development
o Cost reduction strategies
o Electronics industry

o International marketing/sales
o General management/finance
o Start-up operations/organization
o Major client development
o Product management
o Competitive maneuvering
o Expansion/turnaround strategies
o Profit/market share growth
o New product marketing/pricing

CAREER ACHIEVEMENTS

o As Founder and Chief Executive of ABC, Inc., started and built this profitable high-tech electronics company known over 20 years for its innovative products and low-cost volume production: negotiated and executed the lucrative sale of the company to a major corporation.

o Awarded a coveted medal by a foreign government for producing and delivering, in less than 60 days, critically needed communications systems vital to their national defense: crash program cut four months off the schedule.

o More than doubled ABC's revenue by marketing breakthrough products to over 40 countries and major Fortune 500 corporations: developed damage-proof and modular products; introduced concept of placing electronics into clothing; developed communications systems for space projects, carriers, train systems, executive aircraft, and bank machines.

o Became one of the world's largest producers of specialized communication devices by focusing on the high volume global market; instituted "people-based" engineering to extend the life of electronic equipment and produce safety-conscious communications for major clients.

o Turned around out-of-control quality and distribution problems at XYZ Technology increasing on-time shipments from 38% to 95%; also turned around purchasing operations generating $3 million a year in cost reductions while reducing inventory $3 million.

o As Director of Procurement at Acme Company, generated $4 million in annual cost savings and reduced inventory $2 million by resolving serious cost control and material control problems.

CAREER EXPERIENCE

ACME COMPANY, Any City, WA   1996–Present

Director of Procurement
Instituted much needed budget systems; upgraded material control, developed off-shore vendors, reduced materials shortages, and stopped downtime; generated cost savings and reduced inventory.

XYZ TECHNOLOGY CORPORATION, Any Town, WA   1995–1996

Project Director
In a series of manufacturing, technical, and procurement assignments, instituted modern management techniques: improved production quality, cut costs, reduced inventory, and established on-time delivery:

o Upgraded Q.C. operations, policies, and procedures.
o Tightened vendor product quality standards.
o Instituted competitive bidding and second sourcing.
o Introduced Japanese methods of inventory stocking.

ABC, INCORPORATED, Any Town, WA   1974–1995

Chief Executive and Founder
Founded and managed a high-tech company which grew to over 150 employees:

o Expanded through innovation, systems engineering, and cost-effective manufacturing.
o Oversaw product development from inception through design, engineering, and production.
o Established and monitored marketing and pricing objectives.
o Developed client relations with major corporations and numerous countries.
o Continuously expanded into new markets.
o Redesigned and improved products to reduce costs.
o Established rigid quality control standards.
o Designed a plant layout which dramatically improved assembly productivity.
o Consistently met tight delivery schedules.

REFERENCES PROVIDED UPON REQUEST

R&D/Engineering/Project Management

PATRICK A. WILSON

123 Any Street, Any City, CA XXXXX (619) 555-1234

Contact Name   Date
Title
Company
Street Address
City, State Zip

Dear Mr./Ms. _____:

I have applied proficient skills in project management, engineering, product development, client relations, and marketing to develop state-of-the-art systems, execute complex communications studies, turn around out-of-control projects, and generate lucrative accounts for Fortune 500 companies. This has been rewarded with promotions and a reputation for getting the job done.

I am bringing to your attention my skills, achievements, talent for motivating teams, and ability to produce results under intense pressure and out-of-control conditions so that we can discuss my joining _____ as a member of your Project Management Team.

Results achieved to date include:

o As Project Director on a critical $300 million program, directed the development of complex state-of-the-art systems at Acme: sub-systems under my control are among the very few within the total project that are under control and on schedule.

o Turned around relations between Acme Industries and a major client who had stopped payments toward a $300 million project: was singled out by the client for helping Acme to pass a critical Demonstration Review which led to resumption of monthly progress payments.

o As a Project Director at ABC, Inc., generated satisfied clients and substantial revenue by expediting installation of multimillion-dollar space projects for XYZ Company, MCA, and CBS; established productive client rapport and had reputation for delivering on-time projects.

o Played a central role in XYZ Company's efforts to penetrate the closed Asian markets: presented well-received studies to Korea's Ministry of Telecommunications and Osaka Telegraph and Telephone, paving the way for several hundred million dollar deals.

o Upon promotion to Director of ABC's $2 million Space Engineering Unit, stimulated revenue growth, turned around eroding morale, upgraded staff performance, and improved productivity.

It should be to our mutual benefit to meet and determine how I can contribute to your company's bottom-line success.

Sincerely,

Enclosure: Patrick A. Wilson

PATRICK A. WILSON

123 Any Street, Any City, CA XXXXX (619) 555-1234

B.S.   Electrical Engineering   University of Texas   1982

CAREER SKILLS/KNOWLEDGE

- o Project management
- o Product development
- o Communications studies
- o Engineering/administration
- o Planning/scheduling
- o Team motivation
- o Subcontractor relations
- o Cost control/reductions
- o Design/specifications/prototypes
- o Testing/release/support

- o Sales/account management
- o Program management
- o Client development/relations
- o Revenue growth strategies
- o Profit growth strategies
- o Deal-making/negotiating
- o Turnaround strategies
- o Staff supervision/development
- o Productivity improvements
- o International markets

CAREER ACHIEVEMENTS

o As Project Director on a critical $300 million program, directed the development of complex state-of-the-art systems at Acme: sub-systems under my control are among the very few within the total project that are under control and on schedule.

o Turned around relations between Acme Industries and a major client who had stopped payments toward a $300 million project: was singled out by the client for helping Acme to pass a critical Demonstration Review which led to resumption of monthly progress payments.

o As a Project Director at ABC, Inc., generated satisfied clients and substantial revenue by expediting installation of multimillion-dollar space projects for XYZ Company, MCA, and CBS; established productive client rapport and had reputation for delivering on-time projects.

o Played a central role in XYZ Company's efforts to penetrate the closed Asian markets: presented well-received studies to Korea's Ministry of Telecommunications and Osaka Telegraph and Telephone, paving the way for several hundred million dollar deals.

o Upon promotion to Director of ABC's $2.0 million Space Engineering Unit, stimulated revenue growth, turned around eroding morale, upgraded staff performance, and improved productivity.

o Played a pivotal role in ABC's landing the lucrative XYZ Company and MCA accounts: convinced MCA to leave a competitor and turned around negative relations with XYZ.

o Built a reputation at ABC for accomplishing the impossible, receiving numerous accolades from executives at XYZ Company and Essex Communications where one executive voiced his opinion that "Pat is one of the finest Project Managers in the world."

BUSINESS EXPERIENCE

ACME INDUSTRIES, Any Town, CA   2/94–Present

Project Director
Manage client relations and overall planning, scheduling, and staffing for a state-of-the-art system development contract. Direct staff of 50 in executing hardware design, fabrication, and testing.

ABC, INC., Any Town, CA   3/91–2/94

Director—Space Engineering Unit   9/92–2/94
General management responsibility for this engineering services and market research firm:

o Directed staff of 45 sales, marketing, and product management personnel.
o Provided engineering services, interacting with major clients on proposals, price negotiations, and technical issues.
o Delivered critical presentations to Asian clients.

Project Director   3/91–9/92
Primary liaison to XYZ Communications, Essex Communication, MCA, and CBS:

o Established excellent rapport with clientele.
o Conducted complex frequency interference studies of station sites.
o Performed frequency coordination of remote stations, prepared site report, and analyzed field-measurement data.

RIGOR SERVICES COMPANY, Any Town, OR   11/89–3/91

Engineer
Under contract to provide a Mideastern Air Force with on-the-job instruction in F-16 systems troubleshooting.

AVERY COMPANY, Any Town, OH   6/88–11/89

Engineer
Completed rigorous company training at a government facility: managed group on overseas assignment providing technical support for the F-14. Based on results achieved, was requested to stay past the normal pull-out date; such requests are almost never made by the government.

MILITARY CREDENTIALS

Underwater Operations   6/82–6/88
Graduate of the rigorous Nuclear Training Program: ranked near the top of the class and completed long-term assignment aboard a nuclear-powered submarine; substituted for the First Officer; was consulted on major operational decisions.

INTERNATIONAL TRAVEL: Traveled throughout Europe and Asia.

WILLIAM Q. SAMPLE (Version 2)

123 Any Street, Any Town, NJ XXXXX (201) 555-1234

Contact Name   Date
Title
Company
Street Address
City, State Zip

Dear Mr./Ms. _____:

As Executive Vice-President for the U.S. Division of a European-based corporation, I have applied executive skills in operations, materials, engineering, and sales to outmaneuver the competition, deal with volatile exchange rates, accelerate growth of the corporate client base, and achieve a five-fold increase in sales—a revenue level which now accounts for 40% of worldwide sales.

I am presenting for your review my skills, achievements, technical degree, global contacts, and talent for creating productive organizations and achieving aggressive revenue and profit goals so that we can discuss my joining _____ as a member of your senior operations team.

Results achieved to date include:

o Earned multiple promotions up to Executive Vice-President at a U.S. Division of Acme International, one of Europe's largest industrial corporations: created a highly productive sales organization and achieved a fivefold increase in revenue turning the U.S. Division into a $20 million business which now accounts for almost 40% of the subsidiary's global sales.

o In spite of global competition, closed multimillion-dollar clients including Western Electric, AT&T, Boeing, and John Deere: accelerated the AT&T account from zero to $9 million representing half of total sales; generated a ninefold sales increase from the Harvester Division of John Deere; produced an eightfold increase in the Western Electric and Boeing accounts.

o Significantly reduced overhead and logistics expenses and all but eliminated aged receivables and write-offs by creating and enforcing conservative credit policies at Acme; in order to meet scheduled delivery dates through on-time shipments from Europe, also established a first-rate logistics function.

o Earned several promotions up to Director within the Engineering Department of a Florida-based division of Essex Corporation: directed high-quality product designs, upgraded operating systems critical to the production process, and effectively troubleshooted the complex power supply systems.

I look forward to discussing how I can help accelerate or turn around the performance of your international operations.

                                                          Sincerely,

Enclosure: William Q. Sample

WILLIAM Q. SAMPLE

123 Any Street Address, Any Town, NJ XXXXX (201) 555-1234

B.S.	Electrical Engineering	International University	Comprehensive Six-Year Program
B.A.	Business Administration	Lehman College	Managerial Studies

International:	Traveled throughout Europe, Asia, South America, and North America
Languages:	Fluent French and Spanish

CAREER SKILLS/KNOWLEDGE

- o Operations/materials/engineering
- o Purchasing operations
- o Cost controls/reductions
- o Global distribution/logistics
- o Heavy industry clients
- o Aircraft engine market
- o Engineering operations
- o Electrical/systems engineering
- o New product design
- o Plant operating systems design

- o Sales/marketing executive
- o International sales/markets
- o European relations
- o Strategic/marketing plans
- o Market share strategies
- o Major client development
- o Competitive maneuvering
- o Exchange rate strategies
- o Organizational development
- o Staff supervision/development

CAREER ACHIEVEMENTS

o Earned multiple promotions up to Executive Vice-President at a U.S. Division of Acme International, one of Europe's largest industrial corporations: created a highly productive sales organization and achieved a fivefold increase in revenue turning the U.S. Division into a $20 million business which now accounts for almost 40% of the subsidiary's global sales.

o In spite of high turnover and chronically unfavorable exchange rates, which adversely impacted the U.S. Division's pricing structure, generated a 500% increase in Acme's customer base through an accelerated client development program which emphasized quality and service to offset the unfavorable pricing.

o In spite of global competition, closed multimillion-dollar clients including Western Electric, AT&T, Boeing, and John Deere: accelerated the AT&T account from zero to $9 million representing half of total sales; generated a ninefold sales increase from the Harvester Division of John Deere; produced an eightfold increase in the Western Electric and Boeing accounts.

o Significantly reduced overhead and logistics expenses and all but eliminated aged receivables and write-offs by creating and enforcing conservative credit policies at Acme; in order to meet scheduled delivery dates through on-time shipments from Europe, also established a first-rate logistics function.

o Earned several promotions up to Director within the Engineering Department of a Florida-based division of Essex Corporation: directed high-quality product designs, upgraded operating systems critical to the production process, and effectively troubleshooted the complex power supply systems.

CAREER EXPERIENCE

ACME INTERNATIONAL CORPORATION, Any Town, NJ   1984–Present

Executive Vice-President   1987–Present
Direct sales, marketing, strategic planning, client development, import operations, logistics, distribution, and credit.

Vice-President of Sales   1984–1987
Directed sales, marketing, strategic planning, and related functions.

ESSEX CORPORATION, Any Town, FL   1975–1984

Director of Engineering   1980–1984
Earned several promotions based on engineering achievements in directing low-tolerance design and systems engineering projects. Also successfully planned and executed high-visibility manufacturing projects.

MILITARY EXPERIENCE

European Military: Honorably Discharged

Affiliations: Society of U.S. Engineers; Production Engineers of the Northeast
Citizenship: U.S. Citizen

REFERENCES AVAILABLE UPON REQUEST

WILLIAM A. JONES (Version 2)

123 Any Street, Any Town, CA XXXXX Home: (619) 555-1234 Office: (619) 555-2345

Contact Name   Date
Title
Company
Address
City, State Zip

Dear Mr./Ms. _____:

I have applied executive skills in materials management, operations, systems implementation, MRP, procurement, and distribution to turn around out-of-control operations, address and resolve serious inventory problems, implement critically needed MRP systems, institute major quality improvement programs, and generate critically needed project funding for Fortune 500 and smaller companies. Results achieved have been rewarded with promotions and major cross-divisional job offers.

I am bringing to your attention my skills, achievements, talent for generating bottom-line results, and dedication to producing the best so that we can discuss my joining _____ as a member of your Materials/Operations Management Team.

Results achieved to date include:

o As Materials Director at ABC Corporation, turned around out-of-control inventory problems within 15 months reducing inventory by 40%: implemented a critically needed IBM-based MRP system in only six months; created a critically needed Master Scheduling function; restructured and upgraded the previously ineffective Excess and Obsolescence process.

o As Director of Production Systems, took the initiative at a critical time for the beleaguered XYZ Company by initiating and executing a military funded study designed to justify and solicit multimillion-dollar military funding for XYZ's MRP II implementation: study led to funding approval.

o As Project Director for the implementation of the Acme MRP Manufacturing System at XYZ's Printer Division, directed and forced vendor's cooperation in executing design modifications, testing, and debugging of all modules including BOM, INVENTORY, MRP, PURCHASING and all interfaces to shop floor control, data collection, and accounting: loaded over 70,000 part numbers and 50,000 bills of material.

o Chosen from several candidates to direct and execute a high-profile corporate assignment aimed at providing project leadership for the planning and start-up of the Acme MRP II Manufacturing System at XYZ's Systems Division: developed a detailed 24-month plan and organized a 200-person project team earning praise and a major job offer.

I will work hard to achieve bottom-line results and look forward to discussing how I can contribute to your company's future success.

Sincerely,

Enclosure: William A. Jones

Materials Management Executive

WILLIAM A. JONES

123 Any Street, Any Town, CA XXXXX Home: (619) 555-1234 Work: (619) 555-2345

B.A. Honors Pace University Scholarship Recipient 1980

Certifications:
- o American Production and Inventory Control Society
- o Certified in Production and Inventory Management

CAREER SKILLS/KNOWLEDGE

- o Operations/materials management
- o MRP systems expertise
- o IBM/Acme MRP systems
- o Commercial versions
- o Production and inventory control
- o Made /engineered to order /stock
- o Master scheduling/forecasting/planning
- o Excess/obsolescence control
- o Procurement/distribution operations
- o Service operations

- o Systems implementation
- o Manufacturing systems
- o Design/specifications
- o Testing/debugging
- o Alpha /Beta site testing
- o Government guidelines
- o Vendor/user relations
- o Training/development
- o Quality improvement instructor
- o IBM mainframes/DEC minis

CAREER ACHIEVEMENTS

o As Materials Director at ABC Corporation, turned around out-of-control inventory problems within 15 months reducing inventory by 40% implemented a critically needed IBM-based MRP system in only six months; created a critically needed Master Scheduling function; restructured and upgraded the previously ineffective Excess and Obsolescence process.

o As Director of Production Systems, took the initiative at a critical time for the beleaguered XYZ Company by initiating and executing a military funded study designed to justify and solicit multimillion-dollar military funding for XYZ's MRP II implementation: study led to funding approval.

o As Project Director for the implementation of the Acme Manufacturing System at XYZ's Printer Division, directed and forced vendor's cooperation in executing design modifications, testing, and debugging of all modules including BOM, INVENTORY, MRP, PURCHASING and all interfaces to shop floor control, data collection, and accounting: with minimal interruption to business, loaded over 70,000 part numbers and 50,000 bills of material.

o Chosen from several candidates to direct and execute a high-profile corporate assignment aimed at providing project leadership for the planning and start-up of the Acme MRP II Manufacturing System at XYZ's Systems Division: developed a detailed, 24-month plan and organized a 200-person implementation team earning praise and a major job offer.

o As Manager of P&IC at XYZ, accelerated inventory turn rates without impacting product lead times and was selected as an Instructor for the complex Quality Improvement Process: while executing my full-time responsibilities, worked several hours a week overtime to teach this ground-breaking course which impacted every department.

o As Materials Manager within a multi-warehousing environment at XYZ, implemented a critically needed on-line order entry system including a time-phased requirements module; planned and directed the on-schedule relocation of a 100,000 sq. ft. warehouse.

CAREER EXPERIENCE

ABC CORPORATION, Any City, CA   4/92–Present

Materials Director
Implemented IBM-based MRP system in only a few months; established Master Scheduling function; formalized the Excess and Obsolescence process.

XYZ COMPANY, VARIOUS DIVISIONS   5/86–4/92

ESSEX DIVISION, Any City, CA   3/91–4/92

Director of Production Systems
Advisor for implementation of the multimillion-dollar Acme MRP II Manufacturing System. Coordinated and controlled all system changes.

AVERY PRINTER DIVISION, Any City, CA   5/86–3/91

Project Director   1/89–3/91
Projected managed implementation of Acme Integrated Manufacturing System.

Project Consultant   2/88–1/89
Executed this critical corporate assignment: provided project leadership for the implementation planning of the Acme MRP implementation.

Manager P&IC   3/87–2/88
Managed master scheduling, forecasting, and inventory. As an Instructor for the Quality Improvement Process, assumed a central role in instituting this ground-breaking program.

Materials Manager   5/86–3/87
Responsible for customer order through shipping process for parts sales in excess of $80 million: managed procurement, inventory, warehousing, and transportation.

SMART PRODUCTS COMPANY, Any City, CA   6/80–5/86

Manager of Production Control   6/83–5/86
Promoted to this position becoming the youngest supervisor in the company; responsible for the planning, master scheduling, and expediting functions; was chosen for a corporate task force which developed the standards for material control.

Master Scheduling Supervisor   8/81–6/83
Worked long hours to bring a lucrative product into production.

Supervisor   6/80–8/81
Redesigned Bill of Material; instituted uniform methods and procedures.

REFERENCES AVAILABLE UPON REQUEST

JENNIFER A. SMITH

123 Any Street, Any City, WA XXXXX (206) 555-1234

Contact Name   Date
Title
Company
Address
City, State Zip

Dear Mr./Ms. _____ :

I have applied proven skills in HR management, recruiting, redeployment, training, and systems to turn around HR operations, achieve challenging hiring objectives, and institute critically needed systems and training for Fortune 500 corporations. Bottom-line achievements have been rewarded with bonuses and several promotions.

I am bringing to your attention my skills, achievements, high energy, talent for improving job candidate quality, and track record of cost reductions so that we can discuss my joining _____ as a member of your HR Management Team.

Results achieved to date include:

o As HR Director at the Essex Company, upgraded Human Resources for over 3,000 employees: filled over 500 openings annually improving candidate quality while cutting the recruiting cycle in half; reduced excessive benefits operating costs; instituted critically needed cross-training; computerized previously manual systems; directed the upgrade of policies and procedures.

o As HR Manager at ABC Corporation, project managed the start-up of a new headquarters: coordinated the logistics and successfully recruited and hired over 400 employees in only seven months; also directed and accelerated the productivity of the administrative support staff.

o Directed Acme Development Center's Human Resources start-up and operation: achieved first-year staffing goals in less than nine months and instituted comprehensive employee relations programs.

o Turned around Acme's Personnel Redeployment Program achieving over a 90% placement rate through well-received seminars and workshops.

o Directed the highly successful implementation of Acme's critically needed $12 million Human Resource, Benefits, and Payroll system.

I look forward to discussing how I can, likewise, contribute to your company's future success.

Sincerely,

Enclosure: Jennifer A. Smith

Human Resources Management

JENNIFER A. SMITH

123 Any Street, Any City, WA XXXXX (206) 555-1234

B.A.   Honors   Communications   Smith College   GPA 3.7/4.0   1980

CAREER SKILLS/KNOWLEDGE

o Human resources professional
o Recruiting techniques
o Training and development
o Outplacement counseling
o Seminar/workshop development
o Video role playing/feedback
o Payroll/benefits administration
o Performance appraisal/merit guidelines
o Communications/public relations

o Systems implementation
o Systems consulting/design
o Installation troubleshooter
o User training/support
o Computer-based training
o Micro/mainframe applications
o Excel/LOTUS 1-2-3 applications
o Administration
o Staff supervision

CAREER ACHIEVEMENTS

o As HR Director at the Essex Company, upgraded Human Resources for over 3,000 employees: filled over 500 openings annually improving candidate quality while cutting the recruiting cycle in half; reduced excessive benefits operating costs; instituted critically needed cross-training; computerized previously manual systems; directed the upgrade of policies and procedures.

o As HR Manager at ABC Corporation, project managed the start-up of a new headquarters: coordinated the logistics and successfully recruited and hired over 400 employees in only seven months; also directed and accelerated the productivity of the administrative support staff.

o Directed Acme Development Center's Human Resources start-up and operation: achieved first-year staffing goals in less than nine months and instituted comprehensive employee relations programs.

o Turned around Acme's Personnel Redeployment Program achieving over a 90% placement rate through well-received seminars and workshops.

o Directed the highly successful implementation of Acme's critically needed $12 million Human Resource, Benefits, and Payroll system.

o Created and executed job search and redeployment workshops for the homeless in Seattle.

CAREER EXPERIENCE

ESSEX COMPANY, Any Town, WA   7/94–Present

HR Director
Directed recruiting, managed multimillion-dollar benefits plan, computerized operations, instituted aggressive cost-reduction programs, and upgraded policies and procedures.

ABC CORPORATION, Any Town, WA   2/89–7/94

HR Manager
Project managed the logistics and staffing of a new headquarters.

ACME, INC., Any Town, WA   3/84–2/89

Corporate Benefits Administration   1/88–2/89
Performed benefits evaluations and upgraded several outdated HR manuals.

Corporate HR Systems Analyst   12/86–1/88
Project managed the implementation of a major HR system designed to support in excess of 200,000 employees.

Personnel Redeployment   3/85–12/86
Executed well-received Redeployment Programs.

HR Administrator   3/84–3/85
Recruited and hired all staff for the Development Center; established Communications and Benefits Groups; also developed EEO Plans and authored several policies and procedures.

AVERY SERVICE CORPORATION, Any Town, WA   6/80–3/84

HR Administrator
Accelerated cost reduction programs; upgraded and assisted in the administration of relocations, recruiting, terminations, payroll, benefits, and employee orientations.

VOLUNTEER ACTIVITIES

o Created job search seminars for the homeless
o Provided support of the learning disabled
o Taught reading skills to adults

REFERENCES PROVIDED UPON REQUEST

MARTHA A. JONES

123 Any Street, Any City, CA XXXXX (213) 555-1234

Contact Name
Title
Company
Street Address
City, State Zip

Date

Dear Mr./Ms. _____ :

I have applied executive skills in training and development, marketing and management to start up and direct training departments, develop highly marketable training programs, accelerate staff productivity, and turn around the strategic and business planning process for major Fortune 500 corporations.

I am bringing to your attention my skills, achievements, creative energy, and proven talent for satisfying tough clients and achieving bottom-line results so that we can discuss my joining _____ as a member of your Training Management Team.

Results achieved to date include:

o Recruited as the first-ever training director for Acme, Inc.: overcame strong resistance and negativism to establish and direct a cost-effective Training Department offering 80 programs and training over 5000 employees in less than two years.

o As head of training at Acme, initiated and implemented the first-ever senior management business planning and team-building meetings: led to the first team-developed and team-supported business plans and MBOs in the company's history.

o Introduced widely accepted management, technical, and basic skills training programs at Acme: included state-of-the-art systems training as well as proposal development training designed to improve proposal accuracy while cutting the completion time in half.

o As Training Director at XYZ Company, started and managed the Training Department offering 70 management, sales, technical, and basic skills programs—trained over 2,000 people.

o Founded and managed a successful Training Consulting Company, marketing to and servicing major corporate clients including Apple Computer and W.R. Grace: created and produced training programs which were marketed and sold internationally by client companies.

I look forward to discussing how I can contribute to your company's future success.

Sincerely,

Enclosure:

Martha A. Jones

MARTHA A. JONES

123 Any Street, Any City, CA XXXXX (213) 555-1234

CAREER SKILLS/KNOWLEDGE

o Training professional	o Sales/marketing
o Training department management	o Networking strategies
o Training seminar development	o Business development
o Management development	o Independent consultant
o Strategic planning workshops	o Platform skills
o Marketing/technical training	o HR operations
o Trainer instruction	o Redeployment planning
o Basic skills training	o Counseling/development

CAREER ACHIEVEMENTS

o Recruited as the first-ever training director for Acme, Inc.: overcame strong resistance and negativism to establish and direct a cost-effective Training Department offering 80 programs and training over 5000 employees in less than two years.

o As head of training at Acme, initiated and implemented the first-ever senior management business planning and team-building meetings: led to the first team-developed and team-supported business plans and MBOs in the company's history.

o Introduced widely accepted management, technical, and basic skills training programs at Acme: included state-of-the-art systems training as well as proposal development training designed to improve proposal accuracy while cutting the completion time in half.

o Improved communication between Acme's upper and middle management by introducing successful Executive-Communication Meetings offering open and productive dialogue between the senior level executives and middle management.

o As Acme's representative on the Productivity Council, comanaged the Annual Productivity Conferences held to honor the best performing employees.

o As Training Director at XYZ Company, started and managed the Training Department offering 70 management, sales, technical, and basic skills programs—trained over 2,000 people.

o Codirected start-up of a training company: developed and sold state-of-the-art techniques for supervisory level and shop-floor training; trained and managed staff of 40 professionals.

o Founded and managed a successful Training Consulting Company, marketing to and servicing major corporate clients including Apple Computer and W.R. Grace: created and produced training programs which were marketed and sold internationally by client companies.

CAREER EXPERIENCE

ACME, INC., Any Town, CA   6/92–Present

Training Director
Responsibilities executed in support of the company's aggressive growth strategy include:

o Design and implement comprehensive needs evaluation systems.
o Develop and coordinate comprehensive employee development programs.
o Direct the training of all instructors.
o Select and hire outside training resources.
o Coordinate and audit the Educational Aid Program.

XYZ COMPANY, Any Town, CA   3/88–6/92

Training Director
Started and directed Training Department: created, purchased, and instituted 70 programs covering Management Development, Redeployment Planning, Marketing, Technical Training, and Shop-Floor Training.

TRAINING CONSULTING COMPANY, Any Town, CA   12/84–3/88

Founder
Completed major training projects for Fortune 500 clients: designed and produced sales training programs sold nationwide; designed and executed Management Development Workshops; designed and executed Minorities in Management Workshops.

ABC, INC., Any Town, CA   6/80–12/84

Training & Development Manager
Played a central role in the start-up of this firm which authors and publishes custom and standardized management training programs: designed and implemented a wide selection of training programs; recruited and trained staff of professionals.

EDUCATION

B.A.   University of Vienna   1980

PROFESSIONAL AFFILIATIONS

o Member: Board of Directors, Any Town, CA Girl Scouts of America
o Advisor, California Education Group
o Member, American Society for Training and Development

REFERENCES AVAILABLE UPON REQUEST

MATTHEW Q. SAMPLE (Version 2)   Strategic Planning/Sales/General Management

123 Any Street Address, Any Town, TX XXXXX (214) 555-1234

Contact Name   Date
Title
Company
Street Address
City, State Zip

Dear Mr./Ms. _____:

I have combined a top school M.B.A. with executive skills in strategic planning, marketing, sales management, and general management to orchestrate a leveraged buyout, head up a $3 million business, strategically reposition troubled operations, and turn around and accelerate profit growth for weak divisions of the Acme Corporation.

I am bringing to your attention my skills, achievements, talent for stimulating sales productivity, and ability to achieve bottom-line results under the most intense pressure so that we can discuss my joining _____ as a member of your senior planning management team.

Results achieved to date include:

o As Southeastern Sales Director for a troubled division of Acme, turned around profitability becoming the top-ranked Sales Director in the division: instituted aggressive market expansion, national account programs, and strategic planning increasing revenue from $5 million to $23 million in four years; converted a $3 million loss into a $3 million profit.

o Upon promotion to Southwestern Sales Director, accelerated sales productivity and major account development achieving a critically needed 35% growth in sales at a pivotal time for the struggling Acme Corporation, which had lost huge market shares due to poor product pricing strategies: achieved highest sales growth and won a major nationwide sales award.

o Based on a track record of achievements in sales management and strategic planning, was recruited by corporate headquarters to manage a major group's business evaluation function as part of the restructuring of the strategic planning process: improved declining ROIs by upgrading the pricing structure; saved tens-of-millions of dollars by demonstrating the marginal payback of proposed expenditures.

o Negotiated and closed the leveraged buyout of a $3 million service business formerly owned by the Avery Company: developed a solid business plan which was successfully marketed to major financial institutions with whom I negotiated over a million dollars in financing.

o As owner of a Texas-based venture, turned around sales and operations overcoming most roadblocks except the company's lack of liquidity in a recessionary economy: increased sales 60% in 15 months by upgrading service and promotional programs; restructured cash management; reduced aged receivables 75%; negotiated a 20% reduction in product costs; achieved a 60% increase in productivity.

I will work hard to achieve bottom-line results and look forward to discussing how I can contribute to your company's future success.

                                                                Sincerely,

Enclosure: Matthew Q. Sample

MATTHEW Q. SAMPLE   Strategic Planning/Sales/General Management

123 Any Street, Any Town, TX XXXXX (214) 555-1234

CAREER SKILLS/KNOWLEDGE

o Strategic planning
o Business plans/market research
o Market growth/segmentation
o ROI growth strategies
o Profit/investment optimization
o Economic modeling/pricing
o Supply/demand analysis
o Finance/controller operations
o Cash-flow/financing/bank relations

o Marketing/sales management
o Revenue/profit turnaround
o Product management
o National accounts programs
o Sales productivity growth
o Competitor intelligence systems
o Business ownership/leveraged buyouts
o Advertising/promotions
o Operations turnaround

CAREER ACHIEVEMENTS

o As Southeastern Sales Director for a troubled division of Acme, turned around profitability becoming the top-ranked Sales Director in the division: instituted aggressive market expansion, national account programs, and strategic planning increasing revenue from $5 million to $23 million in four years; converted a $3 million loss into a $3 million profit.

o Upon promotion to Southwestern Sales Director, accelerated sales productivity and major account development achieving a critically needed 35% growth in sales at a pivotal time for the struggling Acme Corporation, which had lost huge market shares due to poor product pricing strategies: achieved highest sales growth and won a major nationwide sales award.

o Based on a track record of achievements in sales management and strategic planning, was recruited by corporate headquarters to manage a major group's business evaluation function as part of the restructuring of the strategic planning process: improved declining ROIs by upgrading the pricing structure; saved tens-of-millions of dollars by demonstrating the marginal payback of proposed expenditures.

o Upon promotion to Business Planning Director, orchestrated a multibillion-dollar asset reallocation program which helped triple profits within five years: reallocated over a billion dollars of production assets to growth products; proposed a half-billion-dollar plant conversion which was implemented at half the cost of constructing a new plant.

o Upon being promoted to Product Manager at Acme, created a product management system which accelerated the decision-making process for the pricing, promotion, and distribution of products: increased profits 30% through saturation marketing to growth industries.

o Negotiated and closed the leveraged buyout of a $3 million service business formerly owned by the Avery Company: developed a solid business plan which was successfully marketed to major financial institutions with whom I negotiated over a million dollars in financing.

o As owner of a Texas-based venture, turned around sales and operations overcoming most roadblocks except the company's lack of liquidity in a recessionary economy: increased sales 60% in 15 months by upgrading service and promotional programs; restructured cash management; reduced aged receivables 75%; negotiated a 20% reduction in product costs; achieved a 60% increase in productivity.

CAREER EXPERIENCE

ACME CORPORATION, Any City, TX   1976–1992

Business Planning Director—XYZ Division   1989–1992
Designated to orchestrate the development of corporate strategies and upgrade the planning process.

Business Evaluation Director—ABC Division   1986–1989
Designated to reorganize and turn around strategic planning.

Southwestern Sales Director—ABC Division   1982–1986
Developed and directed a high-producing sales team responsible for national account development.

Product Manager—XYZ Division   1978–1982
Created a product management system which accelerated the decision-making process for the pricing, promotion, and distribution of products.

Southeastern Sales Director—XYZ Division   1977–1978
Implemented a Major Account Program; expanded into growth markets; instituted effective competitor data-gathering procedures; created Division's first comprehensive strategic plan.

Senior Marketing Analyst   1976–1977
Executed comprehensive feasibility studies which resulted in the formation of critically needed account development departments. Developed a well-received business plan for a beleaguered venture.

ESSEX COMPANY, Any City, TX   1992–1994

Senior Consultant
Determined the feasibility of a client's expansion into major European markets: executed comprehensive product demand and competitive studies as a basis for decision-making.

SERVICE VENTURE, Any City, TX   1994–Present

Founder: Directed Marketing, Advertising, Sales, Operations, Finance, and Customer Service.

EDUCATION

M.B.A.	Finance/Marketing	University of Virginia	1976
B.S.	Statistics	UCLA	1974

INTERNATIONAL: Traveled throughout South America and Europe
LANGUAGES: Fluent French, Italian, and Spanish

DAVID A. WILSON   Senior Financial Advisor

123 Any Street, Any City, NJ XXXXX (201) 555-1234

Contact Name   Date
Title
Company
Street Address
City, State Zip

Dear Mr. /Ms. _____ :

I have combined degrees from Stanford and Rutgers with dual careers as a Financial Advisor and Educator to develop expertise in world economics, generate millions in profits for clients, build a loyal client base, teach internationally, and produce Merit Scholars.

I am bringing to your attention my skills, achievements, and special talent for producing financial security for others and myself so that we can discuss my joining _____ as a member of your financial advisory team.

Results achieved to date include:

o As a Registered Broker for Shearson, generated six-figure gross commissions, expanded the customer base to 200 clients, and provided well-researched advice to satisfied customers.

o Based on in-depth research and prudent risk versus reward advice to Shearson clients, recommended several winning stocks which soared as much as 400%; clients continued to seek advice years after I returned to teaching.

o As a well-respected Independent Financial Advisor, created a Risk Avoidance System which has effectively reduced investment risks while producing substantial economic returns for clients.

o Was recruited by a private Academy as Department Chairperson: upgraded the curriculum and faculty, expedited the accreditation process, and produced a record number of Merit Scholars.

o Awarded Aristotle Foundation Award for "Excellence in Teaching Econometric Theory."

I feel it will be to our mutual benefit to meet and discuss how I can contribute to your company's future success.

Sincerely,

Enclosure: David A. Wilson

DAVID A. WILSON

Senior Financial Advisor

123 Any Street, Any City, NJ XXXXX (201) 555-1234

M.A.	History	Stanford University	1974
B.A.	Economics	Rutgers University	1972

Fulbright Grant: Summer study in France

CAREER SKILLS/KNOWLEDGE

- o Finance/economics
- o Financial services
- o Senior investment advisor
- o Registered broker
- o Stock/bond investments
- o Options strategies
- o Insurance annuities
- o Banking industry/operations
- o New account development
- o Competitive analyses
- o Published author
- o International/multilingual

- o Educator
- o Department chairman
- o Educational consulting
- o Upgrading standards
- o Curriculum development
- o Faculty evaluation
- o Workshop development
- o Accreditation expertise
- o Staff supervision
- o Student motivation
- o Counselor/coach
- o International studies

CAREER ACHIEVEMENTS

o As a Registered Broker for Shearson, generated six-figure gross commissions, expanded the customer base to 200 clients, and provided well-researched advice to satisfied customers.

o Based on in-depth research and prudent risk versus reward advice to Shearson clients, recommended several winning stocks which soared as much as 400%; clients continued to seek advice years after I returned to teaching.

o As a well-respected Independent Financial Advisor, created a Risk Avoidance System which has effectively reduced investment risks while producing substantial economic returns for clients.

o Was recruited by a private Academy as Department Chairperson: upgraded the curriculum and faculty, expedited the accreditation process, and produced a record number of Merit Scholars.

o At a private Academy, introduced programs which activated student involvement in community and government affairs: included exposure to low-income communities.

o Selected for prestigious teaching assignment at the Global School in the Mideast where I was Faculty Chairperson and taught an international curriculum.

o Awarded Aristotle Foundation Award for "Excellence in Teaching Econometric Theory."

CAREER EXPERIENCE

A PRIVATE ACADEMY, Any Town, NJ   1995–Present

Chairperson - Economics Department
Responsibilities executed:

o Develop and implement coherent curriculum.
o Recruit, train, and evaluate faculty.
o Teach Economics, History, and Sociology.
o Expedited the accreditation process.

SHEARSON LEHMAN BROTHERS, Any City, NJ   1993–1995

Broker
Increased client base through cold-calling and networking; communicated quality advice to clients based on detailed research and management interviews.

A TOP-RATED SUBURBAN HIGH SCHOOL, Any Town, NJ   1989–1993

Teacher
Instituted seminars to upgrade faculty; taught Social Studies, History, and Economics; introduced course in Value Systems Clarification.

AN INTERNATIONAL SCHOOL IN MIDEAST, Any Town, Mideast   1987–1989

Faculty Chairman
Taught international curriculum of Economics, History, and Sociology.

ANOTHER TOP-RATED SUBURBAN HIGH SCHOOL, Any Town, NJ   1984–1987

Department Chairman
Created new curriculum; supervised and upgraded faculty; initiated programs between different socioeconomic communities.

ANOTHER TOP-RATED SUBURBAN HIGH SCHOOL, Any Town, NY   1974–1984

Teacher
Introduced Economics course study; taught History. Coached championship soccer team.

ADDITIONAL EDUCATION/LICENSES

Post Masters: 30 credits earned from major universities including Columbia
Licenses: Series 7 & 63 Brokerage; NJ State Insurance License

7

Market-Tested Sample Resumes and Cover Letters for Upper-Middle Managers, Professionals, and Technical Specialists

INTRODUCTION

The real-life, market-tested samples in Chapter 7 produced results for upper-middle managers, professionals, and technical specialists with 10 to 25-plus years of experience. This chapter, like the previous one, offers the following unique features designed to give you the same competitive edge that produced quality interviews and job offers for managers just like you:

1. *Superior Quality Sample Resumes and Cover Letters.* Taken directly from almost 30 real-life client case histories, these market-tested and proven resumes and letters are samples of

unmatched quality from which to extract, borrow, and adapt key words, phrases, sentences, and paragraphs as you develop your own power package.

2. *A Strong Focus on Packaging Marketable Skills and Achievements.* This workbook subordinates the narrative job descriptions that clutter most resumes. The market has responded favorably to the skills and achievement-oriented resumes featured in this chapter.

3. *An Unparalleled Emphasis on the Marketing Cover Letter.* This workbook treats the cover letter and resume as *coequal* and *inseparable* components of the total marketing package. A frequently heard comment from my management clients, "The cover letter got me the interview," underscores the importance of the letter. Every sample resume in this book has a corresponding cover letter—*no* other book on the market can make this claim.

4. *A Representative Cross Section of Sample Resumes and Letters.* As reflected in the Chapter Index, I have deliberately excluded many highly specialized, often irrelevant, job positions that provide "filler" for countless resume books. This chapter, instead, presents *seven* major categories and several additional subcategories of mainstream positions into which most managers fall.

5. *An Intense Focus on Market Response.* Simply stated, the following samples achieved the desired results for veteran managers just like you: They produced positive interviews and job offers in an increasingly tough and selective marketplace, which is, of course, the *ultimate* and *only relevant* judge of quality.

THE RESUME AND COVER LETTER HEADERS

As discussed earlier, the sample resume and cover letter packages include, for your optional application, my trademark "headers" which provide the reader with a brief two to five word description of your background/discipline. For your convenience and ease in referencing the samples, I have elevated and boxed in these descriptive headers which are cross-referenced in the Index on pages 158 and 159. Should you choose to include the header in your own resume and cover letter package, you will, of course, position it on the same line as your name.

A WORD ABOUT CLIENT CONFIDENTIALITY

While retaining the full impact and integrity of the real-life marketing packages in this chapter, I have selectively modified and/or otherwise blinded certain confidential information including client names, company names, addresses, specific job titles, employment dates, and other identifying narrative. While education information has also been blinded, colleges and graduate schools of equivalent ranking were substituted where appropriate.

CHAPTER 7 RESUME INDEX

IAN A. SMITH

123 Any Street, Any City, CA XXXXX (619) 555-1234

Contact Name   Date
Title
Company
Address
City, State, Zip

Dear Mr./Ms. _____:

I have formulated and executed expert sales and marketing strategies to outmaneuver the competition, penetrate new markets, and generate record sales in the Los Angeles marketplace during the past decade with a subsidiary of Acme Industries. This has been rewarded with six-figure incomes and number one national ranking.

I am bringing to your attention my skills, achievements, and special talent for identifying, penetrating, and selling even the toughest decision makers so that we can discuss my joining _____ as a member of your senior management team.

Results achieved to date include:

o As Director of Sales for ABC, Inc., a subsidiary of Acme Industries, generated a record $10 million in sales and up to a six-figure annual income during the past 10 years: consistently ranked in the top 10% nationally including three years at number one.

o As a major revenue-producer for ABC, contributed to the company's pivotal milestones over the past decade: included a tripling of gross revenues over six years from $20 million to $60 million; a 600% growth in the value of the stock; and the acquisition of the company.

o Developed and turned around ABC's untapped Los Angeles market during the past 11 years, setting sales records by instituting a cohesive, focused marketing strategy to identify lucrative markets, penetrate key decision makers, and build a loyal client base.

o In a major marketing coup, initiated and closed a half million dollar order selling high-tech processing equipment to all 300 XYZ branches in a market where such multibranch deals for our product line are nearly impossible to close.

It should be to our mutual benefit to meet and determine how I can help accelerate or turn around sales, contributing to your company's future success.

Sincerely,

Enclosure: Ian A. Smith

Sales/Marketing Management

IAN A. SMITH

123 Any Street, Any City, CA XXXXX (619) 555-1234

B.A.   Communications/Psychology   Ohio State University   1980

CAREER SKILLS/KNOWLEDGE

o Sales/marketing management
o Revenue growth strategies
o Competitive maneuvering
o Market identification/penetration
o Decision-maker relations
o Client development
o Expert closer

o Profit growth strategies
o Expert communicator
o Negotiating skills
o Staff supervision/development
o Operations
o Customer service
o Installation/training

CAREER ACHIEVEMENTS

o As Director of Sales for ABC, Inc., a subsidiary of Acme Industries, generated a record $10 million in sales and up to a six-figure annual income during the past decade: consistently ranked in the top 10% nationally including three years at number one.

o As a major revenue-producer for ABC, contributed to the company's pivotal milestones over the past decade: included a tripling of gross revenues over six years from $20 million to $60 million; a 600% growth in the value of the stock; and the acquisition of the company.

o Developed and turned around ABC's untapped Los Angeles market during the past 11 years, setting sales records by instituting a cohesive, focused marketing strategy to identify lucrative markets, penetrate key decision makers, and build a loyal client base.

o In a major marketing coup, initiated and closed a half million dollar order selling high-tech processing equipment to all 300 XYZ branches in a market where such multibranch deals for our product line are nearly impossible to close.

CAREER EXPERIENCE

ACME INDUSTRIES, ABC, INC., SUBSIDIARY, Any Town, CA   1986–Present

Director of Sales
Market sophisticated processing systems to Fortune 500 clients:

o Train, develop, and direct the sales force.
o Emphasize client relations, new account development, and sales force productivity.
o Create innovative and effective presentations; conceptualize productive selling programs.

ESSEX CORPORATION, Any Town, Ohio   1984–1986

Regional Manager
Consulted with and advised financial industry executives regarding the disposition and settlement of defaulted loans: reduced company's loss factor on reclaimed properties from as high as 60% down to only 25% through aggressive resale strategies and negotiations.

AVERY SERVICE COMPANY, Any Town, Ohio   1980–1984

General Sales Manager   1983–1984
Responsible for direct sales, production, and customer service for this business which marketed data processing services to the Fortune 1000: achieved quota, managed and trained employees, and implemented records data processing systems for major financial institutions.

REFERENCES PROVIDED UPON REQUEST

DAVID Q. SAMPLE

123 Any Street, Any City, CA XXXXX (619) 555-1234

Contact Name   Date
Title
Company
Address
City, State Zip

Dear Mr./Ms. _____:

I have combined a top business degree, global experience, and executive skills in sales, finance, banking, and general management to establish and direct new operations which have generated millions in revenue for well-respected international companies. Bottom-line contributions to profit have been rewarded with accelerated promotions, job security, and a six-figure salary package.

I am bringing to your attention my skills, achievements, strategic brainpower, global network, and talent for exceeding profit goals under negative economic conditions so that we can discuss my joining _____ as a member of your senior sales management team.

Major accomplishments to date include:

o As Vice-President of ABC's International Banking Group, produced revenue of $6.5 million in 1994 through aggressive client development and by saving 90% of the seriously at-risk accounts: accelerated the ROA by focusing on corporate finance, investment banking, and asset sales.

o As Vice-President of Corporate Banking at ABC's Southern California headquarters, leveraged my international contacts to market corporate and capital market products generating $5 million in added net income: achieved 250% growth in fees from capital market products.

o Was recruited away and promoted by ABC to start and manage the new International Energy Group: established and directed the lending operation generating over $500 million in new client bookings in only 18 months with an ROA of over 1%.

o As head of Commercial Development in charge of ABC's International Energy Group, initiated and closed several profitable deals including a hard-to-close $600 million project with an international energy company: created and directed a syndicate of major international lenders.

It should be mutually beneficial to meet and assess how I can help accelerate or turn around revenue and profit growth contributing to your company's future success.

Sincerely,

Enclosure: David Q. Sample

DAVID Q. SAMPLE

123 Any Street, Any City, CA XXXXX (619) 555-1234

| M.B.A. Honors | University of Paris Graduate School of Business | 1985 |

International: Bilingual French and English; solid knowledge of Mideastern languages; traveled to over 60 nations

Certifications: Commercial Pilot's License; Black Belt Karate; Championship Skier

CAREER SKILLS/KNOWLEDGE

- o Marketing/sales executive
- o General management
- o Start-up operations
- o Major client development
- o Competitive maneuvering
- o Expansion/turnaround strategies
- o Revenue/profit growth
- o Organizational development

- o Financial executive
- o International banking
- o Investment banking
- o Corporate/capital markets
- o Acquisitions/joint ventures
- o Subsidiary recapitalization
- o Project financing/syndicates
- o Trade financing/foreign exchange

CAREER ACHIEVEMENTS

o As Vice-President of ABC's International Banking Group, produced revenue of $6.5 million in 1994 through aggressive client development and by saving 90% of the at-risk accounts: accelerated the ROA by focusing on corporate finance, investment banking, and asset sales.

o As Vice-President of Corporate Banking at ABC's Southern California headquarters, leveraged my international contacts to market corporate and capital market products generating $5 million in added net income: achieved 250% growth in fees from capital market products.

o Was recruited away and promoted by ABC to start and manage the new International Energy Group: established and directed the lending operation generating over $500 million in new client bookings in only 18 months with an ROA of over 1%.

o As head of Commercial Development in charge of ABC's International Energy Group, initiated and closed several profitable deals including a hard-to-close $600 million project with an international energy company: created and directed a syndicate of major international lenders.

o As Group Officer at Acme International Bank, established and directed operations of a new North American office: achieved and exceeded an aggressive operating plan generating new lending of $300 million and profitability in five months instead of the forecasted ten months.

CAREER EXPERIENCE

ABC BANK, Any Town, CA   3/88–Present

INTERNATIONAL BANKING GROUP, Any Town, CA   2/91–Present

Vice-President
Responsible for major account development emphasizing high-margin corporate finance and in-vestment banking: acquisitions, recapitalization, and collateralized financing. Upgraded asset quality by addressing and restructuring below-par debt.

CORPORATE BANKING, Any Town, CA   3/88–2/91

Vice-President
Created and marketed corporate and capital market products and services to global clients.

ACME INTERNATIONAL BANK, Any Town, Europe   6/85–3/88

Group Officer (Assistant Vice-President), Any Town, British Columbia   4/87–3/88
Managed start-up of a new operation: directed staffing, property selection, facility planning, con-tract negotiations, and purchasing. Also developed marketing policies and operating procedures.

Officer, Any Town, CA   5/86–4/87
Accelerated global account development quadrupling pre-tax net income to over $4 million.

Officer, Any Town, Europe   6/85–5/86
Established a Credit Group generating over $2 million in fees from new business development.

REFERENCES PROVIDED UPON REQUEST

PATRICK A. WILSON

123 Any Street, Any City, CA XXXXX (619) 555-1234

Contact Name   Date
Title
Company
Street Address
City, State Zip

Dear Mr./Ms. _____ :

I have profitably applied skills in sales, client relations, program management, engineering, and product development to generate lucrative accounts, turn around client relations, open up closed markets, and develop state-of-the-art systems for Fortune 500 companies. This has been rewarded with multiple promotions and a reputation for getting the job done.

I am bringing to your attention my skills, achievements, and ability to produce results under intense pressure and out-of-control conditions so that we can discuss my joining _____ as a member of your Sales or Program Management Team.

Results achieved to date include:

o As a Project Director at ABC, Inc., generated satisfied clients and substantial revenue by expediting installation of multimillion-dollar space projects for XYZ Company, MCA, and CBS; established productive client rapport and had reputation for delivering on-time projects.

o Played a pivotal role in ABC's landing the lucrative XYZ Company and MCA accounts: convinced MCA to leave a competitor and turned around negative relations with XYZ.

o Played a central role in XYZ Company's efforts to penetrate the closed Asian markets: presented well-received studies to Korea's Ministry of Telecommunications and Osaka Telegraph and Telephone, paving the way for several hundred million dollar deals.

o Turned around relations between Acme Industries and a major client who had stopped payments toward a $300 million project: was singled out by the client for helping Acme to pass a critical Demonstration Review which led to resumption of monthly progress payments.

o As Project Director on a critical $300 million program, directed the development of complex state-of-the-art systems at Acme: sub-systems under my control are among the very few within the total project that are under control and on schedule.

It should be to our mutual benefit to meet and determine how I can contribute to your company's bottom-line success.

Sincerely,

Enclosure: Patrick A. Wilson

PATRICK A. WILSON

123 Any Street, Any City, CA XXXXX (619) 555-1234

B.S.   Electrical Engineering   University of Texas   1982

CAREER SKILLS/KNOWLEDGE

- o Sales/account management
- o Program management
- o Client development/relations
- o Revenue growth strategies
- o Profit growth strategies
- o Deal-making/negotiating
- o Turnaround strategies
- o Staff supervision/development
- o Productivity improvements
- o International markets

- o Project management
- o Product development
- o Communications studies
- o Engineering/administration
- o Planning/scheduling
- o Team motivation
- o Subcontractor relations
- o Cost control/reductions
- o Design/specifications/prototypes
- o Testing/release/support

CAREER ACHIEVEMENTS

o As a Project Director at ABC, Inc., generated satisfied clients and substantial revenue by expediting installation of multimillion-dollar space projects for XYZ Company, MCA, and CBS; established productive client rapport and had reputation for delivering on-time projects.

o Played a pivotal role in ABC's landing the lucrative XYZ Company and MCA accounts: convinced MCA to leave a competitor and turned around negative relations with XYZ.

o Played a central role in XYZ Company's efforts to penetrate the closed Asian markets: presented well-received studies to Korea's Ministry of Telecommunications and Osaka Telegraph and Telephone, paving the way for several hundred million dollar deals.

o Turned around relations between Acme Industries and a major client who had stopped payments toward a $300 million project: was singled out by the client for helping Acme to pass a critical Demonstration Review which led to resumption of monthly progress payments.

o As Project Director on a critical $300 million program, directed the development of complex state-of-the-art systems at Acme: sub-systems under my control are among the very few within the total project that are under control and on schedule.

o Upon promotion to Director of ABC's $2 million Space Engineering Unit, stimulated revenue growth, turned around eroding morale, upgraded staff performance, and improved productivity.

o Built a reputation at ABC for accomplishing the impossible, receiving numerous accolades from executives at XYZ Company and Essex Communication where one executive voiced his opinion that "Pat is one of the finest Project Managers in the world."

BUSINESS EXPERIENCE

ACME INDUSTRIES, Any Town, CA   2/94–Present

Project Director
Manage client relations and overall planning, scheduling, and staffing for a state-of-the-art system development contract. Direct staff of 50 in executing hardware design, fabrication, and testing.

ABC, INC., Any Town, CA   3/91–2/94

Director—Space Engineering Unit   9/92–2/94
General management responsibility for this engineering services and market research firm:

o Directed staff of 45 sales, marketing, and product management personnel.
o Provided engineering services, interacting with major clients on proposals, price negotiations, and technical issues.
o Delivered critical presentations to Asian clients.

Project Director   3/91–9/92
Primary liaison to XYZ Communications, Essex Communication, MCA, and CBS:

o Established excellent rapport with clientele.
o Conducted complex frequency interference studies of station sites.
o Performed frequency coordination of remote stations, prepared site reports, and analyzed field-measurement data.

RIGOR SERVICES COMPANY, Any Town, OR   11/89–3/91

Engineer
Under contract to provide a Mideastern Air Force with on-the-job instruction in F-16 systems troubleshooting.

AVERY COMPANY, Any Town, OH   6/88–11/89

Engineer
Completed rigorous company training at a government facility: managed group on overseas assignment providing technical support for the F-14. Based on results achieved, was requested to stay past the normal pull-out date; such requests are almost never made by the government.

MILITARY CREDENTIALS

Underwater Operations   6/82–6/88
Graduate of the rigorous Nuclear Training Program: ranked near the top of the class and completed long-term assignment aboard a nuclear-powered submarine; substituted for the First Officer; was consulted on major operational decisions.

INTERNATIONAL TRAVEL: Traveled throughout Europe and Asia.

DENNIS A. CUMMINGS

123 Any Street, Any City, IL XXXXX (312) 555-1234

Contact Name   Date
Title
Company
Street Address
City, State Zip

Dear Mr./Ms. _____:

I have applied proficient skills in product management, marketing, sales, strategic planning, and technical service to help generate over $25,000,000 in revenue for two Fortune 50 corporations during the past 14 years.

I am bringing to your attention my skills, achievements, and talent for improving sales and profits so that we can discuss my joining _____ as a member of your Product Management/Marketing/Sales Team.

Results achieved to date include:

o Product managed XYZ's introduction of major custom product features that ultimately generated $14 million annually.

o Initiated and pushed through major changes to XYZ's product color mix, upstaging the competition with new colors that generated $3 million in added revenue the first two years.

o Directed XYZ's on-schedule implementation of Monitored Service, a program critical to XYZ's future competitiveness.

o Researched, introduced, and marketed the first "residential" specialty feature product that produced $4 million over five years: executed Marketing and Distribution Plan that was rated by key managers as one of the most comprehensive plans ever completed at XYZ.

o Earned multiple promotions at ABC Corporation based on results achieved in sales and technical service: achieved sales quota and managed a field staff that exceeded aggressive service objectives.

A 30-minute exploratory discussion to determine how I can contribute to your future success should be to our mutual benefit.

Sincerely,

Enclosure: Dennis A. Cummings

Product Management/Marketing/Strategic Planning

DENNIS A. CUMMINGS

123 Any Street, Any City, IL XXXXX (312) 555-1234

CAREER SKILLS/KNOWLEDGE

o Product management
o Strategic planning
o New product research
o Competitive strategies/pricing
o Product introduction
o Organizational restructuring
o Business start-up

o Marketing/sales
o Revenue growth strategies
o Direct sales
o Presentations/public speaking
o Technical service management
o Staff supervision/training
o Negotiating skills

CAREER ACHIEVEMENTS

o Product managed XYZ's introduction of major custom product features that ultimately generated $14 million annually; developed marketing plans for all operating companies and over-
came strong internal resistance.

o Directed XYZ's on-schedule implementation of Monitored Service, a program critical to future
competitiveness.

o Initiated and pushed through major changes to XYZ's product color mix, upstaging the competition with new colors that generated $3 million in added revenue the first two years.

o Product managed XYZ's introduction of mobile and voice messaging products that generate
over $4 million a year: evaluated feasibility, determined profitability, established distribution
channels, and negotiated vendor contracts.

o Researched, introduced, and marketed the first "residential" specialty feature product that produced $4 million over five years: executed Marketing and Distribution Plan that was rated by
key managers as one of the most comprehensive plans ever completed at XYZ.

o Earned multiple promotions at ABC Corporation based on results achieved in sales and technical service: achieved sales quota and managed a field staff that exceeded aggressive service
objectives.

CAREER EXPERIENCE

XYZ CORPORATION, Any City, IL   11/87–Present

Senior Product Manager   6/92–Present
Direct the nationwide implementation of Monitored Service:

o Chair program teams at headquarters and operating companies.
o Prepared short- and long-term implementation plans.
o Ensure implementation of monitoring rating and billing systems.

Product Manager   7/89–6/92
Responsibilities executed to introduce mobile and voice messaging products for resale nation-wide:

o Directed headquarters and interdepartmental product teams.
o Established profitability objectives and distribution channels.
o Provided financial and operational requirements for budgeting and strategic planning.

Manager—Forecasting and Pricing   11/87–7/89
Responsibilities executed:

o Developed pricing policy and methodologies for new services.
o Helped plan and implement successful restructing of headquarters and operating companies.

ABC CORPORATION, Any Town, IL   11/82–11/87

Sales Representative   11/84–11/87
Achieved 100% of the annual sales quota in only eight months.

Field Manager   11/82–11/84
Supervised and trained staff; developed and executed operating plans; managed territories.
Named Field Manager of the Quarter.

Reason for leaving: Recruited by an XYZ Department Director.

MILITARY EXPERIENCE   (10/78–10/82)

U.S. Army: Earned multiple promotions and was recommended for Officer Candidate School based on achievements as a Technical Trainer and Mechanical Technician.

TRAINING/VOLUNTEER ACTIVITIES

o Guest speaker in Product Management and Marketing: several colleges including Minnesota State and Drake University
o Instructor: XYZ Management Skills Development Program
o Instructor: ABC's Volunteer Education Program
o Vice Chairman: Chicago Human Relations Commission
o Executive Board: United Way

EDUCATION

B.A.   Ohio State University   1978

REFERENCES PROVIDED UPON REQUEST

MARY A. JOHNSON

123 Any Street, Any City, NJ XXXXX (201) 555-1234

Contact Name   Date
Title
Company
Street Address
City, State Zip

Dear Mr. /Ms. _____:

Having developed and applied strong skills in market research from the design state through analysis and report preparation, I have proven my ability to achieve bottom-line results. I would like to bring my skills, experience, and motivation to your attention.

I am interested in exploring the possibility of joining _____ as a member of your Market Research Team.

Results achieved by applying the market research skills outlined in the attached resume include:

o Completed a well-received year-long research study for the credit card division of a major financial services corporation; resulted in major changes in their strategy for promoting credit card use in discount retail outlets.

o At ABC Company, performed a major product comparison research study which was rated "excellent"; a rating not often given to studies at ABC.

o Prevented serious customer relations problems for a major southwestern bank by identifying the specific negative impacts of closing down local branches; resulted in specific actions to reduce the negative perceptions of customers displaced by the branch consolidations.

o Conducted a research study which outlined the most effective strategy for introducing a new banking package that merged credit card, checking, savings, and money market accounts into a single compact statement—the strategy worked well.

o At ABC, performed a spokesperson research study for a well-known specialty product; resulted in retaining the current celebrity spokesperson, as study results confirmed the correctness of the original selection.

I feel it will be to our mutual benefit to meet and talk face-to-face. You may contact me at the above number to set up an appointment. I look forward to our meeting.

Sincerely,

Enclosure: Mary A. Johnson

Market Research Professional

MARY A. JOHNSON

123 Any Street, Any City, NJ XXXXX (201) 555-1234

EDUCATION

M.B.A.	Marketing	New York University Graduate School of Business	1988
B.A.	Psychology	College of New Rochelle	1980

MARKET RESEARCH SKILLS

o Questionnaire development
o Attribute lists
o Features definition
o Product/service characteristics
o Questionnaire validation
o Client interaction
o Pretest for bid costing
o Response precoding
o Field staff interaction

o Develop/write table shells
o Establish/design tab plan
o Data collection/validation
o Topline analysis
o Analysis of marginals
o Closed-end data analysis
o Open-end data analysis
o Presentation of results
o Draft/final reports

MARKET RESEARCH ACHIEVEMENTS

o Completed a well-received year-long research study for the credit card division of a major financial services corporation; resulted in major changes in their strategy for promoting credit card use in discount retail outlets.

o Prevented serious customer relations problems for a major southwestern bank by identifying the specific negative impacts of closing down local branches; resulted in specific actions to reduce the negative perceptions of customers displaced by the branch consolidations.

o At ABC Company, attention to detail resulted in my uncovering the specific reasons causing a new version of a well-known consumer product to score poorly with institutional buyers.

o At ABC Company, performed a major product comparison research study which was rated "excellent"; a rating not often given to studies at ABC.

o Conducted a research study which outlined the most effective strategy for introducing a new banking package that merged credit card, checking, savings, and money market accounts into a single compact statement—the strategy worked well.

o Significantly upgraded the image of a discount line of widgets through a creative visual marketing campaign showing the widgets in upscale settings.

o At ABC, performed a spokesperson research study for a well-known specialty product; resulted in retaining the current celebrity spokesperson, as study results confirmed the correctness of the original selection.

CAREER EXPERIENCE

ABC COMPANY, Any Town, NJ   7/89–Present

Senior Project Director
Conducted market research studies for major consumer product and financial services industry clients.

XYZ, INCORPORATED, Any Town, NJ   3/87–7/89

Senior Project Director
Conducted research projects as a member of the in-house market research staff of this manufacturer of consumer products.

ACME RESEARCH ASSOCIATES, INC., Any Town, NJ   6/82–3/87

Project Coordinator—Custom Market Research Services
Promoted to this position. Received in-depth training in key aspects of primary consumer market research, learning and experiencing all the steps in conducting a research study from the design state through analysis and report preparation.

Applied skills to produce studies which had bottom-line impact in marketing of our products.

AVERY SERVICE COMPANY, Any Town, NJ   8/80–6/82

Research Analyst
Performed quantitative and administrative functions for this supplier of audit information to Fortune 500 consumer products companies. Prepared weekly posting sheets and sent to field auditors; pulled summary posting sheets when returned; compiled data and performed analytical steps to get monthly calculations; and assisted in report writing.

REFERENCES PROVIDED UPON REQUEST

ALEXIS A. JONES

123 Any Street, Any Town, PA XXXXX (215) 555-1234

Contact Name   Date
Title
Company
Address
City, State Zip

Dear Ms./Mr. _____:

I have applied skills in sales, marketing, administration, customer service, and systems to accelerate profits, strengthen sales networks, turn around weak operations, and help a Fortune 100 company be selected for an international performance award. By directing the turnaround of administrative operations at Acme Business Services, assumed a leadership role in helping the subsidiary to become certified for a prestigious Productivity Award.

I am bringing to your attention my skills, achievements, work ethic, standards of excellence, and talent for achieving bottom-line results so that we can discuss my joining _____ as a member of your administrative management team.

Results achieved to date at Acme Company, Inc. include:

o Upon earning a multilevel promotion to Manager of Administration at Acme Business Services, a $20 million subsidiary, upgraded and turned around administrative operations contributing to the subsidiary being certified for a National Productivity Award.

o As Manager of Administration, took the lead in winning several "Outstanding Group of the Month Awards"—represented the first such awards in over six years: achieved this by significantly improving customer satisfaction, profit contribution, expense control, productivity, billing, inventory control, and systems support.

o Accelerated year-to-date profit performance to 110% of target and top-20 national ranking by reducing expenses and improving productivity: included a half million dollar contribution to profits generated by creating and installing a tracking system to recover outstanding charges.

o As the focal point for customer satisfaction at Acme, turned around a drastic decline in customer satisfaction by creating and enforcing customer service follow-up procedures to expedite corrective actions: within one quarter, customer satisfaction levels accelerated to 95% from a low of 55%.

o Selected for newly created Sales Coordinator position acting as liaison between Acme and its Mid-Atlantic sales agents: introduced critically needed performance reporting systems and controls contributing to Region's top ranking; identified poor performing agents and uncovered gross inefficiencies generating a 60% turnover and a more profitable sales network.

I will work hard to achieve results and look forward to discussing how I can contribute to your company's future success.

Sincerely,

Enclosure: Alexis A. Jones

ALEXIS A. JONES

123 Any Street, Any Town, PA XXXXX (215) 555-1234

M.B.A.	Systems	New York University	GPA 3.8/4.0	1986
B.S.	Marketing	Lehman College	Self-financed	1984

CAREER SKILLS/KNOWLEDGE

- o Marketing support/sales productivity
- o Client development/relations
- o Revenue/profit growth strategies
- o Proposals/pricing/closing
- o Customer service/satisfaction turnaround
- o Administration/controller operations
- o Department set-up/turnaround
- o Budgeting/cost reductions
- o Staff development/productivity growth

- o Management information systems
- o Systems consulting
- o Sales/service support
- o Systems/workstation installation
- o Systems implementation/training
- o IBM PC applications
- o Novell network
- o Excel/Lotus 1-2-3 expertise
- o Graphics/PowerPoint

CAREER ACHIEVEMENTS AT ACME COMPANY, INC.

o Upon earning a multilevel promotion to Manager of Administration at Acme Business Services, a $20 million subsidiary, upgraded and turned around administrative operations contributing to the subsidiary being certified for a National Productivity Award.

o As Manager of Administration, took the lead in winning several "Outstanding Group of the Month Awards"—represented the first such awards in over six years: achieved this by significantly improving customer satisfaction, profit contribution, expense control, productivity, billing, inventory control, and systems support.

o Accelerated year-to-date profit performace to 110% of target and top-20 national ranking by reducing expenses and improving productivity: included a half million dollar contribution to profits generated by creating and installing a tracking system to recover outstanding charges.

o As the focal point for customer satisfaction at Acme, turned around a drastic decline in customer satisfaction by creating and enforcing customer service follow-up procedures to expedite corrective actions: within one quarter, customer satisfaction levels accelerated to 95% from a low of 55%.

o Instituted much needed cross-training while computerizing what had been manually run administrative operations: selected, installed, and troubleshooted several workstations; instituted thorough systems training to maximize productivity of newly installed systems.

o Accelerated productivity by implementing productivity-improving processes that helped the administrative staff to win multiple "Leader of Customer Satisfaction" awards.

o Selected for newly-created Sales Coordinator position acting as liaison between Acme and its Mid-Atlantic sales agents: introduced critically needed performance reporting systems and controls contributing to Region's top ranking; identified poor performing agents and uncovered gross inefficiencies generating a 60% turnover and a more profitable sales network.

CAREER EXPERIENCE

ACME COMPANY, INC., Any City, PA   10/90–Present

Manager of Administration   10/94–Present
Responsibilities include: staff development, systems implementation, customer service, cost control, billing, credit, collection, procurement, accounts payable, cash management, inventory control, and reporting.

Systems Analyst   6/93–10/94
Troubleshot network crashes; installed workstations, processed sales manager compensation including the in-depth auditing of adjustments and exceptions. Ranked as one of the top analysts in the nation.

Sales Coordinator   11/91–6/93
Managed sales systems for a network of sales agents:

o Assumed a leadership role in managing all aspects of the business.
o Developed forecasts and upgraded reporting.
o Formulated strategies for sales promotions.
o Developed sales proposals.
o Managed expenditures and inventory.
o Performed expense analysis; provided pricing input.

Service Analyst   10/90–11/91
Computerized key reports generating more timely and accurate data for management decision-making. The newly automated reports became the standard for the entire corporation.

MAJOR RETAILER, Any City, PA   6/86–10/90

Department Manager
Achieved 300% of plan by profitably directing 20 Departments with a staff of 30 and $2.5 million in inventory; established and directed profitable holiday and special promotion shops producing a 200% increase in sales.

SYSTEMS TRAINING

Systems Seminar; Accelerated Administrator Training; Administrator Training; Lotus 1-2-3; Listing; Graphics; Tables

REFERENCES PROVIDED UPON REQUEST

NANCY A. CUMMINGS

123 Any Street, Any City, MA XXXXX (617) 555-1234

Contact Name   Date
Title
Company
Street Address
City, State Zip

Dear Mr./Ms. _____:

I have profitably applied skills and experience in retailing, store ownership, operations, buying, inventory management, and promotions to start up the first International Merchandise store in the Northeast Region and generate revenue and profit growth as high as 50%.

I am presenting for your review my skills, achievements, and talent for increasing profits even in a declining market so that we can discuss my joining _____ as a member of your Regional/Corporate Staff.

Results achieved to date include:

o Own and manage an International Merchandise franchise outlet: direct operations, attend international buyer shows in major metropolitan areas, and manage the product mix to eliminate slow-moving lines.

o By selecting popular products, instituting aggressive sales, and developing a top staff, made our International Merchandise store profitable from the first year.

o As Outlet Manager at Acme Retailing, Inc., reduced staff turnover and instituted aggressive promotions and inventory management to increase sales in spite of a recessional market.

o As Sales Supervisor at XYZ Corporation, more than quadrupled sales over a seven-year period; contributed to a successful stock offering.

o Generated 50% sales growth in the Domestics Department of a major retailer by upgrading customer relations and identifying and selling off slow-moving merchandise.

A 30-minute discussion to determine how I can contribute to your company's future success might well be to our mutual benefit.

Sincerely,

Enclosure: Nancy A. Cummings

Retail Sales Management

NANCY A. CUMMINGS

123 Any Street, Any City, MA XXXXX (617) 555-1234

B.A.   Business/Psychology   Brunswick College   GPA 3.8   1980

Graduate Courses: Business & Organizational Psychology

CAREER SKILLS/KNOWLEDGE

- o Retail management
- o Franchise ownership
- o Store operations
- o Buying expertise
- o Sales promotion strategies
- o Cash-flow management

- o Marketing/sales
- o Telemarketing/cold-calling
- o Client presentations
- o Closing the sale
- o Customer training/service
- o Computer applications

CAREER ACHIEVEMENTS

o Own and manage an International Merchandise franchise outlet: direct operations, attend international buyer shows in major metropolitan areas, and manage the product mix to eliminate slow-moving lines.

o By selecting popular products, instituting aggressive sales and developing a top staff, made our International Merchandise store profitable from the first year.

o As Outlet Manager at Acme Retailing, Inc., reduced staff turnover and instituted aggressive promotions and inventory management to increase sales in spite of a recessional market.

o Generated 50% sales growth in the Domestics Department of a major retailer by upgrading customer relations and identifying and selling off slow-moving merchandise.

o As Sales Supervisor at XYZ Corporation, more than quadrupled sales over a seven-year period; contributed to a successful stock offering.

CAREER EXPERIENCE

INTERNATIONAL MERCHANDISE STORE, Any Town, MA   8/93–Present

Owner/Manager
Started and operate this high-end specialty store:

- o Executed demographic study to select site location.
- o Set up the store and direct overall operations.
- o Hired and trained the manager and support staff.
- o Execute product mix changes and aggressive promotions.

ACME RETAILING, INC., Any Town, MA   6/89–8/93

<u>Outlet Manager</u>
Managed operations for the Any Town store:

o Hired and trained staff.
o Directed weekly promotions.
o Set up computerized registers.
o Coordinated customer relations.
o Interacted with region management.

AVERY RETAILING, INC., Any Town, MA   11/88–6/89

<u>Department Manager</u>
Responsibilities executed:

o Hired, trained, and supervised staff ranging up to 50 people.
o Specified goods to be purchased based on sales analysis.
o Coordinated customer relations and inventory control.
o Designed and set up window and in-store displays.
o Managed and reported cash.

ESSEX ECOLOGICAL PROGRAM, Any Town, MA   9/87–11/88

<u>Coordinator</u>
Project managed well-received program which introduced students to the world of ecology.

XYZ CORPORATION, Any Town, MA   6/80–9/87

<u>Sales Supervisor</u>
Telemarketed and cold-called to sell sophisticated and expensive high-tech equipment to corporations. Also directed support staff responsible for order processing, customer relations, and receivables.

REFERENCES PROVIDED UPON REQUEST

JOHN Q. SAMPLE

123 Any Street, Any City, CA XXXXX (619) 555-1234

Contact Name   Date
Title
Company
Address
City, State Zip

Dear Mr./Ms. _____:

As a central figure in Acme Corporation's massive restructuring, I applied executive skills in finance, administration, property management, and purchasing to facilitate Acme's turnaround to profitability. I likewise produced multimillion-dollar profits for the ABC Company through productive management of its administration and property management services, receiving accelerated promotions to Director of a $19 million operation.

I am presenting for your review my skills, achievements, and talent for accelerating margins and turning around unprofitable organizations so that we can discuss my joining _____ as a member of your senior management team.

Results achieved to date include:

o Promoted five grade levels during my last four years at ABC Company based on achieving all major P&L goals in directing the $19 million Corporate Administration and Property Management Department.

o As Acme's Corporate Director of Administration & Property Services, generated tens of millions of dollars in cost reductions and cash flow through aggressive property consolidations, upgraded services and procurement, and enforced management accountability.

o Consolidated 29 Acme warehouses down to 4, generating annual savings of $5.8 million; saved $4.6 million by reducing corporate headquarters space 30%; introduced uniform facility standards which reduced total space requirements 20%, generating another $3.4 million in annual cost savings.

o As head of Acme's $230 million purchasing operation, introduced an aggressive multiple-sourcing program which improved the margins of two major product lines by 7% and 9% respectively.

o Productively managed ABC Company's property holdings, achieving 97% occupancy of 800,000 square feet at premium rates; developed a sophisticated model which helped save $7 million on the cost of an out-of-control $40 million building project at ABC.

I look forward to meeting and discussing how I can help accelerate or turn around your company's revenue and profit growth.

                                                          Sincerely,

Enclosure: John Q. Sample

Administration/Finance Executive

JOHN Q. SAMPLE

123 Any Street, Any City, CA XXXXX (619) 555-1234

B.S.   Honors   Finance   Georgetown University   1980

CAREER SKILLS/KNOWLEDGE

o Finance/administration management
o General management
o Strategic/operational planning
o General/administrative services
o Financial planning & analysis
o Procurement operations
o Facilities/telecommunications
o Training operations
o Logistics services
o Global transportation

o Property management
o Development/construction
o Occupancy growth strategies
o Premium rate strategies
o Consolidation strategies
o Lease management/negotiations
o Site selection/space planning
o Budgeting/accountability
o Government regulations
o Environmental guidelines

CAREER ACHIEVEMENTS

o As Corporate Director of Administration & Property Services, assumed a central role in Acme's turnaround to profitability: generated tens of millions of dollars in cost reductions and cash flow through aggressive property consolidations, upgraded services and procurement, and enforced management accountability.

o Promoted five grade levels during my last four years at ABC Company based on achieving all major P&L goals in directing the $19 million Corporate Administration and Property Management Department.

o Consolidated 29 Acme warehouses down to 4, generating annual savings of $5.8 million; saved $4.6 million by reducing corporate headquarters space 30%; introduced uniform facility standards which reduced total space requirements 20%, generating another $3.4 million in annual cost savings.

o As head of Acme's $230 million purchasing operation, introduced an aggressive multiple-sourcing program which improved the margins of two major product lines by 7% and 9% respectively.

o Overcame powerful organizational resistance to produce over $3 million cash and annual savings of $2.1 million by persuading the Chairman to sell off Acme's corporate yacht.

o Generated annual cost savings of over $800,000 by installing a Novell network and upgrading ABC Company's distribution, travel, and other corporate services.

o Productively managed ABC Company's property holdings, achieving 97% occupancy of 800,000 square feet at premium rates; developed a sophisticated model which helped save $7 million on the cost of an out-of-control $40 million building project at ABC.

CAREER EXPERIENCE

ACME CORPORATION, Any Town, CA   3/88–Present

Corporate Director of Administration & Property Services
Direct the overall management, planning, site selection, lease negotiations, consolidations, and disposition for property totaling two million square feet. Additionally direct the $230 million purchasing operation and all corporate administrative services.

ABC COMPANY, Any Town, CA   6/80–3/88

Director of Services & Property   3/85–3/88
Directed services with a staff of 63 and a budget of $19 million: included property management, purchasing, communications, systems, mail, and office equipment placement and maintenance. Reviewed and approved all facilities and construction contracts. Audited almost $100 million in operating expense budgets.

Manager of Administration   2/83–3/85
Developed policies and procedures, negotiated property transactions, and created a model which turned around a $40 million building project.

Senior Facilities Consultant   8/81–2/83
Developed well-received proposals that resulted in the creation of a $12 million Facilities Group.

Senior Consultant   6/80–8/81
Introduced the much needed zero-based budgeting concept to seven major operations.

REFERENCES PROVIDED UPON REQUEST

MARK A. WILSON

123 Any Street, Any City, WA XXXXX (206) 555-1234

Contact Name   Date
Title
Company
Street Address
City, State Zip

Dear Mr./Ms. _____ :

As Treasurer of XYZ Leasing Services, Inc., I played a central role in returning critically needed financial credibility to this out-of-control company. As Division Manager of Acme Corporation's Leasing Subsidiary, I directed its turnaround and major contribution to profits in an otherwise disappointing period for the company.

I am presenting for your review my skills, achievements, ability to turn around treasury operations, and talent for generating bottom-line results within problem organizations so that we can discuss my joining _____ as a member of your financial management team.

Results achieved to date include:

o As one of five key veteran managers remaining after the bankruptcy of XYZ Leasing Services, a nationwide company with revenues of $200 million, was promoted to Treasurer: codirected the company's turnaround and better-than-forecasted $30 million sale.

o As Treasurer and Controller of XYZ Leasing Services, instituted effective post-bankruptcy financial controls returning critically needed credibility to XYZ; also executed a major systems database project critical to the $30 million sale of the company.

o As Division Manager, instituted Acme Corporation's lucrative remarketing program for off-lease equipment generating substantial rentals from the over $4 million in equipment leased to date under the program.

o Investigated and uncovered several million dollars of off-lease equipment that had never been returned to inventory recovering $700,000 in fees for Acme.

o Restructured and turned around Acme's third-party leasing portfolio, upgrading the accounting and administrative controls and creating an accurate database of all equipment.

I look forward to discussing how I can contribute to your company's future success.

                                                            Sincerely,

Enclosure: Mark A. Wilson

MARK A. WILSON

123 Any Street, Any City, WA XXXXX (206) 555-1234

B.B.A.   Accounting   University of Seattle   1986

Certified Public Accountant

CAREER SKILLS/KNOWLEDGE

o Treasury operations
o Portfolio management
o Banking relations
o Finance/accounting
o Controller operations
o Audit operations
o General accounting
o Budgeting/controls
o Collections/taxes

o Leasing industry expertise
o Lease financing cycle
o Division management
o P&L responsibility
o Marketing/sales
o MIS operations
o Personnel/payroll
o Staff supervision/development
o Information security

CAREER ACHIEVEMENTS

o As one of five key veteran managers remaining after the bankruptcy of XYZ Leasing Services, a nationwide company with revenues of $200 million, was promoted to Treasurer: codirected the company's turnaround and better-than-forecasted $30 million sale.

o As Treasurer and Controller of XYZ Leasing Services, instituted effective post-bankruptcy financial controls returning critically needed credibility to XYZ; also executed a major systems database project critical to the $30 million sale of the company.

o As Division Manager of Acme Corporation's Leasing Subsidiary, directed its turnaround and major contribution to profits in an otherwise disappointing period for the corporation.

o Instituted Acme's lucrative remarketing program for off-lease equipment generating substantial rentals from the over $4 million in equipment leased to date under the program.

o Investigated and uncovered several million dollars of off-lease equipment that had never been returned to inventory recovering $700,000 in fees for Acme.

o Restructured and turned around Acme's third-party leasing portfolio, upgrading the accounting and administrative controls and creating an accurate database of all equipment.

o As Program Director at ABC Computer Leasing, introduced critically needed administrative and accounting controls for an affiliated leasing company; thoroughly analyzed the affiliate's portfolio of leases, loans, sale/leasebacks, and remarketing agreements.

CAREER EXPERIENCE

ACME CORPORATION, INC., Any Town, WA   2/95–Present

Division Manager
Responsibilities executed for the Acme Leasing Subsidiary:

o Achieved targeted P&L goals; instituted remarketing program.
o Direct senior staff: Controller, Systems Director, and Operations and Credit Managers.
o Upgraded financial and operational controls and reporting.
o Negotiate, screen, and approve all contracts.
o Upgraded relations with banks.
o Reduced aged receivables; upgraded inventory control.
o Eliminated aged backlog of customer inquiries.

ABC COMPUTER LEASING COMPANY, Any Town, WA   3/94–2/95

Program Director
Audited portfolio of affiliated leasing company from its inception through current status; instituted Equity Tracking System; assisted in transition to new database system.

XYZ LEASING SERVICES, INC., Any Town, WA   6/86–3/94

Treasurer   2/91–3/94
Responsibilities executed:

o Upgraded portfolio management increasing return on $40 million cash.
o Developed relations with major northwestern banks.
o Gained approval for post-bankruptcy exception request.
o Managed Personnel, Payroll, and Collections Departments.

Controller   3/89–2/91
Responsibilities executed:

o Recruited, trained, and supervised several staff accountants.
o Directed the Bookkeeping Department.
o Directed general ledger accounting; prepared consolidations.
o Managed in-depth operational reviews; initiated corrective actions.
o Supervised tax area; reduced equipment property taxes.

REFERENCES PROVIDED UPON REQUEST

SAMUEL A. JONES (Version 1)

123 Any Street, Any Town, CA XXXXX (619) 555-1234

Contact Name   Date
Title
Company
Address
City, State Zip

Dear Mr./Ms. _____:

I have combined in-depth knowledge of Eastern Europe with skills in finance, administration, sales, manufacturing, banking, credit, and management to resolve serious cash shortages, achieve critical cost savings, and accelerate productivity as Director of Finance of an Eastern European operation. Achievements resulted in multiple management promotions in spite of my unwillingness to join the Communist Party.

I am bringing to your attention my skills, achievements, ability to achieve bottom-line results under negative conditions, and talent for executing tough projects including my escape from Eastern Europe so that we can discuss my joining _____ as a member of your International Finance Team.

Major achievements to date include:

o Earned promotion to the much-sought-after position of Director of Finance at a major European operation, the largest such operation in the country, in spite of my negative attitude toward joining the Communist Party: assumed total responsibility for the review and approval of expense outlays for the operation; reduced the multimillion-dollar expense budget 35% while improving overall productivity.

o Upon promotion to Financial Analyst at a European factory, researched and prepared well-conceived financial plans that exceeded cost-reduction targets without sacrificing operational effectiveness; took the lead in negotiating with banks to meet weekly payrolls in the face of critical cash-flow problems.

o Earned rarely achieved first-year promotion within the Cost Department of a European manufacturer based on producing quality multimillion-dollar cost studies: assumed ever-increasing responsibilities with multimillion-dollar signing authority.

o Over a four-year period, planned and executed my escape from the Communist Regime: completed a physical training program; maneuvered access to a waterfront complex; escaped across an inlet and posed as a West German citizen to get to West Germany where the United States granted asylum.

o As a Partner in a San Diego firm, purchase, restore, and successfully market antique furniture; as a Sales Representative for an upscale American business, acted as Assistant Manager and consistently exceeded sales quotas selling $50,000 worth of product in a three-week period: nurtured a loyal client base right up to the unfortunate closing of the business.

I look forward to discussing how I can contribute to your international revenue and profit growth.

                                       Sincerely,

Enclosure: Samuel A. Jones

International Finance/Controller

SAMUEL A. JONES

123 Any Street, Any City, CA XXXXX (619) 555-1234

B.S. Finance/Economics   Finance Institute   1981

Honors:	Chosen to attend selective Institute
	Recipient of major scholarship; Graduated with honors
Citizenship:	U.S.
International:	Eastern Europe Expert
Languages:	Fluent English, German, French, and Italian; some knowledge of Spanish

CAREER SKILLS/KNOWLEDGE

o International relations
o Eastern Europe expertise
o European banking relations
o Credit application/approval process
o European financial/cost controls
o European pricing/capital planning
o Manufacturing/factory operations
o European management techniques

o Financial management
o Controller operations/expense control
o Financial planning
o Forecasting/budgeting
o Cost/pricing studies
o Sales/marketing
o Client development
o Closing/customer service

CAREER ACHIEVEMENTS

o Earned promotion to the much-sought-after position of Director of Finance at a major European operation, the largest such operation in the country, in spite of my negative attitude toward joining the Communist Party: assumed total responsibility for the review and approval of expense outlays for the operation; reduced the multimillion-dollar expense budget 35% while improving overall productivity.

o Upon promotion to Financial Analyst at a European factory, researched and prepared well-conceived financial plans that exceeded cost-reduction targets without sacrificing operational effectiveness; took the lead in negotiating with banks to meet weekly payrolls in the face of critical cash-flow problems.

o Earned rarely achieved first-year promotion within the Cost Department of a European manufacturer based on producing quality multimillion-dollar cost studies: assumed ever-increasing responsibilities with multimillion-dollar signing authority.

o Over a four-year period, planned and executed my escape from the Communist Regime: completed a physical training program; maneuvered access to a waterfront complex; escaped across an inlet and posed as a West German citizen to get to West Germany where the United States granted asylum.

o As a Partner in a San Diego firm, purchase, restore, and successfully market antique furniture; as a Sales Representative for an upscale American business, acted as Assistant Manager and consistently exceeded sales quotas selling $50,000 worth of product in a three-week period: nurtured a loyal client base right up to the unfortunate closing of the business.

INTERNATIONAL EXPERIENCE

Eastern European Operation   6/81–3/86

Director of Finance   1/84–3/86
Audited and exercised final approval for all major expense requests for this manufacturer. Achieved substantial cost reductions while improving productivity.

Financial Analyst   5/83–1/84
Formulated financial plans including detailed forecasts and budgets; interacted with managers to reduce expenses and capital expenditures. Worked with financial institutions to address critical cash-flow problems.

Senior Cost Analyst   6/81–5/83
Formulated detailed cost studies as a foundation for better pricing practices. Interacted with departments to accumulate accurate cost data.

AMERICAN EXPERIENCE

Insurance Firm, Any City, CA   3/95–Present

Sales Representative: Aggressively cold-call and follow-up to close clients.

Investment Firm, Any City, CA   3/90–Present

Cofounder: Purchase, restore, and market antique furniture.

Essex Company, Any City, CA   4/87–3/90

Sales Representative: Sold expensive products and nurtured clients until business closed.

REFERENCES PROVIDED UPON REQUEST

PAUL A. CUMMINGS

123 Any Street, Any City, NJ XXXXX (609) 555-1234

Contact Name   Date
Title
Company
Street Address
City, State Zip

Dear Mr./Ms. _____:

I have applied proficient skills in financial management, planning and analysis, and capital budgeting to generate cost reductions, implement critical systems, expedite budgeting, upgrade controls, and achieve bottom-line results for Fortune 500 companies. Results achieved have been rewarded with multiple promotions.

I am bringing to your attention my skills, achievements, and talent for developing productive, results-oriented relationships with line managers so that we can discuss my joining _____ as a member of your Financial Management Team.

Results achieved to date:

o Completed ABC International's billion dollar fiscal budget in less than three months versus the six months required to complete the previous year's budget: bottoms-up project covered three major Divisions, 14 Departments, 4 Warehouses, and 52 Outlets.

o Based on in-depth review and analysis, generated significant reductions in ABC's 1991 expense budget: reduced utilities expense $3 million, depreciation $400,000, and benefits $300,000.

o Developed, implemented, and was promoted to centrally manage profitability analysis and capital planning systems for XYZ Corporation.

o Codirected cost-savings from $40,000 up to $1.5 million on capital acquisitions at XYZ; coordinated program reviews of major projects identifying problems and corrective actions.

o Earned rapid promotion from Account Executive to Sales Manager at Acme Finance Company based on my top 10% sales performance: qualified for prestigious Performer's Conference, received the Golden Circle Award, and earned the Charter Professional Award.

I look forward to discussions at which we can determine how I can contribute to your company's future success.

                                        Sincerely,

Enclosure: Paul A. Cummings

PAUL A. CUMMINGS

123 Any Street, Any City, NJ XXXXX (609) 555-1234

M.B.A.	Finance	State University of New York	Honors	1985
B.S.	Finance	University of Colorado	Honors	1983

Licenses: NASD Series 6

Languages: Fluent French

CAREER SKILLS/KNOWLEDGE

- o Financial planning and analysis
- o Budget management
- o Forecasting
- o Capital/expense budgeting
- o Variance analysis/reporting
- o Auditing operations
- o Business planning
- o Major program reviews
- o Program management
- o Program controller

- o Line manager interaction
- o Staff supervision
- o Management reporting
- o Capital request approval
- o Payback/discount analyses
- o Lease versus buy
- o Inventory analysis
- o Asset turnover
- o Aged receivables collection
- o Mainframe/micro applications

CAREER ACHIEVEMENTS

o Completed ABC International's billion dollar fiscal budget in less than three months versus the six months required to complete the previous year's budget: bottoms-up project covered three major Divisions, 14 Departments, 4 Warehouses, and 52 Outlets.

o Based on in-depth review and analysis, generated significant reductions in ABC's 1991 expense budget: reduced utilities expense $3 million, depreciation $400,000, and benefits $300,000.

o Developed, implemented, and was promoted to centrally manage profitability analysis and capital planning systems for XYZ Corporation, its Subsidiaries and Strategic Business Units.

o Codirected cost-savings from $40,000 up to $1.5 million on capital acquisitions at XYZ; coordinated program reviews of major projects identifying problems and corrective actions.

o Earned rapid promotion from Account Executive to Sales Manager at Acme Finance Company based on my top 10% sales performance: qualified for prestigious Performer's Conference, received the Golden Circle Award, and earned the Charter Professional Award.

o During my initial 15 months at Acme, achieved what my boss characterized as an almost unheard record of no policy cancellations: also accelerated my close ratio to over 60%, signing up as many as seven business and individual clients out of every ten appointments.

CAREER EXPERIENCE

ACME FINANCE COMPANY, Any Town, NJ   2/93–Present

<u>Sales Manager</u>
Market a full range of financial services including insurance, annuities, pension plans, and mutual funds.

ABC INTERNATIONAL, INC., Any City, NJ   6/90–2/93

<u>Financial Manager</u>
Responsibilities included:

o Developed and coordinated a new budgeting process.
o Managed $20 million pool of cash.
o Prepared and distributed the flash reports.
o Prepared Proxy Statements for the Annual Report and SEC.
o Prepared Pension and Profit-Sharing Plan statements.
o Created comprehensive Policies and Procedures Manual.

XYZ CORPORATION, Any City, NJ   7/85–6/90

<u>Financial Supervisor   9/88–6/90</u>
Promoted to this position; expanded responsibilities included:

o Managed profitability analysis and capital planning systems.
o Delivered major presentations on upgrading capital request and financial reporting controls.
o Liaison between XYZ and Profit Centers.

<u>Capital Supervisor   8/86–9/88</u>
Promoted to this position; responsibilities:

o Analyzed and exercised approval authority for all capital appropriations requests.
o Prepared Five-Year Capital Plan.
o Directed preparation of operating reports.

<u>Senior Analyst   1/86–8/86</u>
Promoted to position; controlled major development programs:

o Instituted comprehensive financial controls.
o Performed variance analysis and formulated corrective actions.
o Forecasted sales, planned manpower, implemented controls, and reviewed capital requests.
o Developed and updated five-year plans.

REFERENCES AVAILABLE UPON REQUEST

AUDREY A. JONES

123 Any Street, Any Town, CA XXXXX (415) 555-1234

Contact Name   Date
Title
Company
Street Address
City, State Zip

Dear Mr./Ms. _____:

I have combined two degrees with skills in credit, customer service, client relations, and sales to upgrade service, improve client retention, reduce aged receivables, and achieve the top sales ranking by generating over $1 million in sales for a Utah based company—a revenue growth which doubled total sales. Results achieved have been rewarded with promotions into credit and sales management as well as an offer to take over as General Manager of the Utah company.

I am bringing to your attention my skills, achievements, creative energy, talent for upgrading service operations, and ability to turn around and retain angry customers so that we can discuss my joining _____ as a member of your customer service/credit management team.

Results achieved to date include:

o As Credit & Collections Manager for an international soda producer, reduced chronically aged receivables and achieved a 94% current status in only a few months by instituting aggressive collection strategies: established constructive dialogue with delinquent customers and made use of stop-shipment leverage; investigated the validity of customer-generated credits recovering 88% of the total.

o Promoted to Sales Manager at a Utah commercial services company based on number one sales ranking and bottom-line contributions in doubling company revenue: cold-called, closed, and serviced lucrative, difficult-to-sell Fortune 500 and smaller clients including Eagle Supermarkets, Bob Smith Restaurants, Hardee's, Inc., Eckerd Drugstores, and Pizza Hut.

o Overcame strong resistance to sell, service, and retain major corporate accounts which generated over $1 million in five years for the Utah commercial services company: circumvented strong union resistance to land the lucrative Eagle account; outmaneuvered the competition by offering and delivering better quality service to land the profitable Bob Smith and Hardee's accounts.

o As liaison to the operations manager and service delivery staff of the Utah services company, significantly upgraded service quality, prevented and resolved customer and employee problems, and enhanced overall morale and productivity: customer complaints dropped 50%; retention of customers with problems increased from 55% to over 93%; employee turnover radically declined.

o Based on bottom-line sales achievements and demonstrated leadership in turning around the service operations, was offered the General Manager position by the owner of the Utah company: was selected from several candidates to fill this key position created by the relocation of the owner.

I will work hard to achieve bottom-line results and look forward to discussing how I can contribute to your company's future success.

Sincerely,

Enclosure: Audrey A. Jones

Credit/Customer Service Management

AUDREY A. JONES

123 Any Street, Any Town, CA XXXXX (415) 555-1234

B.A.	Utah State University	Self-financed	1986
B.S.	Georgia State University	Self-financed	1988

Honors/Awards: Leadership Award (Any Town, CA); Citizenship Award (Any Town, CA)
Leadership Activities: Captain/Varsity Player in several sports
Languages: Strong German; moderate French and Spanish; studied Asian languages

CAREER SKILLS/KNOWLEDGE

- o Customer service/direct sales
- o Client development/retention
- o Credit & collection strategies
- o Cold-calling/telemarketing
- o Competitive maneuvering
- o Presentations/demos
- o Closing/contract negotiations
- o Operations/service/quality control

- o Communications/training
- o Facilitator/leadership skills
- o Platform skills/group presentations
- o Team building/training
- o Staff development/productivity growth
- o IBM/MAC PC applications
- o Excel/Lotus 1-2-3/DBase III
- o PowerPoint/Harvard Graphics/Wordperfect

CAREER ACHIEVEMENTS

- o As Credit & Collections Manager for an international soda producer, reduced seriously aged receivables and achieved a 94% current status in only a few months by instituting aggressive collection strategies: established constructive dialogue with delinquent customers and made use of stop-shipment leverage; investigated validity of customer-generated credits recovering 88%.

- o Promoted to Sales Manager at a Utah commercial services company based on number one sales ranking and bottom-line contributions in doubling company revenue: cold-called, closed, and serviced lucrative, difficult-to-sell Fortune 500 and smaller clients including Eagle Supermarkets, Bob Smith Restaurants, Hardee's Inc., Eckerd Drugstores, and Pizza Hut.

- o Overcame strong resistance to sell, service, and retain major corporate accounts which generated over $1 million in five years for the Utah commercial services company: circumvented union resistance to land the lucrative Eagle account; outmaneuvered the competition by offering and delivering better quality service to land the profitable Bob Smith and Hardee's accounts.

- o As liaison to the operations manager and service delivery staff of the Utah services company, significantly upgraded service, prevented and resolved customer and employee problems, and enhanced overall morale and productivity: customer complaints dropped 50%; retention of customers with problems increased from 55% to over 93%; employee turnover radically declined.

- o Based on bottom-line sales achievements and demonstrated leadership in turning around service operations, was offered the General Manager position by the owner of the Utah company: was selected from several candidates to fill this position created by the relocation of the owner.

- o As a member of the Quality Control group at the Acme Corporation, uncovered potentially serious operational problems that had created serious backlogs which threatened the validity of the shelf-life testing process: formulated and gained approval for $100,000 worth of corrective actions which eliminated the backlog and reinstated the validity of the testing process.

CAREER EXPERIENCE

AVERY SODA COMPANY, Any Town, CA   1993–Present

Manager of Credit & Collection: Accelerated the collection of high-dollar aged receivables by creating receivables tracking reports for chronically slow-paying customers: over a three-month period, reduced average payment days by as much as 43% for large volume clients.

ACME CORPORATION, Any Town, CA   1990–1993

Testing Analyst: Implemented Statistical Process Control in testing areas and designed projects for the Quality Control group: gathered and analyzed data for Q.C.; presented data, conclusions, and recommendations to Quality Assurance management; assisted Q.A., Reliability, Advertising, and Development in acquiring test data; tested production and pilot-line samples.

Investigated and uncovered a serious procedural weakness in the sample testing process that allowed leakage to go undetected: corrected the problem by recommending and instituting procedures to supplement the computer testing.

COMMERCIAL SERVICES COMPANY, Any Town, UT   1988–1990

Sales Manager: Marketed and sold services to Fortune 500 and other businesses: formulated marketing strategies and promotions; developed and presented proposals; negotiated contracts. Also comanaged and upgraded service operations.

Reason for leaving: Relocation to California

GEORGIA STATE UNIVERSITY, Any Town, GA   1987–1988

Worked and earned a B.S. degree while maintaining a straight A average at this multicampus college: planned special events for and delivered 300 presentations to groups of 400 people; supervised the shipping and receiving department; coordinated advertising and direct mailings.

As part of the leadership training, executed challenging exercises in self-reliance: traveled over a thousand miles without transportation and spent the next several days mountain climbing.

ESSEX COUNSELING GROUP, Any Town, GA   1986–1987

Program Manager: Promoted this social service agency to the community, school system, and families. Helped clients network with other agencies and followed up on clients to ensure success. Overcame strong attitudinal barriers to convert and sell school officials and the community on the advantages of our programs.

ADDITIONAL TRAINING : Technical Layout Reading; Professional Carpentry
VOLUNTEER ACTIVITIES : Reading Projects and Centers for the Mentally Retarded

REFERENCES PROVIDED UPON REQUEST

WILLIAM A. JOHNSON

123 Any Street, Any City, NY XXXXX (914) 555-1234

Contact Name   Date
Title
Company
Street Address
City, State Zip

Dear Mr./Ms. _____:

Profitably applying brokerage and client relations skills to rank in the top 10% nationwide and earn promotion to Branch Manager at XYZ Securities by age 25, I have demonstrated the ability to produce bottom-line results by generating millions in revenue.

Based on my skills, achievements, and fast-track experience, I would like to initiate discussions about joining _____ as a member of your brokerage management team.

Bottom-line results achieved at XYZ Securities by aggressively applying the skills detailed on the attached resume include:

o Personally generate up to $2,000,000 annually in "new money."

o Comanaged the turnaround of the Westchester Operation.

o Out of over 1,000 brokers nationwide, consistently ranked near the top.

o Effectively recruit, motivate, and accelerate the productivity of the staff.

I know a face-to-face meeting to determine how I can, likewise, contribute to your firm's future success will be mutually beneficial. I look forward to hearing from you.

                                                    Sincerely,

Enclosure: William A. Johnson

Stockbroker/Branch Manager

WILLIAM A. JOHNSON
---

123 Any Street, Any City, NY XXXXX (914) 555-1234

BROKERAGE/BUSINESS SKILLS

o Branch management
o New account development
o Client relations
o Underwriting

o Staff recruiting/hiring
o Staff development
o Advertising
o Banking/NASD rules

BROKERAGE EXPERIENCE/ACHIEVEMENTS

XYZ SECURITIES, INC., Any Town, NY   6/92–Present

Branch Manager   6/95–Present
Promoted to this position at age 25. Achievements to date:

o Codirected turnaround of Westchester Office.
o Generate up to $2,000,000 annually in "new money."
o Ranked in the top 10% out of over 1,000 brokers nationwide.
o Successfully recruit, motivate, and accelerate productivity of the staff.

EXPERIENCE TO FINANCE EDUCATION
Full-time/Part-time

UNITED DELIVERY SERVICE, Any City, NY   11/88–6/92
Supervisor of Local Operations: Promoted to this position (part-time).

ACME ELECTRIC CORPORATION, Any City, NJ   9/88–6/92
Quality Control: Full-time position during college.

ACADEMIC/CREDENTIALS

B.S.   Business Management   Adelphi University   1992
            Minor: Psychology
            Self-financed 100% of expenses

CERTIFICATIONS

o Registered Full Service Broker Representative (NASD-Series 7)
o Registered Broker Principal (NASD-Series 24)
o The Agent (NASD-Series 63)

REFERENCES PROVIDED UPON REQUEST

BRIAN A. CUMMINGS

123 Any Street, Any City, CA XXXXX (619) 555-1234

Contact Name   Date
Title
Company
Street Address
City, State Zip

Dear Mr./Ms. _____ :

I have applied proficient skills in leasing, financial management, accounting, cash management, and systems to upgrade operations, reduce costs, help win multimillion-dollar contracts, turn around cash-flow problems, start up new operations, and help implement mergers and acquisitions. Results achieved have been rewarded with multiple promotions, pay raises, and bonuses.

I am bringing to your attention my skills, achievements, ability to upgrade staff productivity, and talent for improving cash flow and profit margins so that we can discuss my joining _____ as a member of your financial management team.

Major accomplishments to date include:

o As Director of Finance for a division of XYZ Corporation, generated over a million dollars in annual cost reductions by directing the consolidation of major financial functions from 30 decentralized locations to our San Diego offices.

o During a critically important period at XYZ, earned strong feedback for stepping in and effectively directing financial operations: expedited year-end closing, annual report development, and staff training and productivity.

o Created well-received financial package and upgraded the systems at XYZ: project managed installation of an integrated accounting system using a major General Ledger system and Lotus 1-2-3; also implemented cost-saving Sybron accounting package.

o By instituting critically needed financial credibility, helped ABC Company win a $5 million contract increasing the corporation's market value just prior to its scheduled sale; also helped consolidate and merge several companies into one.

o As Controller at Acme Corporation, executed a product leasing study which led to a profitable shift in marketing strategy; also converted a major acquisition to Acme's policies and procedures.

I will work hard to achieve bottom-line results and look forward to discussing how I can contribute to your company's future success.

Sincerely,

Enclosure: Brian A. Cummings

BRIAN A. CUMMINGS

123 Any Street, Any City, CA XXXXX (619) 555-1234

B.S.   Accounting/Business   University of Texas   1980

CAREER SKILLS/KNOWLEDGE

- Finance/accounting management
- Leasing cycle/financing
- Controller operations
- Operating plan development
- Cash management
- Management reporting
- Budgeting/forecasting
- S.E.C. reporting/compliance
- Software applications/Lotus 1-2-3

- Leasing industry
- Project management
- Business development
- Turnaround strategies
- Margin growth strategies
- Consulting operations
- Franchising operations
- Acquisitions/mergers
- Contract administration

CAREER ACHIEVEMENTS

- As Director of Finance for a division of XYZ Corporation, generated over a million dollars in annual cost reductions by directing the consolidation of major financial functions from 30 decentralized locations to our San Diego offices.

- During a critically important period at XYZ, earned strong feedback for stepping in and effectively directing financial operations: expedited year-end closing, annual report development, and staff training and productivity.

- Created well-received financial package and upgraded the systems at XYZ: project managed installation of an integrated accounting system using a major General Ledger system and Lotus 1-2-3; also implemented cost-saving Sybron accounting package.

- By instituting critically needed financial credibility, helped ABC Company win a $5 million contract increasing the corporation's market value just prior to its scheduled sale.

- As Corporate Controller at ABC, consolidated and merged several companies: issued new stock, integrated the financials, and earned accolades from the outside accounting firm.

- As Controller at Acme Corporation, executed a product leasing study which led to a profitable shift in marketing strategy; also converted a major acquisition to Acme's policies and procedures.

- As Controller at Essex Leasing Services, turned around cash management by instituting better investment strategies and cash utilization.

CAREER EXPERIENCE

XYZ CORPORATION, INC., Any City, CA   7/93–Present

Director of Finance: Supervise staff, systems and reporting, monthly closings, G/L transactions, banking relations, cash flow, investments, payables, and receivables.

ESSEX LEASING SERVICES, Any City, CA   4/91–7/93

Controller: Upgraded lease financing administration and cash management; initiated leasing software implementation.

Reason for leaving: Company's economic downturn.

ABC COMPANY, INC., Any City, CA   3/89–4/91

Controller: Performed revenue-generating consulting assignments; merged several separate companies into one; prepared operating plans, financial statements, payroll and related taxes, and management reports; designed and implemented cost accounting system; directed contract administration and compliance to federal regulations.

Reason for leaving: Company was acquired and relocated.

ACME CORPORATION, Any City, CA   7/87–3/89

Controller: Delivered major presentations to top management. Prepared and analyzed financial statements, operating plans, and cash and sales forecasts.

Reason for leaving: Company relocated to New York.

SMITH INTERNATIONAL SERVICES, Any Town, CA   6/84–7/87

Manager of Accounting: Chosen for start-up management team by the Franchisor of QRS Services which grew from 20 locations to over 600. Managed growth by establishing financial operations and implementing policies, procedures, and systems.

RIS COMPANY, Inc., Any City, CA   6/80–6/84

Accounting Department: Promoted to several positions: upgraded cash management, inventory control, and collections.

REFERENCES PROVIDED UPON REQUEST

Real Estate Brokerage/Property Management

ANN Q. JONES

123 Any Street, Any Town, NJ XXXXX (201) 555-1234

Contact Name   Date
Title
Company
Street Address
City, State Zip

Dear Mr./Ms. _____ :

I have profitably applied skills in real estate brokerage, property management, sales, and marketing to sell $10 million worth of product, earn Million-Dollar-Club status, profitably manage several commercial properties, and generate $5 million in sales in a two-year period.

I am bringing to your attention my skills, achievements, creative energy, work ethic, and ability to sell and achieve bottom-line results even in recessionary markets so that we can discuss my joining _____ as a member of your brokerage team.

Results achieved to date include:

o As a Residential Real Estate Broker for XYZ Real Estate, Inc., sold $10 million worth of modestly priced housing over a four-year period: qualified for the Million-Dollar Club for several consecutive years generating over $5 million in sales in one two-year period alone.

o As a Real Estate Broker, achieved bottom-line results by effectively closing the listing sellers and accurately defining the needs of buyers as a basis for selecting and showing only the best alternative products; effectively balanced the needs and demands of the seller versus the buyer.

o Profitably marketed and managed several apartment buildings over a 12-year period: achieved and maintained a high occupancy rate through aggressive marketing and advertising while attaining a low level of rental income write-offs; directed cost-effective maintenance operations; improved and maintained solid tenant and broker relations.

o As a veteran Representative on a West Coast Zoning Commission, negotiated directly with architects, developers, and builders exercising right of approval for proposed changes to properties.

o Earned multiple promotions during three years with a major retailer; based on sales achievements, was promoted within a year to Department Manager in charge of three high-volume departments; was also promoted into Buying and Human Resources at the flagship operation.

I will work hard to achieve bottom-line results and look forward to discussing how I can contribute to your company's future success.

Sincerely yours,

Enclosure: Ann Q. Jones

Real Estate Brokerage/Property Management

ANN Q. JONES

123 Any Street, Any Town, NJ XXXXX (201) 555-1234

CAREER SKILLS/KNOWLEDGE

o Real estate professional/broker
o Client development/relations
o Cold-calling/telemarketing
o Sale/rental advertising
o Property appraisals
o Proposals/presentations
o Buyer/seller negotiations
o Overcoming objections
o Closing/customer service

o Property management/ownership
o Occupancy rate strategies
o Rent collection strategies
o Maintenance operations
o Administration management
o Staff supervision/training
o Project management/troubleshooting
o Human resources administration
o Recruiting/hiring/benefits

CAREER ACHIEVEMENTS

o As a Residential Real Estate Broker for XYZ Real Estate, Inc., sold $10 million worth of modestly priced housing over a four-year period: qualified for the Million-Dollar Club for several consecutive years generating over $5 million in sales in one two-year period alone.

o As a Real Estate Broker, achieved bottom-line results by effectively closing the listing sellers and accurately defining the needs of buyers as a basis for selecting and showing only the best alternative products; effectively balanced the needs and demands of the seller versus the buyer.

o Profitably marketed and managed several apartment buildings over a 12-year period: achieved and maintained a high occupancy rate through aggressive marketing and advertising while attaining a low level of rental income write-offs; directed cost-effective maintenance operations; improved and maintained solid tenant and broker relations.

o As a veteran Representative on a West Coast Zoning Commission, negotiated directly with architects, developers, and builders exercising right of approval for proposed changes to properties.

o As a Program Director for a West Coast Commission on the Homeless, successfully raised tens of thousands of dollars from area corporations in spite of strong resistance from corporate donors.

o Earned multiple promotions during three years with a major retailer: based on sales achievements, was promoted within a year to Department Manager in charge of three high-volume departments; was also promoted into Buying and Human Resources at the flagship operation.

o Upon promotion to Human Resources administration at a major retailer's flagship store, recruited and hired several hundred employees to staff the main floor and part of the lower level retail operations; also dealt firmly and effectively with strong unions; coordinated new hire training and development; effectively handled benefits administration and other personnel administration.

CAREER EXPERIENCE

XYZ REAL ESTATE, INC., Any City, NJ   1994–Present

<u>Broker:</u> Market and sell residential real estate.

ANOTHER REAL ESTATE INC., Any City, NJ   1989–1994

<u>Broker:</u> Market and sell residential real estate.

COMMISSION ON THE HOMELESS, Any Town, WA   1985–1989

<u>Director:</u> In charge of planning and fund-raising.

PROPERTY MANAGEMENT, Any Town, WA   1987–1989

<u>Management:</u> Managed several apartment buildings: in charge of marketing and operations including rental advertising, tenant relations, maintenance operations, and rent collection.

ZONING COMMISSION, Any Town, WA   1986–1987

<u>Representative:</u> Negotiated with architects, developers, and builders on proposed projects.

REALTY MANAGEMENT COMPANY, Any Town, WA   1983–1986

<u>Human Resources:</u> Recruited staff for the properties managed by the company.

MAJOR RETAILER, Any Town, WA   1980–1983

<u>Department Manager:</u> Managed major departments. Completed well-respected Training Program.

CREDENTIALS

College: Attended University of Seattle   1979–1982

Certifications: Real Estate License (NJ); Graduate Real Estate Institute; Licensed Appraiser

REFERENCES PROVIDED UPON REQUEST

DANIEL A. CUMMINGS

123 Any Street, Any City, CA XXXXX (619) 555-1234

Contact Name   Date
Title
Company
Street Address
City, State Zip

Dear Mr./Ms. _____:

I have applied proficient skills in advertising, marketing, and sales promotion within the travel, cruise line, and transportation industries to achieve bottom-line results. As Director of Advertising and Sales Promotion at a major international cruise line, converted Corporate Advertising into a first-rate $20 million operation which facilitated the company's expansion from 58 to 120 ships.

I am bringing to your attention my skills, achievements, creative energy, and guarantee to generate revenue several times my compensation so that we can discuss my joining _____ as a member of your advertising management team.

Additional results achieved to date include:

o Helped achieve worldwide occupancy rate of over 75% by upgrading the quality, creativity, and payback of Acme Cruise Lines' advertising and sales promotions: instituted local management accountability and significantly improved readership response and marketing analysis.

o Recipient of numerous major advertising and sales promotion awards: we were the only cruise line to ever win a Gold Award from the Art Director's Club, which selected Acme Cruise Lines, Inc., from thousands of entries.

o As Vice President and Account Director at the XYZ Advertising Agency, successfully executed politically sensitive multimillion-dollar campaigns for the San Diego Transportation Authority.

o As a Sales Vice President at a Fortune 500 Corporation, increased annual billing $20 million by signing and managing major accounts including the much sought after Essex Cruise Line.

I look forward to a meeting at which we can focus on how I can contribute to your company's future success.

Sincerely,

Enclosure: Daniel A. Cummings

Advertising Industry Professional

DANIEL A. CUMMINGS

123 Any Street, Any City, CA XXXXX (619) 555-1234

MARKETING SKILLS/KNOWLEDGE

o Advertising/sales promotion	o Travel industry
o Agency operations/relations	o International cruise line industry
o Domestic/international campaigns	o Transportation industry
o Multimedia planning/buying	o Off-peak sales strategies
o Direct marketing	o New market development
o Brochure/catalog development	o Public relations

CAREER ACHIEVEMENTS

o As Corporate Director of Advertising and Sales Promotion at Acme Cruise Lines, converted Corporate Advertising into a first-rate $20 million operation which helped facilitate expansion from 58 to 120 ships worldwide.

o Helped achieve worldwide occupancy rate of over 75% by upgrading the quality, creativity, and payback of Acme Cruise Lines' advertising and sales promotions: instituted local management accountability and significantly improved readership response and marketing analysis.

o Introduced several major changes and innovations to Acme's advertising and promotional material including the use of world-class photographers and illustrators.

o As Vice President and Account Director at the XYZ Advertising Agency, successfully executed politically sensitive multimillion-dollar campaigns for the San Diego Transportation Authority.

o As a Sales Vice President at a Fortune 500 Corporation, increased annual billing $20 million by signing and managing major accounts including the much sought after Essex Cruise Line.

o Significantly improved sales and profit growth at Smith Transportation Company; stimulated off-peak sales achieving a load factor in excess of 87%.

MAJOR ADVERTISING AND PROMOTION AWARDS

o Art Directors' Club Award: Print Advertising
o Magazine Editors Association: Joseph M. Reilly Award
o American Advertising Awards: Consumer Advertising
o Atlantic Travel Association Award: Trade Advertising
o Cruise Line Sales Association Awards: Direct Marketing
o Travel Agents and Travellers Awards: Competitive Surveys

CAREER EXPERIENCE

FREELANCE CONSULTANT, Any Town, CA   1995–Present

Promotional Consultant
Develop and present comprehensive proposals for major cruise lines.

XYZ ADVERTISING AGENCY, Any Town, CA   1989–1995

Vice President and Account Director
Responsible for direct mail programs for the San Diego Transportation Authority; supervised vacation package program for the San Diego Chamber of Commerce. Developed proposals to generate new business from tourism sector. Consultant on Acme Cruise Lines and SRO Cruise Lines.

ACME CRUISE LINES, INC., Any Town, CA   1986–1989

Director of Advertising
Supervised creative staff and administered $20 million budget:

o Worked with outside advertising firms to develop strategies and execute global media plans.
o Monitored activities of European and South American offices.
o Upgraded promotional materials to generate better response.
o Upgraded staff training and development; created and distributed operating manuals.

FORTUNE 500 CORPORATION (ESSEX DIVISION), Any Town, CA   1982–1986

Vice President of Sales & Marketing
Accelerated product acceptance and signed major cruise lines. Managed and accelerated the billings from our largest cruise line account.

SMITH TRANSPORTATION COMPANY, INC., Any City, CA   1978–1982

Manager of Advertising and Public Relations
Directed sales, advertising, communications, and public relations.

EDUCATION

B.S.   Brown University
M.B.A.   UCLA Graduate School of Business Administration

REFERENCES PROVIDED UPON REQUEST

MIS Professional/Systems Consulting

JOANNE A. SMITH

Any Street, Any City, NJ XXXXX (201) 555-1234

Contact Name   Date
Title
Company
Street Address
City, State Zip

Dear Mr./Ms. _____:

I have combined a Stanford M.B.A. with skills in systems consulting, software, client relations, and programming to develop custom software applications, audit and upgrade systems, streamline programs, reduce processing time, produce multilingual software products, and generate lucrative consulting fees from major private and public sector clients.

I am bringing to your attention my skills, achievements, technical prowess, and talent for satisfying the most demanding clients so that we can discuss my joining _____ as a member of your systems consulting team.

Results achieved to date include:

o As a Senior Consultant at XYZ Corporation, project managed the design and development of a German language version of the company's Modified Client Survey: traveled to Frankfurt to document the client's specifications and streamlined the complex conversion procedures.

o Upon graduation from Stanford, was chosen for the selective management development program at Acme Corporation: among other assignments, completed a major systems audit at a Consumer Products Division generating recommendations which upgraded surveillance, improved backup procedures, and helped correct out-of-control financial reporting.

o Received written commendations for streamlining the data input and calculation process for Acme's Executive Benefits Plan—reduced the processing time from several days to only a few minutes; also corrected previously undetected errors in the division financial reports resulting in tens of thousands of dollars in favorable adjustments.

o Earned promotion to Project Head at ABC Corporation based on the on-time development of processing systems for financial institutions: effectively handled tough clients in developing custom back and front office software; generated additional consulting fees by convincing clients to expand the scope of the original projects.

I look forward to discussions at which we can determine how I can contribute to your company's future success.

Sincerely,

Enclosure: Joanne A. Smith

JOANNE A. SMITH

123 Any Street, Any City, NJ XXXXX (201) 555-1234

M.B.A.	Marketing/Finance	Stanford University	Self-financed	1990
B.S.	Quantitative Analysis	University of Chicago	Self-financed	1986

Graduate Studies:	Completed several accelerated computer science courses
Publications:	Article on Computerization: Systems Management Magazine (1983)
International:	Traveled throughout South America and Europe

CAREER SKILLS/KNOWLEDGE

- o MIS/systems consulting
- o Proprietary databases
- o Real-time analysis/graphics display
- o SPSS/DBase III Plus
- o Spreadsheets/Lotus 1-2-3/Excel
- o Design/testing/debugging
- o Fortran/Basic/Pascal/Algol/C

- o Marketing/account management
- o Client relations/development
- o Government relations
- o Corporate relations
- o European relations
- o Market research studies
- o Strategic planning/forecasting

CAREER ACHIEVEMENTS

o As a Senior Consultant at XYZ Corporation, project managed the design and development of a German language version of the company's Modified Client Survey: traveled to Frankfurt to document the client's specifications and streamlined the complex conversion procedures.

o Upon graduation from Stanford, was chosen for the selective management development program at Acme Corporation: among other assignments, completed a major systems audit at a Consumer Products Division generating recommendations which upgraded surveillance, improved backup procedures, and helped correct out-of-control financial reporting.

o Received written commendations for streamlining the data input and calculation process for Acme's Executive Benefits Plan—reduced the processing time from several days to only a few minutes; also corrected previously undetected errors in the division financial reports resulting in tens of thousands of dollars in favorable adjustments.

o Saved Acme expensive outside systems consulting fees by initiating and leading an in-house effort to upgrade and purge the database systems; applied in-depth knowledge of Lotus and complex financial databases to execute this assignment.

o Earned promotion to Project Head at ABC Corporation based on the on-time development of processing systems for financial institutions: effectively handled tough clients in developing custom back and front office software; generated additional consulting fees by convincing clients to expand the scope of the original projects.

o As a programmer on a consulting assignment to Boeing, earned promotion to Senior Associate at Essex, Inc., based on my contribution to the programming on major assignments: helped develop real-time data and graphics display of test information; created software to generate key reports from a confidential database.

CAREER EXPERIENCE

AVERY FINANCIAL GROUP, Any City, NJ   1993–1996

Director
Performed industry research, executed sophisticated supply/demand analyses, and developed economic and financial models.

Reason for leaving: Massive restructuring due to corporation's bankruptcy.

XYZ CORPORATION, Any City, NJ   1991–1993

Senior Consultant
Developed models, statistical data, management reports, and safeguards for proprietary software: designed databases for planning and scheduling corporate consulting assignments; designed and developed multilingual versions of software; conducted industry analyses.

ACME CORPORATION, Any City, NJ   1990–1991

Senior Planner
Upgraded the massive database systems; executed comprehensive systems reviews; generated a research study which documented critically needed marketing, competitive, and demographic information.

ABC CORPORATION, Any City, NJ   1987–1988

Project Head
Promotion. Developed processing systems for financial institutions. Managed a team of analysts.

Reason for leaving: To attend graduate school.

ESSEX, INC., Any City, WA   1986–1987

Senior Associate
Promotion. Programmer on a consulting assignment to Boeing for: development of real-time data and graphics display of test information; creation of software for management reporting from a confidential database.

Reason for leaving: Relocation to New Jersey.

REFERENCES PROVIDED UPON REQUEST

JOHN A. JONES

123 Any Street, Any City, WA XXXXX (206) 555-1235

Contact Name   Date
Title
Company
Street Address
City, State Zip

Dear Mr./Ms. _____:

I have applied executive skills in production, materials management, engineering, and sales to turn around out-of-control operations and build a multimillion-dollar company known for its state-of-the-art products, cost-effective manufacturing, and substantial market shares. Achievements have been rewarded with profit-sharing and awards for the on-time delivery of major systems.

I am bringing to your attention my leadership skills, achievements, ability to turn around problem operations, and proven talent for accelerating profits to produce financial security for others and myself so that we can discuss my joining _____ as a member of your materials management/operations team.

Major accomplishments to date include:

o Turned around out-of-control quality and distribution problems at XYZ Technology increasing on-time shipments from 38% to 95%; also turned around purchasing operations generating $3 million a year in cost reductions while reducing inventory $3 million.

o As Director of Procurement at Acme Company, generated $4 million in annual cost savings and reduced inventory $2 million by resolving serious cost control and material control problems.

o As founder of ABC, Inc., started and built this profitable high-tech electronics company known over 20 years for its innovative products and low-cost volume production: negotiated and executed the lucrative sale of the company to a major corporation.

o More than doubled ABC's revenue by marketing breakthrough products to over 40 countries and major Fortune 500 corporations: developed damage-proof and modular products; introduced concept of placing electronics into clothing; developed communications systems for space projects, carriers, train systems, executive aircraft, and bank machines.

o Became one of the world's largest producers of specialized communication devices by focusing on the high volume global market; instituted "people-based" engineering to extend the life of electronic equipment and produce safety-conscious communications for major clients.

Should we reach mutually agreeable terms, I will work hard to help accelerate or turn around operating performance contributing to your future success.

                                              Sincerely,

Enclosure: John A. Jones

Production/Materials Management

JOHN A. JONES

123 Any Street, Any City, WA XXXXX (206) 555-1235

M.B.A.	Management	Wharton	1974
B.S.	Electrical Engineering	Stanford University	1972
B.A.	Economics	Stanford University	1972

CAREER SKILLS/KNOWLEDGE

- o Operations/materials management
- o Manufacturing/Q.C.
- o Procurement operations
- o Production & inventory control
- o Cost reductions/productivity
- o Cost-effective production
- o R&D/systems engineering
- o Distribution/transportation
- o Electronics industry

- o International marketing/sales
- o General management/finance
- o Start-up operations/organization
- o Major client development
- o Product management
- o Competitive maneuvering
- o Expansion/turnaround strategies
- o Profit/market share growth
- o New product marketing/pricing

CAREER ACHIEVEMENTS

o Turned around out-of-control quality and distribution problems at XYZ Technology increasing on-time shipments from 38% to 95%; also turned around purchasing operations generating $3 million a year in cost reductions while reducing inventory $3 million.

o As Director of Procurement at Acme Company, generated $4 million in annual cost savings and reduced inventory $2 million by resolving serious cost control and material control problems.

o As founder of ABC, Inc., started and built this profitable high-tech electronics company known over 20 years for its innovative products and low-cost volume production: negotiated and executed the lucrative sale of the company to a major corporation.

o Awarded a coveted medal by a foreign government for producing and delivering, in less than 60 days, critically needed communications systems vital to their national defense: crash program cut four months off the schedule.

o More than doubled ABC's revenue by marketing breakthrough products to over 40 countries and major Fortune 500 corporations: developed damage-proof and modular products; introduced concept of placing electronics into clothing; developed communications systems for space projects, carriers, train systems, executive aircraft, and bank machines.

o Became one of the world's largest producers of specialized communication devices by focusing on the high volume global market; instituted "people-based" engineering to extend the life of electronic equipment and produce safety-conscious communications for major clients.

CAREER EXPERIENCE

ACME COMPANY, Any City, WA   1996–Present

Director of Procurement
Instituted much needed budget systems; upgraded material control, developed off-shore vendors, reduced materials shortages, and stopped downtime; generated cost savings and reduced inventory.

XYZ TECHNOLOGY CORPORATION, Any Town, WA   1995–1996

Project Director
In a series of manufacturing, technical, and procurement assignments, instituted modern management techniques: improved production quality, cut costs, reduced inventory, and established on-time delivery:

o Upgraded Q.C. operations, policies, and procedures.
o Tightened vendor product quality standards.
o Instituted competitive bidding and second sourcing.
o Introduced Japanese methods of inventory stocking.

ABC, INCORPORATED, Any Town, WA   1974–1995

Founder
Founded and managed a high-tech company which grew to over 150 employees:

o Expanded through innovation, systems engineering, and cost-effective manufacturing.
o Oversaw new product development from inception through design, engineering, and production.
o Established and monitored marketing and pricing objectives.
o Developed client relations with major corporations and numerous countries.
o Continuously expanded into new markets.
o Redesigned and improved products to reduce costs.
o Established rigid quality control standards.
o Designed a plant layout which dramatically improved assembly productivity.
o Consistently met tight delivery schedules.

REFERENCES PROVIDED UPON REQUEST

ELIZABETH A. JOHNSON

123 Any Street, Any City, VA XXXXX (703) 555-1234

Contact Name   Date
Title
Company
Street Address
City, State Zip

Dear Mr./Mrs. _____:

Combining skills in operations, project management, systems, and technical service with an Engineering degree from M.I.T., I identified and resolved serious systems problems that were costing ABC Company $500 million annually. My ability to achieve bottom-line results has been rewarded with multiple promotions, classification as a high-potential manager, and a salary package in the 70s at age 28.

I am presenting for your review my skills, achievements, and ability to execute high-impact projects so that we can initiate discussions about my joining _____ as a member of your Operations/Project Management Team.

Results achieved at ABC Company by applying the skills detailed on the attached resume include:

o Researched, identified, and developed corrective actions for major problems in the Service System which were costing ABC $500 million annually; created and implemented nationwide a comprehensive training package that will prevent these losses and accelerate profits.

o Due, in part, to the above training package which I designed to prevent massive revenue losses, the Southern Region won ABC's "Excellence Award."

o Created and implemented a marketing campaign to motivate Technicians to sell: achieved 250% of sales objective; was successfully introduced in other districts.

o Codeveloped and implemented nationwide a major Service Program which saved $30 million in 1996.

o In preparing for a major corporate-wide restructuring, established a separate Service Center which became the company's prototype: implemented manual operations, achieving balanced workloads, cost controls, and stable productivity in a crisis environment.

A face-to-face meeting to determine how I can contribute to your company's future success might well be to our mutual benefit.

Sincerely,

Enclosure: Elizabeth A. Johnson

ELIZABETH A. JOHNSON

123 Any Street, Any City, VA XXXXX (703) 555-1234

B.S.   Massachusetts Institute of Technology   Electrical Engineering   Honors   1992

CAREER SKILLS/KNOWLEDGE

- Operations/technical service
- Project management
- Major program implementation
- Marketing campaign development
- Productivity improvements
- Staff management/training
- Training package design
- Negotiating skills
- Expense control/reductions
- Corrective action plans

- Telecommunications
- Installation/maintenance
- Field Service Center set-up
- Field Service Center management
- Crew supervision
- Workload management
- Labor relations
- Systems implementation
- User training
- UNIX Operating System

CAREER ACHIEVEMENTS

- Researched, identified, and developed corrective actions for major problems in the Service System which were costing ABC $500 million annually; created and implemented nationwide a comprehensive training package that will prevent these losses and accelerate profits.

- Due, in part, to the above training package which I designed to prevent massive revenue losses, the Southern Region won ABC's "Excellence Award."

- Codeveloped and implemented nationwide a major Service Program which saved $30 million in 1996.

- Implemented a major program to equip Technicians with portable computers, eliminating the clerical interface between the field and the billing, inventory, and reporting systems; trained personnel in 23 districts including 4,500 Technicians.

- Created and implemented a marketing campaign to motivate Technicians to sell: achieved 250% of sales objective; was successfully introduced in other districts.

- As Manager of one of the largest Service Centers, negotiated a ground-breaking agreement with the local Union permitting ABC to substitute work locations.

- In preparing for a major corporate-wide restructuring, established a separate Service Center which became the company's prototype: implemented manual operations, achieving balanced workloads, cost controls, and stable productivity in a crisis environment.

CAREER EXPERIENCE

ABC COMPANY, Any Town, VA   5/92–Present

L.S.R. HEADQUARTERS, Any Town, VA   8/95–Present

Manager of Operations   3/96–Present
Direct staff responsible for:

o Major field productivity programs designed to generate millions in revenue and cost reductions; also provide support to Service Organizations.
o While on assignment to the Group Director, implemented a major Service Program as well as a program to equip Technicians with portable computers.

Manager of Systems   8/95–3/96
Responsibilities executed:

o Identified and resolved Service System weaknesses costing ABC hundreds of millions.
o Provided applications support for 1,400 field personnel who relied on in-house systems to handle 150,000 maintenance and installation requests weekly.

MANAGEMENT TRAINING, Any Town, VA   5/92–8/95

Marketing Manager   10/94–8/95
Exceeded goals in over 90% of the objectives established: created marketing campaign to accelerate Technician sales; reduced backlog of orders not invoiced from 16,000 to 500.

Service Manager   10/93–10/94
Promotion to manage one of the largest centers:

o Installed and maintained Communication Systems.
o Elevated the responsibility and reliability of Technicians in order to improve productivity.
o Negotiated with the XYZ Union.

Operations   5/92–10/93
Major assignments included:

Center Manager: established the prototype operation.
Supervisor: produced on-time installations and repairs.
Installations Supervisor: Promotion; managed major cutovers.
Foreman: turned around lowest-rated crew; accelerated productivity 48%.
Testing Supervisor: Promotion; ensured on-time service.

REFERENCES AVAILABLE UPON REQUEST

JAMES A. SMITH

123 Any Street, Any City, NY XXXXX (914) 555-1234

Contact Name   Date
Title
Company
Street Address
City, State Zip

Dear Mr./Ms. _____:

I have combined an E.E. degree with management skills in product development, electronics, system engineering, and marketing to create state-of-the-art products, develop high-tech market research devices for the Executive Branch, accelerate revenue and profits, and play a central role in producing one of the most profitable ventures in the history of ABC Company.

I am bringing to your attention my skills, achievements, creativity, technical prowess, and talent for accelerating revenue and profits so that we can discuss my joining _____ as a member of your Product Development/Engineering management team.

Results achieved to date include:

o As Director of a key development group at XYZ, a subsidiary of ABC Company, developed several state-of-the-art communication products in five years creating one of the company's most profitable ventures: ground-breaking systems overcame restrictive limitations permitting peripherals to be located 70 miles away from a computer mainframe.

o As Cofounder of a start-up venture, led development of Single Board Computer, a processor board for industrial applications requiring less coding than other processor boards: protected product through legal means and marketed it to major Fortune 500 clients.

o As Founder of an E.E. consulting firm, developed a proprietary computer-based device called the "XYZ Product" for the Chairman of a market research firm under contract to the Executive Branch: earned fees based on the development, usage, and subsequent sale of the product to the Executive Branch.

o Started and marketed two business ventures during the past year generating six-figure sales: expanded an E.E. consulting firm; started a hazardous material consulting service.

o Directed a software-intensive group in executing state-of-the-art changes to a major machine at Acme Company: led development of coding printer executing all of the complex software and hardware tasks in harnessing the speed-printing technology.

I will work hard to achieve bottom-line results and look forward to discussing how I can contribute to your company's future success.

                                          Sincerely,

Enclosure: James A. Smith

JAMES A. SMITH

123 Any Street, Any City, NY XXXXX (914) 555-1234

B.S.E.E. University of Rochester   Self-financed   1985

Honors: o Earned top grade for Senior project: designed hand-held scanner
            o Who's Who Among Students in American Colleges
            o Graduated with Honors; Dean's List

CAREER SKILLS/KNOWLEDGE

o Product development
o Project management
o System engineering
o Electronics/mechanical
o Digital/analog technology
o PCB design/development
o Computer science/programming
o Biomedical engineering

o Sales/marketing
o Product creation/introduction
o Revenue/profit growth
o Client development
o Cold-calling/telemarketing
o Proposals/presentations
o Closing/customer service
o Business start-up

CAREER ACHIEVEMENTS

o As Director of a key development group at XYZ, a subsidiary of ABC Company, developed several state-of-the-art communication products in five years creating one of the company's most profitable ventures: ground-breaking systems overcame restrictive limitations permitting peripherals to be located 70 miles away from a computer mainframe.

o As Cofounder of a start-up venture, led development of Single Board Computer, a processor board for industrial applications requiring less coding than other processor boards: protected product through legal means and marketed it to major Fortune 500 clients.

o As Founder of an E.E. consulting firm, developed a proprietary computer-based device called the "XYZ Product" for the Chairman of a market research firm under contract to the Executive Branch: earned fees based on the development, usage, and subsequent sale of the product.

o Started and marketed two business ventures during the past year generating six-figure sales: expanded an E.E. consulting firm; started a hazardous material consulting service.

o Directed a software-intensive group in executing state-of-the-art changes to a major machine at Acme Company: led development of coding printer executing all of the complex software and hardware tasks in harnessing the speed-printing technology.

o Successfully developed, for a major automotive company, the 4066 product which provided tape drive channels for customers without dedicated communications facilities: required complete restructuring of XYZ's 6088 product line.

CAREER EXPERIENCE

JAMES SMITH ASSOCIATES, Any Town, NY   1990–Present
E.E. Consulting: Developed feeder mechanism critical to development of a mail machine to be marketed by an electronics firm. Created "XYZ Product" proprietary computer-based data-entry device used to measure responses to words, phrases, and ideas. Worked on a computer-based automated routing system for Essex Corporation.

HAZARDOUS WASTE CONSULTING CORPORATION, Any Town, NY   1994–Present
Started and manage consulting business.

ACME COMPANY, Any City, NY   1992–1994
Directed a product development effort aimed at instituting critical changes to a major machine: introduced speed-printing technology to new code printer.

XYZ SUBSIDIARY, ABC COMPANY, Any Town, NY   1987–1992
Director: Developed high-speed data communications equipment for mainframes; designed PC compatible interface card for serial and parallel transfer to proprietary product. Codeveloped high-speed logic board using FAST series logic and programmable devices; implemented 64K deep high-speed FIFO capable of a 5 Mega word throughput; employed error detection and correction with the RAM array.

COMPUTER START-UP VENTURE, Any Town, NY   1987–1988
Cofounder/Partner: Designed and marketed a single board computer using the Intel 8051 microcomputer: incorporated ROM memory mapping, 8155 I/O ports/RAM/Timers, Electronically Erasable PROM, and RS-232 serial communication using the on-board UART of the 8051.

A FORTUNE 500 ELECTRONICS COMPANY, Any Town, NY   1986–1987
Electronic Engineer: Earned positive feedback for systems testing and authoring critical test sections of major proposal.

A SMALLER ELECTRONICS COMPANY, Any City, NY   1985–1986
Electronic Engineer: Developed control system software for custom molding machines; generated assembly language and PLM programs for the Intel 8085 processor.

REFERENCES PROVIDED UPON REQUEST

DEBORAH A. SMITH

123 Any Street, Any City, CA XXXXX (619) 555-1234

Contact Name   Date
Title
Company
Street Address
City, State Zip

Dear Mr./Ms. _____:

I have applied executive skills in program administration, operations, and marketing to direct the administration of a $300 million project and generate over $1 million in documented cost savings for a major electronics firm. I also started up a multimillion-dollar electronics company, generated half of its total sales, and expanded the client base of another high-tech company.

I am bringing to your attention my skills, achievements, nationwide network of electronics industry contacts, and ability to produce results under crisis management conditions so that we can discuss my joining _____ as a member of your administration management team.

Results achieved to date include:

o As Director of Program Administration for a major $300 million program at ABC Corporation, direct all planning, budgeting, scheduling, and reporting: am recognized for executing crisis projects with little advance notice including critical Design Reviews for the Board.

o As administrative manager for a $60 million project at ABC, generated over $1 million in documented cost savings by recommending alternative vendors who offered better prices, quality, and service.

o As Manager of Administration for a $500 million ABC system, acted as liaison to a foreign government interacting up to the Cabinet level: enforced security, coordinated state visits and relocations, and expedited shipment of top priority hardware.

o Recipient, for the third consecutive year, of the "ABC Service Award" which is awarded based on "outstanding service and contributions by individuals to ABC and important team projects."

o As Cofounder and Sales Vice President for Acme Electronics, Inc., accelerated revenue growth and directly generated 60% of the gross sales for this high-tech multimillion-dollar company.

I look forward to discussing how I can contribute to your company's future success.

                                                            Sincerely,

Enclosure: ·   Deborah A. Smith

R&D Program Administration

DEBORAH A. SMITH

123 Any Street, Any City, CA XXXXX (619) 555-1234

B.S.	University of Colorado	1980
M.S. Candidate	University of San Diego	1997

CAREER SKILLS/KNOWLEDGE

- R&D program administration
- Project management
- Liaison to officials
- Planning/budgeting
- Scheduling/reporting
- Senior program reviews
- Cost reduction strategies
- Corrective action plans
- Internal consulting

- Sales/marketing
- Market expansion strategies
- Cold-calling/telemarketing
- Client development/relations
- Overcoming objections/closing
- Entrepreneurial start-ups
- Operations/manufacturing
- Staff development/productivity
- Materials/procurement

CAREER ACHIEVEMENTS

- As Director of Program Administration for a major $300 million program at ABC Corporation, direct all planning, budgeting, scheduling, and reporting: am recognized for executing crisis projects with little advance notice including critical Design Reviews for the Board.

- Recipient, for the third consecutive year, of the "ABC Service Award" which is awarded based on "outstanding service and contributions by individuals to ABC and important team projects."

- As administrative manager for a $60 million project at ABC, generated over $1 million in documented cost savings by recommending alternative vendors who offered better prices, quality, and service.

- As Manager of Administration for a $500 million ABC system, acted as liaison to a foreign government interacting up to the Cabinet level: enforced security, coordinated state visits and relocations, and expedited shipment of top priority hardware.

- Overcame strong resistance to persuade ABC's Layout Manager to designate our project location a "test site"; resulted in a total renovation of our facility greatly improving productivity.

- As Cofounder and Sales Vice President for Acme Electronics, Inc., accelerated revenue growth and directly generated 60% of the gross sales for this high-tech multimillion-dollar company.

- Directed Acme Electronics' operations, instituting better training which accelerated productivity and upgrading procurement which improved quality and reduced cost of materials 30%.

- As Sales Account Specialist for XYZ Distributors, Inc., generated major multimillion-dollar accounts expanding the client base 40%.

PROJECT MANAGEMENT/ADMINISTRATION EXPERIENCE

ABC CORPORATION, Any City, CA   5/88–Present

Director of Program Administration ($300 million project)   3/90–Present
Coordinate inter-departmental planning, budgeting and reporting:

o Assure cooperation; avoid duplication of effort; foster communication.
o Identify prime and supporting objectives; prepare schedules; participate in progress reviews.
o Prepare status reports; recommend and implement corrective actions.

Manager of Administration ($500 million project)   5/88–3/90
Liaison to clients and upper management; established procedures to insure performance compliance; developed and administered plan to monitor objectives and manpower utilization.

SALES/OPERATIONS EXPERIENCE

ACME ELECTRONICS, INC., Any Town, CA   4/86–5/88

Cofounder/Vice President of Sales and Operations
Directed Sales and Operations for this electro-mechanical company: Developed client network, cold-called and closed deals; directed production; instituted second sourcing; negotiated contracts.

HIGH-TECH MANUFACTURER, Any City, CA   10/84–4/86

Regional Sales Manager
Sold panel meters to test equipment companies, military electronics companies and medical instrumentation companies.

A.B. ENTERPRISES, INC., Any Town, CA   9/82–10/84

Sales Representative: Sold electro-mechanical products.

XYZ DISTRIBUTORS, INC., Any City, CA   8/81–9/82
Sales Representative: Sold electronic components and test equipment.

A SMALL ELECTRONICS FIRM, INC., Any Town, CA   6/80–8/81

Sales Representative
Managed almost 100 accounts, specializing in OEMS, military electronics companies and medical equipment companies; worked with engineers to spec out components/meters/test equipment.

CERTIFICATE PROGRAMS

Accounting for the Non-Accounting Manager	San Diego State	1989
Managing for Growth	San Diego State	1990
Three-month Management Course	ABC Corporation, Inc.	1992
Negotiating Skills	San Diego State	1994

Human Resources Professional

VINCENT A. JONES

123 Any Street, Any City, WA XXXXX (206) 555-1234

Contact Name   Date
Title
Company
Street Address
City, State Zip

Dear Mr./Ms. _____:

> Written quote from a Group President of Acme Corporation:
>
> "It's not easy for a marketing guy, like myself, to run a company like Acme, Inc. Because of Vincent (Jones), we have a better understanding of the work that is required in staffing a growing organization. I learn every day, that is every day I find someone whom I respect for their talents and would like to emulate. Vincent Jones is one of those people."

I have applied diverse skills in human resources management to achieve bottom-line results in corporate staffing, sales force staffing and development, productivity growth, turnover reduction, accident prevention, and cost control. I am presenting for your review my skills, achievements, and proven track record so that we can discuss my joining _____ as a Human Resources Manager.

Results achieved by persistently applying the skills detailed on the attached resume include:

o Successfully staffed the sales force for selected Acme dealerships which generate a substantial portion of total company revenue.

o Developed and implemented accelerated training programs at a regional XYZ Company: significantly improved manager/employee relations and measurably upgraded individual performance.

o Through aggressive yet selective staffing techniques, reduced average unfilled requisitions at Acme from 20 per month to 8 per month.

o Established a new regional record for "Accident Free Days" at a regional XYZ Company through the aggressive efforts of the accident prevention committee which I instituted.

I look forward to a face-to-face meeting which will give us the opportunity to discuss how I can contribute to your company's future success.

Sincerely,

Enclosure: Vincent A. Jones

VINCENT A. JONES

123 Any Street, Any City, WA XXXXX (206) 555-1234

> "Recruiting good people is always difficult at best.
> Through Vince Jones' staffing effort, we were able to
> hire excellent prospective sales people. All of us
> here at Acme look forward to the next opportunity
> of working with Vince."
>
> —Corporate Vice President

CAREER SKILLS/KNOWLEDGE

o Human resources management	o Sales force staffing
o Employee relations	o Sales force development
o Staffing strategies	o Dealer relations
o Wage/salary administration	o Training programs
o Benefits administration	o Recruiting: exempt/non-exempt
o Affirmative action plans	o Monthly reporting
o Accident prevention programs	o Extensive travel
o Outplacement counseling	o Newsletter publication
o Unemployment cost control	o Community affairs
o Suspensions/terminations	o Counseling-outreach program
o Worker compensation	o Correctional counseling

SELECTED ACHIEVEMENTS

o Successfully staffed the sales force for selected Acme dealerships which generate a substantial portion of total company revenue.

o Through aggressive yet selective staffing techniques, reduced average unfilled requisitions at Acme from 20 per month to 8 per month.

o Developed and implemented accelerated training programs at a regional XYZ Company: significantly improved manager/employee relations and measurably upgraded individual performance.

o Researched and implemented major wage scale revisions at a regional XYZ Division: substantially reduced company turnover.

o Established a new regional record for "Accident Free Days" at a regional XYZ Company through the aggressive efforts of the accident prevention committee which I instituted.

o Organized and executed Acme's participation in Career Days at various Employment Fairs: screened an average of 40 candidates in four days, hiring an average of 5.

o Researched and wrote Acme's well-received 1986 Equal Employment Opportunity Program.

CAREER EXPERIENCE

ACME CORPORATION, Any Town, WA   9/93–Present

HR Manager
Responsibilities executed include:

o Employee staffing—exempt and non-exempt
o Sales force recruiting/branch relations
o Wage and salary administration
o Benefits administration
o Unemployment cost control
o Worker compensation
o Affirmative action plans
o Outplacement counseling

XYZ COMPANY, INC., Any Town, CA   6/86–9/93

HR Manager—XYZ Division, Any Town, KY   6/90–9/93
Managed Human Resources for over 500 employees. Generalist functions executed included staffing, employee relations, training and development, salary administration, orientations, accident prevention, benefits administration, and unemployment cost control.

HR Supervisor—XYZ Division, Any Town, CA   5/88–6/90
Managed personnel functions for over 1,500 employees at one of XYZ's largest operations. Responsibilities included: staffing, terminations, unemployment cost control, and accident prevention.

EDUCATION/CREDENTIALS

B.A. Philosophy/English	San Diego State University	1986
Certified HR Training	University of California	1986

Additional Training: Completed several comprehensive Human Resource Management courses and workshops.

REFERENCES PROVIDED UPON REQUEST

JENNIFER A. SMITH

123 Any Street, Any City, WA XXXXX (206) 555-1234

Contact Name   Date
Title
Company
Address
City, State Zip

Dear Mr./Ms. _____:

I have applied proven skills in training and development, HR management, recruiting, redeployment, and systems to turn around training and development operations, institute critically needed training programs, and achieve challenging HR recruiting objectives for Fortune 500 corporations. Bottom-line achievements have been rewarded with bonuses and several promotions.

I am bringing to your attention my skills, achievements, high energy, and talent for upgrading the training process and accelerating worker productivity so that we can discuss my joining _____ as a member of your training and development management team.

Results achieved to date include:

o As HR Director at the Essex Company, upgraded Human Resources for over 3,000 employees: filled over 500 openings annually improving candidate quality while cutting the recruiting cycle in half; instituted critically needed training programs as well as comprehensive cross-training; reduced benefits operating costs; upgraded systems, policies, and procedures.

o As HR Manager at the ABC Corporation, project managed the start-up of a new headquarters: coordinated the logistics and successfully recruited, hired, and directed the training and development of over 400 employees in only seven months; also directed and accelerated the productivity of the administrative support staff.

o Directed Acme Development Center's Human Resources start-up and operation: achieved first-year staffing and training objectives in less than nine months and instituted comprehensive employee relations programs.

o Turned around Acme's Personnel Cross-Training and Redeployment Program achieving over a 90% placement rate through well-received seminars and workshops.

o Directed the highly successful implementation of Acme's critically needed $12 million Human Resource, Benefits, and Payroll system.

I look forward to discussing how I can, likewise, contribute to your company's future success.

Sincerely,

Enclosure: Jennifer A. Smith

Training and Development Professional

JENNIFER A. SMITH

123 Any Street, Any City, WA XXXXX (206) 555-1234

B.A.   Honors Communications   Smith College   GPA 3.7/4.0   1980

CAREER SKILLS/KNOWLEDGE

- Human resources professional
- Training and development
- Recruiting techniques
- Seminar/workshop development
- Video role playing/feedback
- Payroll/benefits administration
- Performance appraisal/merit guidelines
- Communications/public relations
- Outplacement counseling

- Systems implementation
- Systems consulting/design
- Installation troubleshooter
- User training/support
- Computer-based training
- Micro/mainframe applications
- Excel/LOTUS 1-2-3
- Administration
- Staff supervision

CAREER ACHIEVEMENTS

- As HR Director at the Essex Company, upgraded Human Resources for over 3,000 employees: filled over 500 openings annually improving candidate quality while cutting the recruiting cycle in half; instituted critically needed training programs as well as comprehensive cross-training; reduced benefits operating costs; upgraded systems, policies, and procedures.

- As HR Manager at the ABC Corporation, project managed the start-up of a new headquarters: coordinated the logistics and successfully recruited, hired, and directed the training and development of over 400 employees in only seven months; also directed and accelerated the productivity of the administrative support staff.

- Directed Acme Development Center's Human Resources start-up and operation: achieved first-year staffing and training objectives in less than nine months and instituted comprehensive employee relations programs.

- Turned around Acme's Personnel Cross-Training and Redeployment Program achieving over a 90% placement rate through well-received seminars and workshops.

- Directed the highly successful implementation of Acme's critically needed $12 million Human Resource, Benefits, and Payroll system.

- Created and executed job search and redeployment workshops for the homeless in Seattle.

CAREER EXPERIENCE

ESSEX COMPANY, Any Town, WA   7/94–Present

HR Director
Directed recruiting, managed multimillion-dollar benefits plan, computerized operations, instituted aggressive cost-reduction programs, and upgraded policies and procedures.

ABC CORPORATION, Any Town, WA   2/89–7/94

<u>HR Manager</u>
Project managed the logistics and staffing of a new headquarters.

ACME, INC., Any Town, WA   3/84–2/89

<u>Corporate Benefits Administration   1/88–2/89</u>
Performed benefits evaluations and upgraded several outdated HR manuals.

<u>Corporate HR Systems Analyst   12/86–1/88</u>
Project managed the implementation of a major HR system designed to support in excess of 200,000 employees.

<u>Personnel Redeployment   3/85–12/86</u>
Executed well-received Redeployment Programs.

<u>HR Administrator   3/84–3/85</u>
Recruited and hired all staff for the Development Center; established Communications and Benefits Groups; also developed EEO Plans and authored several policies and procedures.

AVERY SERVICE CORPORATION, Any Town, WA   6/80–3/84

<u>HR Administrator</u>
Accelerated cost reduction programs; upgraded and assisted in the administration of relocations, recruiting, terminations, payroll, benefits, and employee orientations.

VOLUNTEER ACTIVITIES

o Created job search seminars for the homeless
o Provided support of the learning disabled
o Taught reading skills to adults

REFERENCES PROVIDED UPON REQUEST

WILLIAM Q. SAMPLE   International Marketing Executive

123 Any Street Address, Any Town, NJ XXXXX (201) 555-1234

Contact Name   Date
Title
Company
Street Address
City, State Zip

Dear Mr./Ms. _____:

As a follow-up to our recent discussion, I am forwarding the information about which we spoke. As Executive Vice-President for the U.S. Division of a European corporation, I have applied skills in international sales, marketing, client development, and operations to outmaneuver the competition, deal with volatile exchange rates, accelerate growth of the corporate client base, and achieve a fivefold increase in sales—a revenue level which accounts for 40% of global sales.

I am presenting for your review my skills, achievements, technical degree, global contacts, and talent for creating productive marketing organizations and achieving aggressive revenue goals so that we can discuss my joining _____ as a member of your senior management team.

Results achieved during the past decade with Acme International include:

o Earned multiple promotions up to Executive Vice-President of Sales at a U.S. Division of Acme International, one of Europe's largest industrial corporations: created a highly productive sales organization and achieved a fivefold increase in revenue turning the U.S. Division into a $20 million business which now accounts for almost 40% of the subsidiary's global sales.

o In spite of high turnover and chronically unfavorable exchange rates, which adversely impacted the U.S. Division's pricing structure, generated a 500% increase in Acme's customer base through an accelerated client development program which emphasized quality and service to offset the unfavorable pricing.

o In spite of global competition, closed multimillion-dollar clients including Western Electric, AT&T, Boeing, and John Deere: accelerated the AT&T account from zero to $9 million representing half of total sales; generated a ninefold sales increase from the Harvester Division of John Deere; produced an eightfold increase in the Western Electric and Boeing accounts.

o Significantly reduced overhead and logistics expenses and all but eliminated aged receivables and write-offs by creating and enforcing conservative credit policies at Acme; in order to meet scheduled delivery dates through on-time shipments from Europe, also established a first-rate logistics function.

I look forward to discussing how I can help accelerate or turn around the performance of your international operations.

Sincerely,

Enclosure: William Q. Sample

Over-50 Manager Marketed to Career Position

WILLIAM Q. SAMPLE   International Marketing Executive

123 Any Street Address, Any Town, NJ XXXXX (201) 555-1234

B.S.   Electrical Engineering   International University Comprehensive Six-Year Program
B.A.   Business Administration Lehman College   Managerial Studies

International: Traveled throughout Europe, Asia, South America, and North America
Languages: Fluent French, and Spanish

CAREER SKILLS/KNOWLEDGE

- o Sales/marketing executive
- o International sales/markets
- o European relations
- o Strategic/marketing plans
- o Market share strategies
- o Major client development
- o Competitive maneuvering
- o Exchange rate strategies
- o Organizational development
- o Staff supervision/development

- o Operations/materials/engineering
- o Purchasing operations
- o Cost controls/reductions
- o Global distribution/logistics
- o Heavy industry clients
- o Aircraft engine market
- o Engineering operations
- o Electrical/systems engineering
- o New product design
- o Plant operating systems design

CAREER ACHIEVEMENTS

o Earned multiple promotions up to Executive Vice-President of Sales at a U.S. Division of Acme International, one of Europe's largest industrial corporations: created a highly productive sales organization and achieved a fivefold increase in revenue turning the U.S. Division into a $20 million business which now accounts for almost 40% of the subsidiary's global sales.

o In spite of high turnover and chronically unfavorable exchange rates, which adversely impacted the U.S. Division's pricing structure, generated a 500% increase in Acme's customer base through an accelerated client development program which emphasized quality and service to offset the unfavorable pricing.

o In spite of global competition, closed multimillion-dollar clients including Western Electric, AT&T, Boeing, and John Deere: accelerated the AT&T account from zero to $9 million representing half of total sales; generated a ninefold sales increase from the Harvester Division of John Deere; produced an eightfold increase in the Western Electric and Boeing accounts.

o Significantly reduced overhead and logistics expenses and all but eliminated aged receivables and write-offs by creating and enforcing conservative credit policies at Acme; in order to meet scheduled delivery dates through on-time shipments from Europe, also established a first-rate logistics function.

o Earned several promotions up to Director within the Engineering Department of a Florida-based division of Essex Corporation: directed high-quality product designs, upgraded operating systems critical to the production process, and effectively troubleshooted the complex power supply systems.

CAREER EXPERIENCE

ACME INTERNATIONAL CORPORATION, Any Town, NJ   1984–Present

Executive Vice-President of Sales   1987–Present
Direct the Sales Organization with responsibility for direct sales, marketing, strategic planning, client development, import operations, logistics, distribution, and credit.

Vice-President of Sales   1984–1987
Directed sales, marketing, strategic planning, and related functions.

ESSEX CORPORATION, Any Town, FL   1975–1984

Director of Engineering   1980–1984
Earned several promotions based on engineering achievements in directing low-tolerance design and systems engineering projects. Also successfully planned and executed high-visibility manu-facturing projects.

MILITARY EXPERIENCE

European Military: Honorably Discharged

Affiliations: Society of U.S. Engineers; Production Engineers of the Northeast
Citizenship: U.S. Citizen

REFERENCES AVAILABLE UPON REQUEST

Entrepreneur Marketed to Top Brokerage Firm

DANIEL A. JOHNSON   **Brokerage Candidate**

123 Any Street, Any City, CA XXXXX (619) 555-1234

Contact Name   Date
Title
Company
Street Address
City, State Zip

Dear Mr./Ms. _____:

Having profitably applied skills in sales, marketing, client development, and dealer relations, I have consistently demonstrated the ability to start up and grow high-risk ventures which have generated substantial revenue and profits over the past decade.

I am very interested in exploring the possibility of joining _____ as a member of your brokerage team.

Specific results achieved by applying the skills detailed in the attached resume:

o Founded a highly profitable publishing firm, producing and marketing sophisticated how-to books which are highly marketable supplements to a popular how-to series marketed by Time-Life; consistently achieved aggressive, six-figure revenue goals.

o Authored the initial how-to book and through creative and persistent sales techniques, overcame intense resistance to form an international distribution network for my book series: retail distributors sold included such major chains as Barnes & Noble, Lauriats, and Doubleday.

o Cofounded and assumed the marketing and sales leadership role in a successful renovation business; substantial revenue growth well into six figures was achieved by aggressively marketing our contract services to Fortune 500 and smaller clients.

o Consistently exceeded targeted sales and profit goals throughout all stages of my business and entrepreneurial career.

A face-to-face meeting will afford us the opportunity to determine how I might be of service. You may contact me at your earliest convenience to set up an appointment. I look forward to our discussion.

Sincerely,

Enclosure: Daniel A. Johnson

DANIEL A. JOHNSON   Brokerage Candidate

123 Any Street, Any City, CA XXXXX (619) 555-1234

CREDENTIALS

B.A.   Drew University   GPA 3.5/4.0   1986

Honors/Activities: Graduated with Honors; College Varsity Sports; Class President; Editor-in-Chief; Authored and scored plays; Studied with well-known artists

MARKETING SKILLS/KNOWLEDGE

o Sales/marketing
o Direct sales/client development
o Product distribution/dealer relations
o Brochure development
o Corporate client interaction
o Cold-calling/telemarketing
o Proposal development/presentations
o Closing the sale
o Entrepreneurial/business owner

o Marketing strategies
o Creating markets
o Product piggybacking
o Product development
o Staff supervision/development
o Budgeting/finance/accounting
o Cost control
o Author/editor
o PC applications

CAREER ACHIEVEMENTS

o Founded a highly profitable publishing firm, producing and marketing sophisticated how-to books which are highly marketable supplements to a popular how-to series marketed by Time-Life; consistently achieved aggressive, six-figure revenue goals.

o Authored the initial how-to book and through creative and persistent sales techniques, overcame intense resistance to form an international distribution network for my book series: retail distributors sold included such major chains as Barnes & Noble, Lauriats, and Doubleday.

o Cofounded and assumed the marketing and sales leadership role in a successful renovation business; substantial revenue growth well into six figures was achieved by aggressively marketing our contract services to Fortune 500 and smaller clients.

o Created and implemented effective marketing strategies to promote the concept of floor renovation as a cost-effective substitute for replacement—successfully sold services to large corporate clients as well as smaller companies.

o Codeveloped a new floor renovation product composed of a special mixture of penetrating oils; resulted in improved customer servicing.

o Consistently exceeded targeted sales and profit goals throughout all stages of my business and entrepreneurial career.

CAREER EXPERIENCE

ACME PUBLISHING CORPORATION, Any Town, CA   8/93–Present

Founder/President
Started firm; directed global marketing of how-to books:

o Formulated and implemented overall marketing and operational strategies.
o Authored and coauthored books.
o Established international distribution network including Barnes & Noble and Doubleday.
o Used PC applications for word processing, graphics, and transmission.
o Instituted tight financial and accounting controls.

ABC RENOVATION CORPORATION, INC., Any Town, CA   6/86–8/93

V.P. of Sales and Marketing/Cofounder
Responsible for the start-up and marketing of this floor renovation company:

o Developed marketing and sales strategies.
o Scoped out and tapped new markets.
o Directed sales to Fortune 1000 and smaller clients.
o Coordinated staffing and supervision.
o Executed new product development.
o Instituted effective cost controls.

REFERENCES AVAILABLE UPON REQUEST

Military Officer to Private Sector

JOHN A. JOHNSON   Sales/Marketing

---

123 Any Street, Any City, NY XXXXX (212) 555-1234

Contact Name   Date
Title
Company
Street Address
City, State Zip

Dear Mr./Ms. _____:

I have combined proven leadership with skills in communication, strategic planning, organization, training, and logistics to restructure multimillion-dollar operations, turn around out-of-control situations, upgrade performance standards, direct record-setting campaigns, and accomplish what had been described as "the toughest challenges." Results achieved have been rewarded with top performance reviews and rapid promotion.

I am bringing to your attention my skills, achievements, talent for overcoming obstacles, ability to achieve bottom-line results, and desire to contribute to your revenue growth so that we can discuss my joining _____ as a member of your professional sales team.

Results achieved to date include:

o As Company Commander with responsibility for a rapid deployment force and $500 million in equipment, significantly improved unit's combat readiness by restructuring the training, maintenance, fitness, and property accountability: achieved operational readiness rating of 96%.

o As Brigade Logistics Officer for an Air Assault Division, was cited for making lasting contributions to Brigade's combat readiness: upgraded unit movement plans, directed motorpool reorganization, fielded several hundred High Mobility Vehicles, and directed the logistics for successful no-notice Emergency Deployment Exercises.

o Directed one of the most successful fund-raising drives ever conducted at Fort XYZ; exceeded established goals by orchestrating television and print media campaigns, mailing over 20,000 marketing letters, and developing automated control systems.

o Upon promotion to Operations and Training Officer, a position normally held by a higher ranking officer, authored the first documented Post Defense Plan, upgraded Special Forces training, streamlined Alert Notification Procedures, and radically revised NCO training programs achieving 30% better test scores.

I will work hard to achieve bottom-line results and look forward to discussing how I can contribute to your company's future success.

                                        Sincerely,

Enclosure: John A. Johnson

JOHN A. JOHNSON

Sales/Marketing

123 Any Street, Any City, NY XXXXX (212) 555-1234

ACADEMIC/MILITARY CREDENTIALS

B.S.   Distinguished Graduate   Ohio State University   1984

Additional Studies

o Completed graduate marketing courses toward Masters Degree
o Graduate of Combined Arms and Services Staff School
o Completed 20 comprehensive military courses including Advanced Officer Courses

CAREER ACHIEVEMENTS

o As Company Commander with responsibility for a rapid deployment force and $500 million in equipment, significantly improved unit's combat readiness by restructuring the training, maintenance, fitness, and property accountability: achieved operational readiness rating of 96%.

o As Brigade Logistics Officer for an Air Assault Division, was cited for making lasting contributions to Brigade's combat readiness: upgraded unit movement plans, directed motorpool reorganization, fielded several hundred High Mobility Vehicles, and directed the logistics for successful no-notice Emergency Deployment Exercises.

o Directed one of the most successful fund-raising drives ever conducted at Fort XYZ; exceeded established goals by orchestrating television and print media campaigns, mailing over 20,000 marketing letters, and developing automated control systems.

o Upon promotion to Operations and Training Officer, a position normally held by a higher ranking officer, authored the first documented Post Defense Plan, upgraded Special Forces training, streamlined Alert Notification Procedures, and radically revised NCO training programs achieving 30% better test scores.

o Upon promotion to Executive Officer, upgraded operations directly contributing to Company B's much improved readiness position: reorganized supply system increasing accountability; upgraded maintenance program achieving higher availability; developed equipment loading plans which considered all possible contingency missions.

o Introduced zero-based budgeting in developing the Division's current and long-range training budgets: authored budgeting book which became the model and developed a program which created much greater understanding of the Training Management System.

o Turned around a tactically and logistically poor performing mortar platoon instituting combat readiness: proved that what had been considered impossible was possible by creating and executing a concept for mortar employment in rough terrain.

CAREER EXPERIENCE

UNITED STATES ARMY   10/84–Present

Officer in Charge, Fort XYZ, GA   4/95–Present
Doubled the number of training courses and instructional hours at no additional cost.

Brigade Logistics Officer, Fort XYZ, GA   6/92–4/95
Coordinated logistical support for the training exercises and contingency plans.

Company Commander, Fort XYZ, GA   3/90–6/92
Maintained a combat ready force capable of rapid deployment.

Operations and Training Officer, Fort ABC, FL   9/88–3/90
Created and developed effective mobilization and Post Defense.

Executive Officer/Captain, Fort GHI, OR   2/88–9/88
Responsible for logistical, administrative, and maintenance operations of an infantry company.

Platoon Leader, Fort GHI, OR   7/87–2/88
Planned and coordinated rough terrain survival training.

Platoon Leader, Fort DEF, OR   6/85–7/87
Formulated well-received fighting positions; significantly upgraded poor performing platoon.

Project Officer/1st Lieutenant, Fort ABC, FL   10/84–6/85
Managed production of visual aids; coordinated logistics for production in rough terrain.

REFERENCES PROVIDED UPON REQUEST

SAMUEL A. JONES (Version 2)   International Sales/Finance

123 Any Street, Any Town, CA XXXXX (619) 555-1234

Contact Name   Date
Title
Company
Address
City, State Zip

Dear Mr./Ms. _____ :

I have combined in-depth knowledge of Eastern Europe with skills in sales, finance, manufacturing, banking, credit, and management to generate revenue, resolve serious cash shortages, achieve critical cost savings, and accelerate productivity for American and Eastern European operations. Achievements at a major European company were rewarded with multiple management promotions in spite of my unwillingness to join the Communist Party.

I am bringing to your attention my skills, achievements, ability to achieve results under negative conditions, and talent for executing tough projects including my escape from Eastern Europe so that we can discuss my joining _____ as a member of your International Sales or Finance Team.

Major achievements to date include:

o Earned promotion to the much-sought-after position of Director of Finance at a major European operation, the largest such operation in the country, in spite of my negative attitude toward joining the Communist Party: assumed total responsibility for the review and approval of expense outlays for the operation; reduced the multimillion-dollar expense budget 35% while improving overall productivity.

o Upon promotion to Financial Analyst at a European factory, researched and prepared well-conceived financial plans that exceeded cost-reduction targets without sacrificing operational effectiveness; took the lead in negotiating with banks to meet weekly payrolls in the face of critical cash-flow problems.

o Earned rarely achieved first-year promotion within the Cost Department of a European manufacturer based on producing quality multimillion-dollar cost studies: assumed ever-increasing responsibilities with multimillion-dollar signing authority.

o Over a four-year period, planned and executed my escape from the Communist Regime: completed a physical training program; maneuvered access to a waterfront complex; escaped across an inlet and posed as a West German citizen to get to West Germany where the United States granted asylum.

o As a Partner in a San Diego firm, purchase, restore, and successfully market antique furniture; as a Sales Representative for an upscale American business, acted as Assistant Manager and consistently exceeded sales quotas selling $50,000 worth of product in a three-week period: nurtured a loyal client base right up to the unfortunate closing of the business.

I look forward to discussing how I can contribute to your international revenue and profit growth.

Sincerely,

Enclosure: Samuel A. Jones

SAMUEL A. JONES   International Sales/Finance

123 Any Street, Any City, CA XXXXX (619) 555-1234

B.S.   Finance/Economics   Finance Institute   1981

Honors: Chosen to attend selective Institute
                  Recipient of major scholarship; Graduated with honors

Citizenship: U.S.
International: Eastern Europe Expert
Languages: Fluent English, German, French, and Italian; some knowledge of Spanish

CAREER SKILLS/KNOWLEDGE

o International relations
o Eastern Europe expertise
o European banking relations
o Credit application/approval process
o Manufacturing/factory operations
o European management techniques
o European financial/cost controls
o European pricing/capital planning

o Sales/marketing
o Client development
o Closing/customer service
o Financial management
o Controller operations/expense control
o Financial planning
o Forecasting/budgeting
o Cost/pricing studies

CAREER ACHIEVEMENTS

o Earned promotion to the much-sought-after position of Director of Finance at a major European operation, the largest such operation in the country, in spite of my negative attitude toward joining the Communist Party: assumed total responsibility for the review and approval of expense outlays for the operation; reduced the multimillion-dollar expense budget 35% while improving overall productivity.

o Upon promotion to Financial Analyst at a European factory, researched and prepared well-conceived financial plans that exceeded cost-reduction targets without sacrificing operational effectiveness; took the lead in negotiating with banks to meet weekly payrolls in the face of critical cash-flow problems.

o Earned rarely achieved first-year promotion within the Cost Department of a European manufacturer based on producing quality multimillion-dollar cost studies: assumed ever-increasing responsibilities with multimillion-dollar signing authority.

o Over a four-year period, planned and executed my escape from the Communist Regime: completed a physical training program; maneuvered access to a waterfront complex; escaped across an inlet and posed as a West German citizen to get to West Germany where the United States granted asylum.

o As a Partner in a San Diego firm, purchase, restore, and successfully market antique furniture; as a Sales Representative for an upscale American business, acted as Assistant Manager and consistently exceeded sales quotas selling $50,000 worth of product in a three-week period: nurtured a loyal client base right up to the unfortunate closing of the business.

INTERNATIONAL EXPERIENCE

Eastern European Operation   6/81–3/86

Director of Finance   1/84–3/86
Audited and exercised final approval for all major expense requests for this manufacturer. Achieved substantial cost reductions while improving productivity.

Financial Analyst   5/83–1/84
Formulated financial plans including detailed forecasts and budgets; interacted with managers to reduce expenses and capital expenditures. Worked with financial institutions to address critical cash-flow problems.

Senior Cost Analyst   6/81–5/83
Formulated detailed cost studies as a foundation for better pricing practices. Interacted with departments to accumulate accurate cost data.

AMERICAN EXPERIENCE

Insurance Firm, Any City, CA   3/95–Present

Sales Representative: Aggressively cold-call and follow-up to close clients.

Investment Firm, Any City, CA   3/90–Present

Cofounder: Purchase, restore, and market antique furniture.

Essex Company, Any City, CA   4/87–3/90

Sales Representative: Sold expensive products and nurtured clients until business closed.

REFERENCES PROVIDED UPON REQUEST

LAURA A. JONES   **Professional Sales**

123 Any Street, Any City, PA XXXXX (215) 555-1234

Contact Name   Date
Title
Company
Street Address
City, State Zip

Dear Mr./Ms. _____ :

Having recently been promoted to Assistant Sales Manager in a computer industry corporation, a role in which I have responsibility for both a direct sales quota and sales management, I have proven my ability to achieve bottom-line results. Sales skills which I have developed and applied to achieve quota include: aggressive cold-calling; telemarketing; effective presentations; overcoming objections; closing; customer training; effective follow-through to promote future sales.

I am very interested in discussing the possibility of joining _____ as a professional salesperson.

Specific results achieved to date include:

o Rank among the top revenue-producers with Telco Corporation, a computer industry company; earned promotion to Assistant Sales Manager while retaining an aggressive sales quota.

o Quote from the President of Telco: "Ms. Jones has generated more prospects and sales appointments and produced more custom proposals for prospects than anyone in the company with equivalent time and experience. After only seven months, she is performing at the level of a two-year veteran."

o Selected as the first salesperson at Telco to break into the tough, highly competitive Philadelphia market; made significant inroads and accelerated unit sales through persistent cold-calling and telemarketing combined with disciplined follow-up and persuasive closes.

o Received strong feedback and lucrative deals from Telco customers who characterized my overall approach from initial contact to proposal presentation as thorough and professional.

I feel that it will be mutually advantageous to meet and talk face-to-face. You may contact me at the above number so that we can make the necessary arrangements. Thank you in advance for your consideration.

                                             Sincerely,

Enclosure: Laura A. Jones

LAURA A. JONES   Professional Sales

123 Any Street, Any City, PA XXXXX (215) 555-1234

CREDENTIALS

M.S.	University of Pennsylvania	1985	GPA 3.8/4.0
B.S.	State University of New York	1983	Self-financed

Courses at Studies for Professional Women (Philadelphia, PA 1989):

- o The Successful Marketing of High-Tech Products
- o Proven Strategies in Achieving Corporate Objectives

Attended Workshops on "Prospecting and Cold-calling Tactics"

Honors: Earned Commendation for Master's Thesis; Graduated with Honors
Member: National Association of Computer Professionals
                 Pennsylvania Women and Men in Computer Sales

SALES/MARKETING ACHIEVEMENTS

o Rank among the top revenue-producers with Telco Corporation, a computer industry company; earned promotion to Assistant Sales Manager while retaining an aggressive sales quota.

o Quote from the President of Telco: "Ms. Jones has generated more prospects and sales appointments and produced more custom proposals for prospects than anyone in the company with equivalent time and experience. After only seven months, she is performing at the level of a two-year veteran."

o Selected as the first salesperson at Telco to break into the tough, highly competitive Philadelphia market; made significant inroads and accelerated unit sales through persistent cold-calling and telemarketing combined with disciplined follow-up and persuasive closes.

o Received strong feedback and lucrative deals from Telco customers who characterized my overall approach from initial contact to proposal presentation as thorough and professional.

o As an Account Executive for a Philadelphia-based Personnel Firm, achieved and exceeded placement quotas.

SALES SKILLS/KNOWLEDGE

- o Cold-calling/telemarketing
- o Decision-maker contact/client development
- o Effective proposals/presentations
- o Cost-benefit studies development
- o Overcoming objections
- o Negotiations/closing
- o Follow-up/training/support

SALES EXPERIENCE

TELCO, INC. (COMPUTER INDUSTRY), Any Town, PA   2/96–Present

<u>Assistant Sales Manager   4/96–Present</u>
Promotion. Responsibility for both direct sales and sales management:

o Recruiting, hiring, and training and development including: prospecting, overcoming objections, proposals, presentations, and closing.
o Continue to generate sales through aggressive client development.

<u>Sales Representative   2/96–4/96</u>
Chosen as the first salesperson assigned to the tough South Philadelphia territory. With the goal of establishing an initial client base, cold-called, prospected, and followed-up leads. Worked with clients as a computer consultant to close sales. Received on-going product and sales training.

ABC PERSONNEL, INC., Any Town, PA   7/95–2/96

<u>Account Executive</u>
Responsibilities executed:

o Developed and maintained new business in downtown Philadelphia; designed sales strategies; cold called; formulated sales tactics.
o Scoped out and assessed prospect needs; prepared tailored sales presentations; interacted with decision makers; negotiated agreements; monitored service quality.
o Maintained sales reports and records; analyzed sales results; assisted in the design and development of sales literature.
o Demonstrated strength in overcoming obstacles; received excellent feedback based on results.

OTHER EXPERIENCE

<u>Metropolitan Health Care, Inc., Any Town, PA   8/88–7/95</u>

<u>Director of Activities</u>
Directed the support staff in the creation and execution of the Activities Programs.

<u>The Essex Center, Any Town, PA   6/85–8/88</u>

<u>Activities Director</u>
Created and instituted Activities Programs for the mentally challenged.

REFERENCES AVAILABLE UPON REQUEST

WALTER A. CUMMINGS   MIS/Systems Professional

123 Any Street, Any City, NJ XXXXX (201) 555-1234

Contact Name   Date
Title
Company
Street Address
City, State Zip

Dear Mr./Ms. _____:

Having developed a full command of the EDP Operations of both large and small data centers during the last nine years, I have demonstrated the ability to apply technical and managerial skills to consistently meet tight deadlines and achieve bottom-line results. I would like to bring my skills, accomplishments, and take-charge attitude to the attention of your company.

I am very interested in exploring the possibility of joining _____ as a member of your systems management team.

Specific MIS skills applied to meet even the most aggressive production schedules and achieve other targeted goals (related to my multiple DP supervisory and technical roles) include: operations management; production planning; production scheduling; tape library management; IBM System 3033 management; negotiation of management priorities; and additional EDP technical and supervisory skills.

I feel it will be to our mutual benefit to meet and talk face-to-face. You may contact me at the above number to set up an appointment. I look forward to our meeting.

Sincerely,

Enclosure: Walter A. Cummings

WALTER A. CUMMINGS   MIS/Systems Professional

123 Any Street, Any City, NJ XXXXX (201) 555-1234

CAREER SKILLS/KNOWLEDGE

o Operations management—System 32
o Tape library supervision
o Scheduling supervision/negotiation
o IBM System 3033
o IBM Systems 360/370
o Job Control Language (JCL)
o Peripheral equipment usage

o UCCI Tape Management System (TMS)
o ROSCOE application
o Abend analysis
o JCL maintenance
o Knowledge of utilities
o Table development
o Retention management

CAREER EXPERIENCE/ACHIEVEMENTS

A FORTUNE 100 CORPORATION, Any City, NJ   4/92–Present

Production Planning Supervisor
Promoted to this position; responsibilities include:

o Develop and implement realistic systems output schedules based on user requirements, optimum systems usage, and lead-times.
o Negotiate compromises to accommodate conflicting user objectives.
o Screen all new program packages to verify programmer meets standards relative to JCL—will accept or reject packages.
o Access two IBM 3033s via ROSCOE terminal.
o Monitor schedule for projects to be processed for next-day completion; retrieve scheduled jobs from Partitioned Data Set to set up for running based on notes and commentary in the JCL.
o Perform maintenance/changes to JCL; run utilities—copy tapes, scratch files, catalog files, etc.

Results achieved to date include:

o Consistently meet scheduled completion dates relative to major project output.
o Implemented UCC1 on-line system for tape library management—a major productivity improvement.
o Designed and implemented corporate wide a critically needed disaster recovery program.
o Successfully developed and applied computer, human-interaction, and negotiating skills to achieve targeted goals.

ANOTHER FORTUNE 100 CORPORATION, Any City, NJ   6/88–4/92

Scheduling Supervisor
Promoted to this position. Responsibilities included: supervised tape library and scheduled computer time; analyzed and corrected JCL and system abends.

Improved on-time performance by over 30%; significantly improved departmental efficiency.

ABC COMPANY, Any Town, NJ   7/86–6/88

Operations Supervisor
Responsibilities included:

o Supervised and trained operations staff.
o Operated IBM System 32 minicomputer.
o Performed system maintenance.
o Implemented department standards and procedures.

Significant improvements were achieved in processing turnaround time and overall productivity.

Reason for leaving: Company discontinued operations.

OTHER EXPERIENCE

XYZ SALES COMPANY, Any City, NJ   6/85–7/86

Credit Analyst
Promotion. Researched financial background of prospective accounts and compiled detailed financial profiles for management review. Collected past due interest totaling $150,000.

ESSEX CORPORATION, Any City, NJ   3/84–6/85

Tape Librarian
Developed training manual for new tape librarians and implemented department standards and procedures. Supported and maintained on-line tape library management system.

QRS SYSTEMS, Any City, NY   1/82–3/84

Service Support
Maintained portfolios for individuals and banks; updated transaction reports.

EDUCATION

College: 57 hours of college credits: data processing, programming, and general business

Training: o JCL/Utilities Course by IBM
o Credit Financial Analysis by Dun & Bradstreet
o Speed Reading Course

REFERENCES PROVIDED UPON REQUEST

Part II

Launching a Job Search Campaign in the Twenty-First Century

REALITY CHECK

In the career and job search game, the only thing that really matters is results. As demonstrated through real-life case histories, clients who combined our market-tested resume and cover letter packages with our patented Expansionist Theory have enjoyed a placement success rate that far surpassed the outplacement industry norm.

8

Predatory Greed: A Workforce Betrayed and under Fire

REALITY CHECK

Despite the best job market in 25 years, the downsizing ax continues to swing freely. Although the 434,000 layoffs in 1997—announced by such notables as AT&T, Eastman Kodak, and Boeing—did not match the 477,000 announced in 1996, the fourth quarter of 1997 represented the greatest number of layoffs since the fourth quarter of 1993 when downsizing peaked (Daniel S. Levine, "www.disgruntled.com/downsize198," 31 January 1998).

Although capitalism and self-interest have served America well during much of the past 200 years, greed reminiscent of the late-nineteenth-century robber barons has clouded the late twentieth century. Relentless downsizing, boardroom mischief, and calculated transfers of income and wealth—bordering on class warfare—have seriously undermined the American workforce. Even as workers acceded to the role of expendable asset, boardrooms across the nation gorged at the corporate trough. Executive perks and short-term expediency reigned supreme as job security was consigned to history. While pink slips flowed, the "ratio between the earnings of chief executives and those of the average workers in their companies exploded from 41 to 1 in the 1970s to 225 to 1 in the 1990s" (*New York Times Magazine,* 11 September 1996). Corporate excess, coupled with upward shifts in income that accompanied trickle-up tax cuts of the 1980s, caused a historic redistribution of wealth and income. While most workers experienced two decades of economic stagnation, declining real wages, and record numbers of bankruptcies, the richest 1% of families almost doubled their share of the nation's wealth—from 22% in 1976 to 42% in 1992. The richest 20% of families captured 80% of the total wealth. This premeditated—and elitist—transfer of the nation's resources depleted the middle class and gave America a first: The United States now harbors the biggest gap between rich and poor among the top 15 industrial nations (*New York Times Magazine,* 11 September 1996; *Philadelphia Inquirer,* 29 September 1996).

The magnitude of the problem created by these radical shifts in wealth and income is clearly evidenced in my home state. Recent income studies, reported in the *Hartford Courant,* 24 February 1998, recount a full-fledged assault on Connecticut's middle class. According to economist James Stodder, "Nearly half of Connecticut's residents saw a drop in *real* income between the latter part of the recession and 1996. Real income for the state's median households fell a record 11.3% during the first half of this decade—from $47,117 in 1991/92 to $41,775 in 1995/96." This explains why its housing and cost of living remain a burden to a struggling middle class. The working poor fared no better. Says economist William McEachern, "During the past five years, Connecticut experienced the highest percentage increase in households with annual income below $15,000." This explains why its underfunded food programs continue to face record demand.

REALITY CHECK

History shows that those with nothing to lose are the most dangerous people in society. Predatory greed has fueled growth of an uneasy middle- and underclass with little to lose . . . creating a society plagued by de facto class warfare and an increasingly hostile workplace where six million people are threatened each year and two million acts of violence are committed annually (David Reed & Associates, "www.reedassoc.com/viol," 10 March 1998 and *Forum: An Epidemic of Workplace Violence,* Harvard Medical Institutions, February 1995, p. 1).

Chronic insecurity and declining real incomes have produced an unsettled, hostile, and increasingly violent workforce harboring record-low morale and eroding loyalty. In the past few years, two high-profile executives became poster boys for this hostility. Albert J. Dunlap, aka "Chainsaw" Al, was the more vilified, even by his peers, who often branded him the most egomaniacal executive in America. Dunlap's slash-and-burn cost-cutting earned him a fast $100 million at Scott Paper Company where he fired 11,000 people and sold the company. This was followed immediately by another big payday as the new CEO of Sunbeam Corporation where he fired 50% of its 12,000 people. Even if these layoffs were justified in the name of competitive survival, this excuse gets lost in Dunlap's narcissistic outbursts and incessant self-promotion. His affinity for ruthless cost-cutting, for example, was garishly exhibited in a 1996 publicity photo in which he was outfitted with assault weapons and across-the-shoulder ammunition belts like the movie character Rambo (*USA Today*, 30 September 1996). This provocative photo made him look cruel and reckless at a time when a stressed-out workforce—armed with 200 million handguns—commits more than two million acts of workplace violence annually (*Forum: An Epidemic of Workplace Violence*, Harvard Medical Institutions, February 1995, p. 1). This epidemic of on-the-job violence has been graphically displayed in a myriad of news reports that do not spare the blood and guts. Al Dunlap—and other self-anointed masters of the universe—should be forewarned that the American workforce is increasingly fed up with the role of expendable asset.

In early 1998, Al Dunlap launched Sunbeam's $1.95 billion takeover of The Coleman Company, Mr. Coffee parent Signature Brands USA, and First Alert, Inc. In responding to queries about possible layoffs at the three companies, he crudely retorted, "We never do anything half-hearted" (*Stamford Advocate*, 3 March 1998). CNN reported that Mr. Dunlap's letterhead actually read "From the desk of GOD." Even if this was meant to be funny, "Chainsaw" Al would have been well advised to improve his image or bolster his personal security.

In a surprising—and auspicious—turn of events, "Dunlap (finally) got a taste of his own medicine." According to a front page article in the *Wall Street Journal* (15 June 1998), he was fired by five directors on Sunbeam Corporation's board, who had seen the company's stock plummet from a high of $53 to a 52-week low of $18. Dunlap's cost-cutting tactics had "failed to deliver long-promised results." In orchestrating and timing his departure, the board, not Dunlap, called the shots. Rather than accepting his recent face-saving offer to "take a severance package and leave," several board members "assured him of their support." Four days later they ousted him during a "short and to the point" five-minute conference call. In response to his demand to "know the reasons," the board simply "advised Mr. Dunlap to have his attorneys contact Sunbeam's attorneys to work out the details." "Chainsaw" Al was momentarily powerless. In the expected "battle over the terms" of his dismissal, the board was "determined not to award Dunlap a severance package." Even if he ultimately walked away with millions, as it seemed likely he would, Dunlap was on the receiving end of the very downsizing that he so ruthlessly inflicted on tens of thousands of workers over the course of two decades. Sometimes justice does prevail.

REALITY CHECK

Workplace violence is now the second leading cause of on-the-job fatalities. This was graphically illustrated on 6 March 1998 when an aggrieved employee, armed with a 9-millimeter handgun and military-style knife, stalked and killed the president and three other top executives at the headquarters of Connecticut Lottery Corporation. Two weeks later, on 23 March 1998, a 55-year-old suspended employee committed a triple murder-suicide that took the life of two supervisors. America's killing fields have invaded the workplace.

The next most celebrated target of worker hostility was former AT&T Chairman Robert Allen whose tenure was recently eclipsed by a two-year barrage of bad press and internal strife. According to CNN's *Democracy in America* series, Allen never recovered from controversy sparked in late 1995 when he announced another 40,000 mostly white-collar layoffs—necessitated, in part, by billion-dollar losses from a disastrous acquisition of NCR Corporation (*CNN Presents: Democracy in America*, 22 September 1996). That layoff announcement was accompanied by "leaks of tightly wrapped news revealing the Chairman's $9.7 million cut from restructuring-related stock options" (*Associated Press*, 5 March 1996; *Fortune*, 1 April 1996). The ensuing backlash and scathing publicity targeted Allen whose appearance on the cover of *Newsweek* turned him into an international symbol of corporate greed (*Newsweek*, 15 January 1996).

The internal backlash against Allen was exacerbated by the fact that former AT&T employees were having difficulty securing new jobs that paid as much as their old ones. Facing a crisis mirrored nationwide, only 33% of all workers laid off between 1982 and 1992 had secured new jobs paying as much or more. The other 67% had taken pay cuts (*CNN Presents: Democracy in America,* 22 September 1996). Despite efforts to delay the inevitable, two years of unrelenting attacks finally ended with Allen's "retirement" on 1 November 1997 (*AT&T Press Release,* 20 October 1997). Though not the only causal factor in Allen's demise, it was clear that a hostile workforce had exercised its will. It was long overdue payback time for the American worker.

In the category of what goes around comes around, there is an ironic new twist to the AT&T saga (reported in the *Stamford Advocate,* 20 February 1998). In response to another round of layoffs for 1998, C. Michael Armstrong, Robert Allen's successor, is facing unexpected dissent—from some of his best high-tech managers who are saying, "Take my job, please." These coveted managers—belonging to groups *ineligible* for lucrative buyout packages—are crying foul. Instead of being gratified by the company's desire to retain them, they have expressed a desire to be transferred to the eligible list so they can take the early retirement package and leave. Armed with a "suddenly booming job market that's created unusual demand for high-tech talent," Ma Bell's finest know they "could easily get new jobs after essentially being paid to leave." This would allow them to bank the whole retirement package. Speaking on condition of anonymity, veteran managers expressed little remorse for wanting to stick it to AT&T. They were merely exercising their right to be as greedy and treacherous as the company. Says David Kalish, "To be sure, the situation mirrors the broader psychological impact of corporate cutbacks. Many workers are likely to take buyouts because they don't want to stick around a company that's cutting jobs. Those that remain may be uneasy about their prospects even if their jobs are safe" (*Stamford Advocate*/AP, 20 February 1998).

REALITY CHECK

Paradoxically, the surging job market and low unemployment of the late 1990s have done little to appease an increasingly angry and disaffected workforce. Instead, the improved job market has provoked a record-high voluntary turnover by white-collar professionals seeking retribution (*Wall Street Journal,* 5 March 1998).

In what must be deemed a hopeful sign for the American workforce, a global giant has been taught some hard lessons in human resource management. AT&T learned that a dissident workforce could neutralize—and ultimately depose—a well-entrenched chairman. It also learned that endless layoff announcements accompanied by a healthier job market could make it vulnerable to a mass exodus of its best and brightest—a loss that could jeopardize its future growth. The potential severity of this problem was acknowledged by AT&T through spokesperson Ruthlynn Newell who admitted, "The company recognizes the danger of losing coveted managers and will work hard to retain them" (*Stamford Advocate,* 20 February 1998). It's refreshing to witness a corporate icon twisting in the wind. It's equally rousing to see a beleaguered workforce assert its power by forcing a bureaucracy to deal with its failed leadership. AT&T will not be the last company to pay a price for alienating its workforce. It's payback time for the American worker—stay tuned.

As the American workforce enters the twenty-first century, its tenuous relationship with corporate leadership—alarmingly echoed in a wave of workplace violence—continues to deteriorate. Boardroom gluttony, together with trickle-up tax laws disguised and sold as trickle-down during the 1980s, has depleted, downsized, and alienated a workforce that has resorted to antisocial behavior to retaliate against those answerable for the upward transfers of wealth and income. Based on the premise that success is really the best revenge, the American workforce can exact retribution by taking control of their professional life. As demonstrated through real-life case histories featured throughout the text, clients who took control by coupling our power marketing packages with our patented Expansionist Theory (detailed in Chapter 10) achieved their targeted career and job search goals. While the competition dallied, clients got results. You will too.

9

Top Ten Rules of the Job Market: What Worked for Satisfied Clients

_____ **REALITY CHECK** _____

In the career and job search game, the only thing that matters is results. As demonstrated through the real-life case histories featured throughout this text, clients who combined our choice marketing packages with Montag Associates' patented Expansionist Theory achieved their targeted career and job search goals.

As a preface to the discussion of our patented Expansionist Theory in Chapter 10, here are ten market-tested rules that helped clients and readers produce job offers even in the worst job markets of the past two decades. While the competition dawdled, clients of Montag Associates were busy outmarketing them by applying the following principles:

> _Rule 1. Failure to Take Control of Your Career and Job Planning Forfeits Control to Others._ In the final analysis, each one of us is, and should have always been, responsible for our own job satisfaction and security. Yet, as we approach the next century, this take-charge philosophy—and the tools to implement it—continue to

elude a workforce whose servitude to corporate America has left it short of the professional job search skills required to take control. This skills deficit spurred hundreds of blue-chip managers to pay thousands of dollars each to the author of this text—which is dedicated to rectifying this deficiency.

Rule 2. Taking Control of Your Career and Job Life Is Anything but a Straightforward Task. How naive is our workforce regarding the effort required to conduct a competent search? This is best answered by saying that I will scream bloody murder if I hear one more job seeker tell a network news reporter, "I've done everything possible to get a job. I mailed out 100 resumes in the past six months." Admitting in front of several million viewers that it took six months to do three days' work makes the American workforce look absurd. Here and now, let it be understood that a search is equal to a full-time job, period.

Rule No. 3. To Take Advantage of Luck and Timing, Your Paperwork Must Be in the Right Hands at Exactly the Right Moment. The search process is, and will always be, a numbers game. Universal failure to play the numbers game—buoyed by logic that says 100 contacts are somehow just as good as 2,000—is so baffling that it makes the workforce look asinine. Speaking selfishly on behalf of clients and readers, this widespread folly is good news since it gives a huge competitive edge to those who do play the game. Clients of Montag Associates have repeatedly outdistanced the competition with a winning formula that says power packaging plus *high-volume marketing* equals multiple interviews and job offers.

Rule No. 4. You Can't Get an Invitation to Interview with Your Resume and Cover Letter in Your Briefcase. This rule was born one night long ago when I shouted these words across the room to a client who had just arrived after a 12-hour day at a job she hated. She was so angry at her obnoxious advisor that she immediately accelerated her stalled campaign. Within six weeks, we were celebrating a great job offer from 3M Corporation.

Rule No. 5. There Are Smart Ways to Work, But No Shortcuts to the Right Interviews. This rule has given clients a major competitive edge that resulted in multiple job offers.

Rule No. 6. The Real Power in a Job Search Is the Power to Say No. Anyone can say yes to the first job offer. Producing multiple job offers affords the freedom to turn down bad ones. This is power. This is taking control of your career and job life. (Exception: Accepting the first offer in order to pay the bills and finance your on-going job search is, of course, an exception to the rule. Buying time to achieve career goals is certainly taking control.)

Rule No. 7. In an Era of Fleeting Job Security, the Twenty-First-Century Workforce Must Cast Off Traditional Definitions of Employment and Security. Old ideas about job security have been rendered null and void. Most of the workforce has yet to accept this reality. This mass denial—and corresponding inaction—is good news for those who can exploit the possibilities accompanying change.

Rule No. 8. The Circa 2000 Global Economy Mandates That Contract Job Openings Be Treated as a Near-Equivalent of Permanent Employment. The growth in outsourcing and executive temp services—offering high-paying, long-term assignments—reflects a historic growth in demand for contingent workers who now make up more than one-third of the total workforce. According to the prestigious Washington, DC-based *Conference Board,* managerial and professional contract workers will assume an ever-increasing role in the twenty-first century. It's readily apparent that contract jobs are now only marginally less secure than permanent jobs in a corporate world addicted to downsizing.

Rule No. 9. Never Underestimate the Mega-Power of the Internet/ World Wide Web (WWW). Those of you who have yet to harness the power of the Web should realize that you are aiding and abetting the competition—who are already using this tool to replace the research library, post office, typing service, copy shop, and hard-copy classifieds. Want ads from around the globe can now be accessed, researched, and answered within minutes at "www. CareerPath.com," and "www.CEWeekly.com" as well as other great Web sites. America Online and other Internet service providers make accessing the WWW easy—log on now.

Rule No. 10. Recognize the Exceptional Power of the Telephone to Produce Results. This rule is designed to encourage those fearless enough to tap the singular power of the telephone. A case in point is a client who literally phoned his way into a major corporation that had all but frozen new hiring. Determined to join this recovering blue-chip, George exercised his skills as a top-ranked sales manager to telephone his way up the chain of command at IBM. Refusing to accept no for an answer, he cold-called, circumvented, and neutralized a dozen bureaucrats before unearthing the right connection. After the initial interview, George followed with more calls that produced more interviews that, in turn, produced a lucrative job offer. For those with fortitude, the telephone can work miracles.

These proven principles combined with our power packaging and patented Expansionist Theory (discussed in the next chapter) will give you the same competitive edge that has produced thousands of satisfied clients and readers—who took control of their work lives.

10

Launching the Search: The Patented Expansionist Theory

REALITY CHECK

In comparing restrictive search theories to our patented Expansionist Theory, remember this simple truth: You can never be guilty of making too many contacts, but you can certainly be guilty of making too few. Widespread failure to heed this fact has ceded a big competitive edge to our clients who surpass the competition with high-volume marketing that gets job offers.

INTRODUCTION: A WINNING FORMULA

Armed with the market-tested resume and cover letter packages drafted in Part I, you already hold a competitive edge that will facilitate and expedite your job search. While it's true that the resume alone will not get you a job, it's equally certain that quality marketing packages can produce the right interviews, including many that our clients would have otherwise failed to land. Power packaging coupled with our patented Expansionist Theory and use of the World Wide Web has been a winning formula for clients of Montag Associates—who repeatedly outmarket, outsmart, and outdistance the competition.

THE EXPANSIONIST THEORY:
NO RESTRICTIONS, NO DUPLICITY

First, let's separate the wheat from the chaff. The literary chaff of the career genre is the harmfully restrictive guidance that imposes arbitrary limits on the job search process. Although exclusionary advice comes from many sources, the disciples of networking have effected the most damage on a workforce already stifled by its servitude to corporate America. Sometimes employing scare tactics regarding breaches of confidentiality that could endanger your present job, the networking gurus have persuaded millions to reject direct company contact and other equally viable search methods—that are relegated to secondary status. Speaking selfishly on behalf of readers and clients—85% of whom got results through means other than networking—this widespread inertia is good. It gives an enormous competitive edge to those who understand that networking is just one step of a multistep, high-volume process that we call the Expansionist Theory. While their peers bow to the gurus, clients of Montag Associates are busy outmarketing them by at least 1,000%—achieving a placement success rate that buries the competition.

REALITY CHECK

In order to capitalize on luck and timing, your marketing package must be in the hands of the decision maker at exactly the right moment. A job search is, and will always be, a numbers game. Widespread failure to play the game has benefited those who do, including clients of Montag Associates who simply outclass the competition.

EXPANSIONIST THEORY, STEP ONE:
DIRECT COMPANY CONTACT

The unqualified success of direct company contact stands as the sharpest rebuke to the irresponsible disciples of networking. Ignoring unsubstantiated drivel about breaches of confidentiality and overexposure, over half of the executives and professionals served by our firm in the past decade achieved career moves through this method.

FIGURE 10.1a. The Power of Direct Company Contact: A Case History

---

Client: Robert A. Gordon

Volume of direct company contacts: over 1,300 packages mailed/e-mailed/faxed (continuous process)

Results achieved within three months:

Favorable responses (phone):	73 (plus 1 to 2 calls/day going into the fourth month)
Formal telephone interviews:	38 (calls still coming in going into the fourth month)
Formal in-person interviews:	19 (calls still coming in going into the fourth month)
Formal job offers received:	8 (formal offer letters)

Companies extending job offers:	Behemoth Capital Corporation (pseudonym)
	Accepted
	Mont Blanc Capital Corporation (pseudonym)
	Electronic Industries, Inc. (pseudonym)
	Babcock Industries, Inc.
	Bowater, Inc.
	Irving Trust Company
	Perkin-Elmer Corporation
	U.S. Concord Corporation

The bottom line: Within three months this client had generated eight good offers through direct contact.

Armed with power packaging, CD-ROM listings, the *Directory of Corporate Affiliations,* and the Web, clients have researched, selected, and queried thousands of executive decision makers, who have responded very well to our skills and achievement-oriented packages. Clients have been told repeatedly that the first paragraph of the letter *hooked* the reader, enticing him/her to review the entire package, so never underestimate the power of the words that you drafted in Part I. At the end of the day, the sheer magnitude and quality of our marketing campaigns have produced extraordinary results for clients, period.

A Definitive Case History

The power of direct contact is exemplified in the fast-track career of Bob Gordon, who is now the youngest executive in a financial services division of a European giant. As a long-time client who has conducted three searches in the past decade, Bob has progressed from a recent graduate of a state university to a financial manager with a six-figure salary (one of several offers that emerged from his latest search). As shown in Figure 10.1a, his most recent campaign included mass mailing customized packages (Figures 10.1b to 10.1d) to more than 1,300 companies. Armed with CD-ROM listings obtained from Web sites like "www.reedref.com" and "www.nwbuildnet.com," Bob completed the mailing in under three weeks. The responses were immediate and positive. In order to eliminate nonstarters, Bob screened callers more rigorously than they screened him. Within three months, our direct campaign had generated countless phone calls, 73 positive responses, 38 phone interviews, 19 on-site interviews, and 8 good job offers (Figure 10.1a). As always, this client, whose talent and charisma yield an imposing interview-to-offer ratio, was firmly in control of his career and work life. Power packaging combined with high-volume marketing had once again produced results.

EXPANSIONIST THEORY, STEP TWO: RECRUITER CONTACTS

Clients of Montag Associates deal with the maligned recruiting industry for one reason—they have job orders. But our clients deal from strength. Since recruiters are only one step of a process, clients never have to depend on an industry whose loyalty naturally lies with their client companies. The bottom line is that recruiters are vital to any search as long as you don't rely on them. Although the retainer firms—represented by such icons as Korn/Ferry International and Heidrick & Struggles—are often considered more reputable, the contingency firms should not be overlooked. Recruiters in both categories have helped our clients. Armed with CD-ROM or floppy-disk versions of the *Directory of Executive Recruiters* (available at 1-800-531-1026 or "www.kennedyinfo.com"), our clients outmarket the competition by contacting at least 500 search firms. Volume counts, period.

A Definitive Case History

The power of recruiter contacts is illustrated in the career of Leslie Barnes, a training and development executive whose talent has been rewarded with endless company awards and a vice presidency. Another long-time client of ours, she recently encountered the indiscriminate wrath of a new executive who was equally vile to all. Realizing it was time to take action, Leslie called to update her marketing package and initiate a search that would include recruiters, direct contact, the classifieds, and networking. As shown in Figure 10.2a, she sent custom resume and cover letter packages (Figures 10.2b to 10.2d) to more than 700 search firms. Armed with the *Directory of Executive Recruiters* on floppy disk, she completed the mailing in just a few weeks. Within

ROBERT A. GORDON   Auditing/Finance/Management/Consulting

One Sutton Place, New York, NY 10022 Telephone: (212) 555-1234 e-mail: rgmanager@aol.com

Contact Name   Date
Title
Company
Street Address
City, State Zip

Dear Mr./Ms. _____:

As the division's youngest department director—reporting to an executive vice-president—I assumed full responsibility for restructuring, automating, and expanding the corporate audit department at Global Resource Corporation. Results achieved over the past five years were rewarded with rapid promotions and a 220% growth in salary.

I am presenting for your review my skills, P&L accomplishments, and talent for turning around weak operations so that we can discuss my joining _____ as a member of your corporate finance/audit management team.

Results achieved during the past five years at Global Resource Corporation (GRC) include:

o Promoted from Manager to Director of Corporate Audit after profitably redefining and expanding our corporate charter: shifted focus from routine compliance audits to unstructured operational reviews designed to identify and resolve high-impact problems within GRC; the immediate payback of these in-depth audits led to further expansion of our charter as corporate audit was elevated to chief investigatory arm of GRC's top management.

o Reinforced our growing credibility by investigating and stopping potential crises including legal and financial exposures related to our non-compliance with state and local tax laws (applicable to customer lease payments): corrective actions included automating out-of-control manual processes; also recommended critically needed systems integration, as well as organizational changes that ultimately produced a major staff realignment.

o Worked directly with GRC and C&L top management to effect major cost savings in year-end audit fees: saved tens of thousands of dollars in charges by developing new CAAT applications for use by C&L; created an automated account confirmation process for GRC/GR of Quebec; provided strong technical support generating special reports and complex analyses; expanded year-end audits to include other financial service subsidiaries.

o Exposed and corrected control problems related to multimillion-dollar streams of cash flowing back and forth between GRC and its vendors: stopped big dollar overpayments to vendors caused by poorly trained staffers who had failed to net current/overdue amounts owed to GRC by vendors against amounts owed to vendors by GRC.

It should be to our benefit to meet and discuss the possibilities. I look forward to discussing how I can contribute to your company's future success.

Best Regards,

Enclosure: Robert A. Gordon

ROBERT A. GORDON   Auditing/Finance/Management/Consulting

One Sutton Place, New York, NY 10022   Telephone: (212) 555-1234 e-mail: rgmanager@aol.com

CAREER SKILLS/KNOWLEDGE

o Auditing operations/internal consulting
o Department management/turnaround
o Annual audit plan development/budgeting
o Computerized audit department start-up
o Manpower planning/staff development
o Major cost reductions/productivity growth
o Major operational/financial audits
o Process improvement/compliance audits
o Services/manufacturing/government/defense
o Year-end audits/outside auditor fee savings
o Major report writing/communications
o Easytrieve/Panaudit Plus/ACL

o Financial/administration/leasing
o Financial controls/collections turnaround
o Leasing and financing revenue audits
o Asset remarketing/maturity programs
o Dealer activity and control audits
o Upgraded wholesale flooring controls
o Upgraded dealer rate participation controls
o Upgraded sales/property tax administration
o MIS/EDP operational reviews/security
o Hardware/software policy development
o Lotus macros/databases/utilities
o MVS (TSO, ISPF, JCL)

CAREER ACHIEVEMENTS AT GLOBAL RESOURCE CORPORATION (GRC)

o Earned rapid promotions by significantly improving the image, credibility, and productivity of corporate audit: introduced state-of-the-art auditing techniques and upgraded our obsolete systems in spite of strong resistance from senior systems management; ultimately enlightened the MIS Director who implemented required software upgrades; project managed the implementation and instituted training seminars to accelerate the conversion.

o In our new role as the President's chief investigatory arm, identified and reported high-dollar/legal exposures that led to major corrective actions in several areas including commodity validation/dealer guarantee programs.

o Exposed high-dollar problems in the lease/remarketing program that led to the formation of a corporate office, as well as upgraded staffing and systems at GR of Quebec: found virtually no controls over repossessed inventory, asset disposal, and loss recovery; over a 10-month period, the inventory of repossessed items aged over 120 days increased from 17% to 56% of total assets; poor loss recovery led to a doubling of write-offs.

o Expanded our region audit coverage—and reviewed $450 million in credit transactions—by creating a library of standard CAAT applications for sample selections, data integrity tests, analytical reports, and IRR calculations; further improved coverage by auditing big dollar exposures including dealer interest and charge delinquencies; this audit led to immediate corrective actions and collection of nearly a million dollars in overdue payments.

o Based on an interest rate verification program designed and programmed in Easytrieve/Panaudit Plus, exposed numerous deviations from customer finance program guidelines: because unexplained variances were detected in 44% of the contracts issued during a one-month period, IA issued company-wide bulletins, prepared monthly reports for top management, and worked with the regions to institute critically needed manual/systems controls.

o Sanctioned immediate corrective actions to address the absence of centralized strategic planning and controls within MIS: forced its management to define GRC's systems requirements, justify multimillion-dollar budgets, and correct poor budget controls—that had caused at least a million dollars in unwarranted expenditures.

ROBERT A. GORDON   Page 2

CAREER EXPERIENCE

GLOBAL RESOURCE CORPORATION, New York, NY   4/91–Present

Director of Corporate Audit   2/95–Present
As the company's youngest department director, assumed full P&L responsibility for corporate audit.

Manager of Corporate Audit   3/93–2/95
As the company's youngest department manager, assumed coresponsibility for the corporate audit staff.

Audit Leader   8/92–3/93
Major promotion. In charge of planning, staff development, and auditing operations.

Senior Audit Specialist   4/91–8/92
Promotion with significant salary increase.

SUNBEAM CORPORATION, Miami, FL   4/89–4/91

Senior Operational Auditor   11/89–4/91
Double promotion. In auditing a major division, found millions in committed-yet-unapproved appropriations, out-of-control inventory, and unjustified project delays; uncovered millions of dollars in purchases without valid PO numbers as well as weak competitive bidding. During a major manufacturing audit, ordered a product disassembly that disclosed serious and costly discrepancies between the actual parts, BOM, and engineering drawings.

Associate Auditor/Corporate Management Training Program   4/89–11/89
Chosen for one of six training slots. After just a few months, acted as in-charge auditor for an unstructured review of a problem division: created the audit plan and uncovered millions of dollars in cannibalized company property.

EDUCATION

BS Accounting   University of Illinois   Dean's List   Self-financed   1989

CREDENTIALS/MANAGEMENT TRAINING

o Active Member: Institute of Internal Auditors (IIA)
o Zenger-Miller: Front-line Leadership Development Program
o French and Spanish Languages: semi-fluent

COMMUNITY/VOLUNTEER ACTIVITIES

o Active Advisor/Consultant: Junior Achievement (Teach Economics/Entrepreneurialism)
o Active Volunteer: Harbor/River Watch Program (water testing project)

FIGURE 10.2a. The Power of Recruiter Contacts: A Case History

---

Client: Leslie A. Barnes

Volume of recruiter contacts: over 700 packages mailed / e-mailed / faxed (continuous process)

Results achieved within four months:

Recruiters responding (by phone):   129 (plus activity going into the fifth month)
Client company interviews—phone: 26 (calls still coming in going into the fifth month)
Client company interviews—on-site: 29 (calls still coming in going into the fifth month)
Formal job offers received: 4 (bona fide offer letters)

Companies extending job offers: Grumman Corporation (pseudonym)   Accepted
     General Reinsurance Corporation
     Philips Medical
     General Electric Corporation

The bottom line: Within four months this client had generated four good offers through recruiter contacts.

---

four months, our recruiter campaign produced countless phone calls, 26 formal telephone interviews, 29 on-site interviews and 4 good job offers (Figure 10.2a). She accepted a job as Vice President of Training and Development for a high-tech division of a Fortune 500 company. A quality, high-volume campaign got the job done once again.

EXPANSIONIST THEORY, STEP THREE: THE CLASSIFIED ADS

The World Wide Web has virtually nullified all the old excuses for failing to answer classified ads promptly. It has ended the agony of reading, analyzing, and sorting hard-copy classifieds—whose tiny print has all but blinded readers of the Sunday edition of the *New York Times*. Using on-line classifieds is so easy that it's hard to make a mistake. Clients simply sign on to America Online or other Internet service providers, initiate a Web search, and type in "www.CareerPath.com" to get instant access to the help-wanted sections of more than 50 leading newspapers. Once they have selected applicable publications, clients simply enter key words and job classifications to pinpoint relevant job openings that are then conveniently listed on a separate report. They have finished a task that once took days or even weeks, and they can transmit their responses to the ads in record time.

LESLIE A. BARNES   Human Resources/Training Executive

199 Washington, Briarcliff Manor, NY 10510 Telephone: (914) 555-1234 e-mail: tdmanager@aol.com

Contact Name   Date
Title
Company
Address
City, State Zip

Dear Mr./Ms. _____:

As Director of Training and Development, I earned awards for achieving strategic goals within tight budgets. Tough vendor negotiations and judicious use of internal resources allowed T&D to achieve bottom-line results including Daytron's first-ever: middle-management TQM; self-managed production teams; technical skills inventory; and off-site strategic planning.

As an achiever who has survived a 75% reduction in staff, I am presenting for your review my skills and talent for getting the job done so that we can discuss my joining one of your client companies as Vice President of T&D.

Results achieved during the past several years at Daytron Systems include:

o As director of our cross-functional Training Council, ensured that T&D did everything possible to meet business plan requirements within limited budgets: met all functional requirements and employee development needs by identifying and resolving any and all shortfalls in training and basic education; stretched our budget dollars by initiating and directing after-hours and state-funded courses at nominal cost to the corporation.

o At the request of Daytron's Chairman, restructured and directed the strategic business review process: drafted members of the Chairman's senior staff to lead teams accountable for resolving issues critical to the survival of the business; led to corrective actions that increased productivity and generated high dollar cost savings.

o As part of Daytron's desperate search for additional operating capital, initiated and directed over 11 months of intense and hard fought negotiations that produced a $2 million commitment from the State of New York.

o Chosen by the Vice President of Human Resources to head a steering committee chartered to create TQM teams composed of cross-functional middle managers addressing management-level business issues: facilitated the definition of specific business issues around which some 20 teams were formed; among other major process improvements, these teams significantly reduced the cycle for producing multimillion-dollar proposals from 75 to 19 days.

o Recruited to build Daytron's first training department: overcame initial barrage of opposition and cynicism to start and direct a cost-effective department that has offered hundreds of programs to thousands of employees.

I look forward to discussing how I can contribute to one of your clients' future success.

                                                   Sincerely,

Enclosure: Leslie A. Barnes

LESLIE A. BARNES   Human Resources/Training Executive

199 Washington, Briarcliff Manor, NY 10510   Telephone: (914) 555-1234   e-mail: tdmanager@aol.com

CAREER SKILLS/KNOWLEDGE

- o T&D management/HR senior staff
- o Budgeting/cost controls/corrective actions
- o Training department start-up
- o Management/staff development
- o Strategic planning process
- o Succession planning/manpower planning
- o Marketing/sales professional
- o Business start-up/independent consulting

- o Self-managed production teams
- o Process improvement teams/ISO-9000
- o Needs analysis/skills inventory system
- o Diversity/sexual harassment
- o Surveys and culture change
- o Technical training
- o Basic skills training
- o Multiple computer applications

CAREER ACHIEVEMENTS AT DAYTRON SYSTEMS

o As T&D Director, earned sundry management awards for creating and managing a state-of-the-art department that achieved and exceeded major business goals: in spite of downsizing and budget cuts, achieved results through good people, tough vendor negotiations, and optimum use of internal and government resources.

o Exceeded the hours of training per employee target by 50%; earned corporate commendation for implementing first-ever technical skills inventory; scored highest among all divisions in diversity training; also implemented automated tracking systems adopted by other business units; doubled participation in basic education classes.

o Won the Chairman's Citation for facilitating adoption and implementation of self-managed production teams: fully trained and prepared the facilitators and team members for this important transition.

o Initiated and facilitated Daytron's first-ever senior staff off-site strategic planning and team-building meetings: produced the first group-developed and group-supported strategic plans and MBOs.

o Initiated and implemented state-of-the-art missile systems training, as well as proposal development training that materially improved the accuracy of our proposals while streamlining the cumbersome development cycle.

o Initiated corrective actions to address deteriorating communication between senior and middle management: introduced and facilitated a series of Chairman-interchange meetings that encouraged open dialogue between the Chairman's staff and our normally reticent middle managers.

o As Daytron's representative on a headquarters employee relations council, codirected several events including an annual gathering that honored the corporation's top performing employees and vendors.

LESLIE A. BARNES   Page 2

CAREER EXPERIENCE

DAYTRON SYSTEMS, INC., White Plains, NY   11/91–Present

Director of Training and Development: Human Resources
Implement management, technical, and basic skills training in support of our strategic plan; secure commitment and financial support from management; direct company-wide needs assessment and skills inventory; facilitate implementation of self-managed work teams and strategic business review process; identify and implement cost reductions; direct vendor negotiations; facilitate and expedite employee development dictated by annual reviews; review and update instructor training; and communicate Daytron's business plan and leadership philosophy.

HOLLINGER ENGINEERING, New York, NY   9/88–11/91

Director of Training
Created, organized, and directed T&D for this electronics firm. Trained over 3,000 employees; introduced 81 programs, 80% of which were designed and implemented in-house. These broad-based training programs covered such critical areas as management development, succession planning, sales, technical, and basic skills.

BARNES CONSULTING, White Plains, NY   2/87–9/88

Founder and Trainer
Created, marketed, and provided customized training programs to such clients as Texaco, Citgo, General Motors, Peat Marwick, SCM Corporation, IBM, and GTE. Designed and conducted numerous Women in Management programs for IBM. Initiated, designed, and produced sophisticated training packages for PM's interactive videotex subsidiary. Designed an advertising training program marketed nationwide by IBM.

TRAINING TECHNOLOGY, INC., Webster, NY   6/84–2/87

Manager Training and Development
Comanaged start-up and operation of this company which designed and published both customized and off-the-shelf training products. Created, marketed, and executed innovative management and basic skills training. Also recruited, directed, and trained a talented staff of 30 professionals.

CAREER AWARDS AT DAYTRON SYSTEMS

Chairman's Award: for initiating adoption and implementation of self-directed work teams
Leadership Awards: based on outstanding achievements throughout the 1990s
Excellence in Performance Program (EIP) Awards: exceeded major goals established by senior management
Corrective Action Awards: for leadership in improving Daytron's work environment

EDUCATION: BA   Hunter College   1984

A Definitive Case History

The one-two punch of classified ads and custom packaging is illustrated in the career of Ken Allen, a veteran entrepreneur who achieved his goal of transitioning to the Fortune 500. In the midst of direct mailings, recruiter contacts, and networking, Ken saw some on-line ads that persuaded him to try the big corporations, where he wanted to be a division sales director. Operating under the premise of "no-guts, no-glory," we tailored his package (Figures 10.3a to 10.3c) to accomplish three things: meet the ad specifications, stress bottom-line results, and boldly assert Ken's unabashed pride in being an entrepreneur although he is thoroughly qualified to be a corporate department head. (Employed judiciously, this in-your-face, never-apologize strategy does work.) The ten special packages initially sent produced two good interviews. We had gotten him in the door. As a powerful communicator with a gift for neutralizing opposition, Ken survived the standard callbacks and gauntlet of bureaucratic interviews, where his entrepreneurial background was viewed with skepticism. He received and accepted an offer and is doing very well. A combination of astute packaging and a talented client had beaten the system.

EXPANSIONIST THEORY, STEP FOUR: NETWORKING

REALITY CHECK

Exploit networking for all it's worth, but assume that you must achieve a career move on your own. At the end of the day, we must rely primarily on ourselves.

As one step of a process, networking is obviously vital. Although many networking books offer excellent guidance and strategies regarding the relationship-building process, others have detoured into duplicitous tactics. They endorse bogus schemes to gain access to decision makers so that the topic of jobs can be broached at a later more "opportune" time. Those amenable to these roundabout tactics can certainly employ them. In the past decade, I have had few clients who would comfortably abide this subterfuge. Our clients have instead adopted forthright tactics including third-party introductions which can be extremely effective as shown in our case history below. While nurturing and sustaining work and social relationships is a top priority, the fact remains that 85% of our clients achieved career moves

KENNETH A. ALLEN Sales Executive/General Management

11 Tunic Road, Larchmont, NY 10538 Telephone: (914) 555-1234 e-mail: kamanager@aol.com

John Smith   Date
Senior Vice President of Sales
Division of a Fortune 500 company
118 Wilmot Avenue
Paramus, NJ 05432

Dear Mr. Smith:

I have exercised skills in sales, marketing, operations, and general management to start, expand, and manage two million-dollar businesses that were later sold at a sizable profit. I have repeatedly outmaneuvered the competition, penetrated new markets, and expanded operations to achieve financial security both for others and myself. I can and will accomplish these same bottom-line results as a division sales director in your Fortune 500 company.

I am bringing to your attention my skills, achievements, and talent for thwarting competitors to achieve sales goals so that we can discuss my joining your Fortune 500 division as Director of Sales.

Results achieved to date include:

o Rapidly promoted to Vice President of Sales and Operations at United Spring Water Company after achieving a nine-fold increase in revenue within a highly competitive market: increased our sales from less than $100,000 to almost $1,000,000—setting the stage for the company's acquisition by the largest Eastern distributor of Pepsi-Coca.

o Profitably competed within the ruthless soft-drink industry by outmaneuvering the competition and penetrating new markets: introduced 24-hour service; expanded narrow product lines; formed and nurtured new territories; created and administered combative marketing campaigns; and helped reduce unfair industry practices.

o Surmounted potentially disastrous competitive threats from the majors: drafted a marketing plan that secured critically needed capital funding from two New York City banks; purchased and installed state-of-the-art equipment that allowed United Spring Water to enter the lucrative concentrated syrup market.

o As the founder and CEO of a building and remodeling business, increased revenue from $78,000 in 1989 to almost $2.1 million in fiscal 1995: ultimately sold the company at a premium to a $50 million corporation.

o More than tripled company sales between 1993 and 1995 through strategic changes to our organization and marketing: formed a partnership; expanded our facilities; developed a client base of large builders; emphasized lucrative commercial work; participated in major home shows; and computerized our operation.

As an entrepreneur and rainmaker who never acquired the less desirable habits of corporate America, I am fully qualified to join your company. I would like an appointment to discuss how I can accelerate your sales growth.

Sincerely,

Enclosure: Kenneth A. Allen

KENNETH A. ALLEN   Sales Executive/General Management

11 Tunic Road, Larchmont, NY 10538   Telephone: (914) 555-1234 e-mail: kamanager@aol.com

Bachelors Degree Cum Laude Illinois Institute of Technology 1985

CAREER SKILLS/KNOWLEDGE

o Marketing/Sales	o General management
o Revenue/profit growth	o Start-up venture
o Competitive maneuvering	o Operations/cost control
o Product/market development	o Business planning/budgeting
o Turnaround strategies	o Funding/capitalization
o Pricing/market penetration	o Negotiating/acquisitions
o Advertising/direct mail	o Productivity improvements
o Networking/promotions	o Staff development/supervision
o Service strategies	o Computerization/PC applications
o Territory planning/management	o Inventory management/control

CAREER ACHIEVEMENTS

o As Vice President of Sales and Operations at United Spring Water Company, achieved a several-fold increase in revenue within a highly competitive market: increased sales from $100,000 to almost $1,000,000—setting the stage for our acquisition by the largest East Coast distributor of Pepsi-Cola.

o Competed within the cut-throat soft-drink industry by outsmarting the competition and penetrating untapped markets: introduced 24-hour service, expanded product lines, developed new territories, executed effective marketing campaigns, and helped mitigate unfair industry practices.

o Surmounted potentially disastrous competitive threats from the major soft-drink companies: drafted a business and marketing plan that secured needed funding from New York City banks to finance the installation of state-of-the-art electronic equipment needed for expansion into concentrated syrups.

o As the founder and CEO of a $2 million building and remodeling business, negotiated the lucrative sale of the company to a $50 million corporation.

o Initiated actions that nearly quadrupled company sales between 1993 and 1995: formed partnership, expanded facilities, developed a client base of large builders, focused on commercial work, participated in home shows, and computerized operations.

o Accelerated revenue growth between 1989 and 1993 through aggressive marketing and expansion: emphasized lucrative kitchen renovations, targeted high-end markets, developed network of architects, created productive ad campaigns, and expanded our facilities and staff.

KENNETH A. ALLEN   Page 2

CAREER EXPERIENCE

WHITE PLAINS BUILDERS, INC., New York, NY   1995–Present

Vice-President of Sales and Marketing
Initiated, researched, and negotiated a deal to sell Technical Builders, Inc., to this $50 million company in 1993. Currently honoring a four-year contact to manage the company.

TECHNICAL BUILDERS, INC., Larchmont, NY   1993–95

Cofounder/President/Marketing VP
Organized and directed this building and remodeling partnership:

o Created and staffed organization; tripled size of facility.
o Developed network of high-end builders; focused on commercial work.
o Planned and executed participation in lucrative home shows.
o Directed operations; computerized all planning and administration.

ALLEN'S BUILDING & REMODELING, INC., Larchmont, NY   1989–93

Founder/President/Marketing VP
Founded and directed growth of this building and remodeling company:

o Created and executed marketing/advertising campaigns.
o Developed network of architects; focused on kitchen renovations.
o Instituted professional cold-calling, proposal writing, and closing.
o Directed operations; upgraded and expanded staff and facilities.

UNITED SPRING WATER COMPANY, Port Chester, NY   1985–89

Vice President of Sales and Operations
Directed all sales, marketing, operations, and administration:

o Supervised department heads composed of production manager, route manager, and service director.
o Established and monitored sales and profit objectives.
o Expanded product line introducing new cocktail mixers.
o Restructured product line to include full-line syrups.
o Designed marketing campaigns including direct mail.
o Evaluated and expanded territories; established/monitored routes.
o Negotiated and purchased all materials and equipment.
o Established inventory and quality control systems.
o Established credit and collection procedures; supervised financials.
o Reduced transportation costs through truck fleet conversion.

REFERENCES PROVIDED UPON REQUEST

KATHERINE POWERS   Presenting Lawrence V. Chambers

Telephone: (212) 555-1234 ext. 567 e-mail: kpmanager@gcc.com

Confidential Eyes Only: Presenting Mr. Lawrence V. Chambers

Ross Murdoch   Date
President and CEO
Global Communications Corporation
One Park Avenue
New York, NY 10016

Based on discussions with a long-time business associate, I am introducing Mr. Lawrence V. Chambers.

As per the attached curriculum vitae, Mr. Chambers might well be able to expedite our circa 2000 goals.

As Executive Vice President reporting to the Board of a global financial services firm, Mr. Chambers planned and directed the turnaround of its ailing international division—that is once again a significant earnings contributor. He added some $275 million in revenue by leveraging his extensive global network and accelerating cross-regional business development. He contributed over $56 million to profits by restructuring product development strategies.

At the Chairman's request, Mr. Chambers orchestrated the same organizational changes at the Geneva headquarters that marked his profitable tenure at the North American operation. He transformed the corporation into an investment-banking and deal-oriented business committed to management by objectives and bottom-line accountability. His rise to one of the firm's top executives reflects of his singular abilities and brainpower.

As an investment banker and global deal-maker with the drive and spirit of a chief executive, Mr. Chambers is interested in shifting to a corporate setting within global communications. He covets international assignments—and would gladly perform such for our company.

Mr. Chambers is working stateside for the next month. He would be glad to meet at a time convenient to both your calendars. He is confident that he can make important contributions to our international growth plans.

I will call you on Friday to follow-up.

Best Regards,

Enclosure: Katherine Powers
                                                          Corporate Vice President

LAWRENCE V. CHAMBERS	**Global Marketing/Management/ Business Development**

West Swedeland Road, Geneva, Switzerland Telephone: (0114122) 555-1234 e-mail: lvcmanager@aol.com

Confidential Curriculum Vitae: Presenting Mr. Lawrence V. Chambers

CAREER EXPERIENCE

GLOBAL FINANCIAL SERVICES OF GENEVA, Geneva, Switzerland   9/90–Present

Executive Vice President and General Manager/International Division   3/95–Present
Reporting to the Board, helped return the international division to profitability. Added $275 million in revenue by leveraging global contacts and expanding business development. Added $56 million to profits by restructuring marketing and product development. Enhanced global marketing by ensuring that players like Microsoft received equal attention in Europe and Asia. Ensured that reciprocal tax treaties were integrated into financing solutions.

Strengthened our balance sheet by exploiting profitable market developments. Cognizant that investment bankers can no longer compete by excelling on the advisory, structuring, underwriting, and financing side, shifted focus to the distribution side by expanding product development to encompass the entire product chain. Also eliminated all underperforming assets by packaging and selling them off to third-party investors.

Appointed by the Chairman to orchestrate the same organizational transformation that reshaped North American operations. Achieved P&L goals by cultivating inter-divisional teams that required employees to act as CEOs in order to better define customers' needs. Changed attitudes from that of a traditional lender to that of an investment-banking and deal-oriented operation committed to maximizing revenue opportunities.

Representing all of the Swiss financial institutions, negotiated with the IMF and former Iron Curtain governments. Reduced a potential $2.75 billion loss to $550 million by minimizing debt forgiveness and optimizing the mix of exchanged debt instruments for maximum trading appreciation. Established a LDC bond portfolio that produced an average ROC of 195%—representing one of our most successful desks.

Assumed regional responsibility for Africa and the Middle East.

Managing Director—Corporate Finance: North American Operations   1/93–3/95
Directed staff of 94. As chief architect of a total turnaround in the North American operations, accelerated income and orchestrated radical shifts in our tarnished image. Recast the operation as a global player by generating a 265% growth in return while tripling its asset base to $8.6 billion. Gained market penetration by opening offices in the Midwest and South. Converted weak South American unit to capital market/M&A advisors.

Senior Vice President—Corporate Finance: North American Operations   6/91–1/93
Rebuilt organization. Recruited ten VPs and formed five marketing teams. Expanded client base via strategy that required new VPs to act as CFOs through adoption of a value-added, activist, and proactive marketing philosophy.

LAWRENCE V. CHAMBERS

Confidential Curriculum Vitae: Presenting Mr. Lawrence V. Chambers

CAREER EXPERIENCE

GLOBAL FINANCIAL SERVICES OF GENEVA, Geneva, Switzerland 9/90–Present

Vice President—Corporate Finance: North American Operations 9/90–6/91
Recruited by the Board to plan and direct crucial changes to the motivation and focus of the entire North American operation. Achieved a record 260% growth in return (on risk-adjusted capital employed) by totally restructuring the organization, staffing, marketing, and product mix. With carte blanche support from the Board, planned and executed a ground-breaking reorganization that transformed the North American group to an investment-banking and deal-oriented operation committed to management by objectives and bottom-line accountability.

CHASE MANHATTAN BANK, New York, NY 1/87–9/90

VP Global Merchant Banking, 2/89–9/90: Generated $11 million in revenue by saving 80% of the at-risk accounts. Increased fees/ROA by focusing on corporate finance and asset sales.

VP Corporate Banking, 8/88–2/89: Leveraged contacts to market corporate and capital market products. Generated $5 million in added NI and achieved a 330% growth in fees.

Manager Business Development—European Energy Group, London, England, 1/87–8/88: Recruited to start and direct new BD group. Established productive project finance and lending operation that generated $400 million in new business within two years with a ROE of 17%. Closed lucrative deals including a much sought after $400 million project with a global energy company.

GLOBAL FINANCIAL SERVICES OF CANADA, Calgary 9/85–1/87

Division Head, 2/86–1/87: Started office and exceeded goals by generating new business of $180 million.

Principal Lending, 9/85–2/86: Expanded multinational accounts tripling pretax NI to $2.95 million.

EDUCATION AND OTHER CREDENTIALS

Education: BS Finance with honors; University of Virginia   1985
Languages: Fluent in French, Spanish, and Swedish

through means other than networking. Even the best networking is no substitute for our multistep, high-volume search process that out-classes the competition by applying a truth that the workforce invari-ably sidesteps, namely, that you can never be guilty of making too many contacts, but you can certainly be guilty of making too few.

A Definitive Case History

The power of networking and third-party introductions is shown in the career of Lawrence V. Chambers, a long-time client who has tripled his annual compensation during our seven-year association. The chal-lenge of his most recent search was to balance a need for aggressive-ness with a need for caution due to his high profile within global finance. We resolved this quandary by employing a discreet version of the Expansionist Theory. In order to secure pledges of confidentiality, we called company contacts and recruiters before sending packages. Unblinded classifieds were also contacted; blind ads were jettisoned. Our networking included discreet phone calls by Larry and third-party introductions by past clients who were well-connected in their companies. The latter produced results. Another long-time client, Katherine Powers, submitted Larry's package (Figures 10.4a to 10.4c) to the CEO of her company. It produced an important first interview that led to follow-up interviews and a lucrative offer that Larry ulti-mately accepted.

EXPANSIONIST THEORY, STEP FIVE: RADICAL TELEPHONY (optional)

This optional step is based on the success of a minority of clients who are fearless enough to tap the advanced power of the telephone. Such a client was George Henderson, whose mastery allowed him to talk his way into a corporation that had all but stopped hiring. Determined to join this recovering blue-chip, George exercised his skills as a top-ranked sales manager to telephone his way up the chain of command at IBM. Refusing to accept no for an answer, he cold-called, circum-vented, and nullified a dozen bureaucrats before finding the right con-nection. After an initial interview, he followed with more calls that produced more interviews that, in turn, produced a job offer. George recently celebrated his second anniversary with IBM. For those with fortitude, the telephone can work miracles.

The bottom-line is that the Expansionist Theory works, period.

Appendix I

Conversion from the Recommended
Combination Functional and
Chronological Format
to a Chronological Format

JAMES A. SMITH   R&D/Engineering/Marketing

123 Any Street, Any City, NY XXXXX (914) 555-1234

B.S.E.E.   University of Rochester   Self-financed   1985

Honors: o Earned top grade for Senior project: designed hand-held scanner
           o Who's Who Among Students in American Colleges
           o Graduated with Honors; Dean's List

CAREER SKILLS/KNOWLEDGE

o Product development
o Project management
o System engineering
o Electronics/mechanical
o Digital/analog technology
o PCB design/development
o Computer science/programming
o Biomedical engineering

o Sales/marketing
o Product creation/introduction
o Revenue/profit growth
o Client development
o Cold-calling/telemarketing
o Proposals/presentations
o Closing/customer service
o Business start-up

CAREER ACHIEVEMENTS

o As Director of a key development group at XYZ, a subsidiary of ABC Company, developed several state-of-the-art communication products in five years creating one of the company's most profitable ventures: ground-breaking systems overcame restrictive limitations permitting peripherals to be located 70 miles away from a computer mainframe.

o As Cofounder of a start-up venture, led development of Single Board Computer, a processor board for industrial applications requiring less coding than other processor boards: protected product through legal means and marketed it to major Fortune 500 clients.

o As Founder of an E.E. consulting firm, developed a proprietary computer-based device called the "XYZ Product" for the Chairman of a market research firm under contract to the Executive Branch: earned fees based on the development, usage, and subsequent sale of the product.

o Started and marketed two business ventures during the past year generating six-figure sales: expanded an E.E. consulting firm; started a hazardous material consulting service.

o Directed a software-intensive group in executing state-of-the-art changes to a major machine at Acme Company: led development of coding printer executing all of the complex software and hardware tasks in harnessing the speed-printing technology.

o Successfully developed, for a major automotive company, the 4066 product which provided tape drive channels for customers without dedicated communications facilities: required complete restructuring of XYZ's 6088 product line.

CAREER EXPERIENCE

JAMES SMITH ASSOCIATES, Any Town, NY   1990–Present

E.E. Consulting: Developed feeder mechanism critical to development of a mail machine to be marketed by an electronics firm. Created "XYZ Product" proprietary computer-based data-entry device used to measure responses to words, phrases, and ideas. Worked on a computer-based automated routing system for Essex Corporation.

HAZARDOUS WASTE CONSULTING CORPORATION, Any Town, NY   1994–Present

Started and manage consulting business.

ACME COMPANY, Any City, NY   1992–1994

Directed a product development effort aimed at instituting critical changes to a major machine: introduced speed-printing technology to new code printer.

XYZ SUBSIDIARY, ABC COMPANY, Any Town, NY   1987–1992

Director: Developed high-speed data communications equipment for mainframes; designed PC compatible interface card for serial and parallel transfer to proprietary product. Codeveloped high-speed logic board using FAST series logic and programmable devices; implemented 64K deep high-speed FIFO capable of a 5 Mega word throughput; employed error detection and correction with the RAM array.

COMPUTER START-UP VENTURE, Any Town, NY   1987–1988

Cofounder/Partner: Designed and marketed a single board computer using the Intel 8051 microcomputer: incorporated ROM memory mapping, 8155 I/O ports/RAM/Timers, Electronically Erasable PROM, and RS-232 serial communication using the on-board UART of the 8051.

A FORTUNE 500 ELECTRONICS COMPANY, Any Town, NY   1986–1987

Electronic Engineer: Earned positive feedback for systems testing and authoring critical test sections of major proposal.

A SMALLER ELECTRONICS COMPANY, Any City, NY   1985–1986

Electronic Engineer: Developed control system software for custom molding machines; generated assembly language and PLM programs for the Intel 8085 processor.

REFERENCES PROVIDED UPON REQUEST

JAMES A. SMITH   R&D/Engineering/Marketing

123 Any Street, Any City, NY XXXXX (914) 555-1234

B.S.E.E.   University of Rochester   Self-financed   1985

Honors: o Earned top grade for Senior project: designed hand-held scanner
           o Who's Who Among Students in American Colleges
           o Graduated with Honors; Dean's List

CAREER EXPERIENCE

JAMES SMITH ASSOCIATES, Any Town, NY   1990–Present
E.E. Consulting: One of two ventures started during the last year. Developed feeder mechanism critical to development of a mail machine to be marketed by an electronics firm.

Also developed a proprietary computer-based device called the "XYZ Product" for the Chairman of a market research firm under contract to the Executive Branch: earned fees based on the development, usage, and subsequent sale of the product.

HAZARDOUS WASTE CONSULTING CORPORATION, Any Town, NY   1994–Present
Started and manage consulting business.

ACME COMPANY, Any City, NY   1992–1994
Directed a product development effort aimed at instituting critical changes to a major machine.

Led development of coding printer executing all of the complex software and hardware tasks in harnessing the speed-printing technology.

XYZ SUBSIDIARY, ABC COMPANY, Any Town, NY   1987–1992
Director: Developed high-speed data communications equipment for mainframes; designed PC compatible interface card for serial and parallel transfer to proprietary product. Codeveloped high-speed logic board using FAST series logic and programmable devices; implemented 64K deep high-speed FIFO capable of a 5 Mega word throughput; employed error detection and correction with the RAM array. Selected accomplishments include:

o As Director of a key development group, developed several state-of-the-art communication products in five years creating one of the company's most profitable ventures: ground-breaking systems overcame restrictive limitations permitting peripherals to be located 70 miles away from a computer mainframe.

o Successfully developed, for a major automotive company, the 4066 product which provided tape drive channels for customers without dedicated communications facilities: required complete restructuring of XYZ's 6088 product line.

COMPUTER START-UP VENTURE, Any Town, NY   1987–1988
Cofounder/Partner: Designed and marketed a single board computer using the Intel 8051 micro-computer: incorporated ROM memory mapping, 8155 I/O ports/RAM/Timers, Electronically Erasable PROM, and RS-232 serial communication using the on-board UART of the 8051.

Processor board for industrial applications required less coding than other processor boards: protected product through legal means and marketed it to major Fortune 500 clients.

A FORTUNE 500 ELECTRONICS COMPANY, Any Town, NY   1986–1987
Electronic Engineer: Earned positive feedback for systems testing and authoring critical test sections of major proposal.

A SMALLER ELECTRONICS COMPANY, Any City, NY   1985–1986
Electronic Engineer: Developed control system software for custom molding machines; generated assembly language and PLM programs for the Intel 8085 processor.

REFERENCES PROVIDED UPON REQUEST

Appendix II

Time-Tested Observations about the Job Interview

REALITY CHECK

Be yourself, inform yourself, and subtly take control. Remember that the interviewer is not God and that you are not a slave—it's a 50–50 dialogue, period.

As a brief supplement to the plethora of interview books, audiotapes, videos, and on-line guidance, the following are time-tested observations regarding the interview process.

1. At the risk of sounding naive, it's my strong opinion that the truth is the best interview script. Being prepared, truthful, and forthright in responding to questions eliminates the need to "get your story straight." It also mitigates the need to role-play and "act" your way through interviews. Not getting the job is a secondary problem compared to the problems created by pretending to be somebody you're not. Be yourself, period.

2. Remember that the interviewer isn't God and you're not a slave. Be respectful, but recognize that interviews are a 50–50 proposition. You're also there to screen them. It's better to identify the worst now. Prevention is much less painful than the cure.

3. Regarding salary negotiations, remember that if they try to nickel and dime you now, they will nickel and dime you later. If at all possible, discuss salary last so that you can properly assess the value of the job. Once you know that they are interested, you can request a fair to premium salary based on the job's scope of responsibility.

4. Turn rejection into alternative opportunities. If the offer is dead, ask about other jobs in the company or other leads. You have nothing to lose and everything to gain.

5. In follow-up letters or calls, communicate interest, restate contributions you'll make, and, most importantly, reference specific key points from the interview. Never send a boilerplate letter. It should be from the heart. Failure to do so can cost you the job.

6. Don't become discouraged. Learn from, but try not to obsess about, interview gaffes. You will do better in future interviews.

7. Always remember that you have a major competitive edge. Unlike most interviewees, you are conducting an aggressive, multistep job search campaign armed with market-tested resumes and cover letter packages. The Expansionist Theory works, period.

A FINAL THOUGHT: INTERVIEWER QUESTIONS

Candidates sometimes encounter off-center questions designed to test their temperament—don't take the bait. Here are a dozen examples heard over the years.

1. Are we just a stopover for you? Does this job really measure up to your goals?
2. Isn't the team player stuff a lot of nonsense? Contrast cooperation with taking charge.
3. What negatives soured you on past employers? How do you know we're any better?
4. What past criticism really angered you? How did you resolve your hostility?
5. How do you correct lousy morale? When push comes to shove, isn't theory X better?
6. What types of personalities rub you the wrong way? How do you react emotionally?

7. Contrast working smarter with working harder. How do you really feel about overtime?
8. How do you respond to intense pressure, deadlines, or adversity? How angry do you get?
9. How do you feel about constant fire fighting? constant crises? midnight meetings?
10. Would you take a cut in pay? Don't you agree that it's cheaper to live in the South?
11. What can you do that other more skilled candidates can't? Why should we hire you?
12. Don't you think that you might be better off in another company?

Appendix III

Career Planning,
Job Search, and
Interview Preparation
Research Sources

This section will facilitate use of the library and World Wide Web. Reference librarians and Internet service providers (such as America Online and Netcom) will be your support team in researching and conducting a campaign.

Our sampling of research sources—many of which are available on CD-ROM or floppy disk—is organized into five categories:

1. National directories
2. Local directories
3. Interview preparation sources
4. Trade publication sources
5. Almanacs

1. NATIONAL DIRECTORIES

Directory of Corporate Affiliations: The big red book lists companies on the major stock exchanges and the Fortune 1000. Each entry includes subsidiaries, divisions, names and titles of executives, addresses, phone numbers, sales, and number of employees.

Wards Business Directory: Excellent multivolume set complements the above directory.

Standard & Poor's Register of Corporations, Directors and Executives: This three-volume set lists companies alphabetically. Each entry includes SIC codes, addresses, names and titles of officers, phone numbers, sales, exchange listing, divisions, and subsidiaries.

Dun & Bradstreet Reference Book: Three-volume set lists firms by city and state; includes SIC codes and financials. Because data is coded, must reference index in each volume.

Dun & Bradstreet Million-Dollar Directory: Three-volume set includes a master index referencing volume and page of entries. Companies are arranged according to net worth.

Directory of Executive Recruiters: Lists approximately 4,000 retainer and contingent search firms cross-indexed by functions, industries, and geography. (Kennedy Information at 1-800-531-1026 or www.kennedyinfo.com.)

SearchSelect© For Windows: Directory of Executive Recruiters database in software format. (Kennedy Information at 1-800-531-1026 or www.kennedyinfo.com.)

Directory of Executive Temporary Placement Firms: Lists over 200 firms in the United States and Europe. (Kennedy Information at 1-800-531-1026 or www.kennedyinfo.com.)

International Directory of Executive Recruiters: A companion directory to the last three publications. (Kennedy Information at 1-800-531-1026 or www.kennedyinfo.com.)

Directory of Legal Recruiters: Lists 800 recruiters in 320 firms indexed into 33 legal specialties. (Kennedy Information at 1-800-531-1026 or www.kennedyinfo.com.)

Directory of Franchising Organizations: Each entry in this directory has franchiser name and address, line of business, and approximate investment required.

Business Organizations and Agencies Directory: Lists business and commercial organizations, government agencies, chambers of commerce, data banks, computerized services, and more. Each listing includes address, phone number, contact names, and membership data.

Trade Names Dictionary: Two-volume set contains an alphabetical listing of more than 100,000 trade names. Entries include product descriptions, manufacturer's addresses, and names of distributors and importers. This dictionary documents sources to simplify additional research. Use this directory when you know the brand name but not the manufacturer.

Reference Book of Corporate Managements: Offers profiles of the directors and officers of companies with sales exceeding $20 million or employee headcount of 1,000.

Encyclopedia of Associations: National organizations arranged into 14 sections. Entries include address, phone, membership, contacts, and a brief description of the organization.

Directory of Directories: Includes two indexes—one lists directory names alphabetically, the other lists them by subject. Entries include publisher names, addresses, compilers, number of listings in each directory, and type of businesses covered in each directory.

Klein's Guide to American Directories: Lists major U.S. and some global directories. Listed directories are published by business and reference book publishers; magazines; trade associations; chambers of commerce; and city, state, and federal government agencies.

2. LOCAL DIRECTORIES

Contact your Chamber of Commerce regarding local directories available in your area.

SACIA Guide
Southwestern Connecticut Business Directory, Fairfield County, CT. (203) 359-3220

Golden Apple Guide
Chamber of Commerce, Westchester County, New York. (914) 683-8855

The Source
Chamber of Commerce, New Haven, CT. (203) 787-6735

Chamber of Commerce Directory
Southeastern Connecticut Chamber of Commerce, New London, CT. (203) 443-8332

Top Companies in Greater Hartford and Companies Employing 500 People or More
Chamber of Commerce, Hartford, CT. (203) 525-4451

3. INTERVIEW PREPARATION SOURCES

In addition to the directories listed above, employ these sources for preinterview research.

Value-Line Investment Survey: Offers superior one-page profiles of companies; includes multiyear financials, key statistics, pro forma projections, and credible narrative about its prospects. Names of executive officers, addresses, and phone numbers are also included. These routinely updated reports also include stock performance history and projections.

F&S Index of Corporations and Industries: Cross-references companies with articles in major trade, business, and financial journals. Allows researcher to retrieve the articles.

Standard & Poor's Stock Reports: Quarterly reviews of stock exchange and over-the-counter firms. Good supplement to *Value-Line,* which does not cover all public firms.

Annual Reports: A company's audited annual report is an excellent resource.

4. TRADE PUBLICATION SOURCES

Trade publications cover products, services, trends, innovations, successes, and failures. They are vital for networking and identifying job opportunities via articles and classified ads. Those covering your field are listed in the *Standard Rate and Data Service* publication.

Standard Rate and Data Service (SRDS): This monthly business publication provides up-to-date information on U.S. and international trade publications including industrial, merchandising, and professional periodicals. All listings are organized alphabetically.

5. ALMANACS

The Hammond Almanac: Lists the following: directors of federal departments and agencies; companies with largest number of common stockholders; the largest universities and colleges in the United States; and the 30 largest university libraries in the United States.

The World Almanac and Book of Facts: Lists the following: all chambers of commerce; the 500 largest U.S. corporations with addresses, names of CEOs, subsidiaries, products, and parent companies; state governors and mayors of large U.S. cities; U.S. government agencies and addresses; associations and societies with addresses and membership statistics.

Information Please Almanac: Overview of business and economics: includes definitions and explanations of Gross Domestic Product (GDP), Leading Economic Indicators (LEIs), and other commonly used business jargon. Also includes charts depicting status and trends of business. It also lists companies with the largest number of stockholders.

Everybody's Business and Almanac: Profiles companies; information and data cover sales, earnings, stock performance, rankings, and a history of the company.